Boy 11963

An Irish Industrial School Childhood and an Extraordinary Search for Home

John Cameron overcame tragic beginnings to become a respected schoolteacher, working for over 35 years in West Dublin. Now 85, he lives at home in Gorey with his wife of 58 years, Treasa. He has five grown-up children and five grandchildren and likes nothing more than having the family sitting around the kitchen table.

Having developed Parkinson's Disease with Lewy body dementia in recent years, John lives a quiet but contented life. He enjoys spending time with his grandchildren, tinkering in his work shed, and volunteering his woodworking and crafting expertise in the local Men's Sheds Association. *Boy 11963*, the story of John's early life and his search for his origins, is his first book.

Kathryn Rogers has worked as a journalist and columnist for national newspaper titles including the *Sunday Press, Sunday Tribune, Irish Independent* and *Irish Daily Star* for more than two decades.

As a ghost-writer and co-author, she has written memoirs, autobiographies and self-help books for clients whose stories have been published in Ireland and the UK.

She lives in Clontarf in Dublin with a long-suffering husband and three cats.

With love and eternal gratitude
to the women who changed my life:
Treasa, Nell, Fran, Una, Betty, Ada, Marie and Joan.

Contents

Foreword

While we were growing up, my siblings and I never knew anything about our father's past. We had heard a vague story that his father died in a car crash in America and, as a result, Dad had grown up in an orphanage. We didn't ask questions because we knew his past was something we weren't supposed to speak about.

As children, we didn't give it much thought anyway. Our mother was the youngest of ten children, so we lived in a huge extended family with fifty-two cousins. With such a big family, we rarely gave our dad's side a thought.

We grew up in a very happy home. We were reared in the country, where we climbed trees, made forts with hay bales and picked wild mushrooms and berries. Mam was the disciplinarian, seldom Dad, but we grew up knowing we were loved.

It was only when the shameful treatment of children in institutional care was exposed in the years before the 2009 Ryan Report that Dad began to open up about his past. It was a slow unravelling of stories. Even then, every time we gleaned another bit of information, we were sworn to secrecy. It was for the family's ears only. As we absorbed the magnitude of what had happened to him as a child, it shocked us that he could have endured so much. It is a testament to his gentle nature that he tried to never let the demons of his past affect our family life.

Regardless of why it happened, Dad's early life was one of hardship and adversity. Despite this, he rose like the phoenix from the ashes. He fought hard to become someone, to carve out a decent and honourable life, and to raise a family.

All his life, he has had a fervent love of politics and architecture, and in another life, he might have followed a different career path from teaching. He may not have become a great politician or architect, but when you read his story, you will see that our dad is a great man, nonetheless.

Boy 11963 is our father's story, but the writing of it has been a family affair. We had many discussions about whether or not he should write the book at all. Dad sought seclusion and valued his privacy all his life. We were concerned that he might be overwhelmed by the process of laying himself bare and digging up painful memories of his past. But it was Dad who decided, in his eighties, that it was time. He needed to tell his story, lay some old ghosts to rest, and enable his family to know and understand his past. It has been therapeutic for him to tell his story, but it has also been a cathartic process for the family.

Despite his suffering, and intense, prolonged psychological distress, he not only survived but succeeded in every aspect of his life.

Now, by telling his story, a lifetime of secrecy, shame and denial is behind him at last.

John Cameron is both an ordinary and an extraordinary man. Above all, he is one of life's unsung heroes whose medals of accolade are all the many people, his children included, who deeply love and admire him.

Aileen Rogers

Author's Note

At the conclusion of many of the following chapters, I have added a few notes and facts that may offer the reader a greater insight into the background to or the context of this story. Ireland of the 1930s and 1940s was a very different country, and I aim to give a clearer understanding of some of the cultural, social or political issues of the day.

Prologue

On the day that changed my life, the rain drummed so hard on the windows that my daughter Niamh hardly heard the phone ringing in the hall. It was a call that we might have missed or that might never have come at all, yet it was the most important phone call of my life.

All through my childhood and adulthood, I had fought to unravel the truth about who I was. I had been a boy who grew into a man who had no past. I had no mother, no father, no siblings, no idea of who I was or where I came from. That side of our family was a vacuum, a series of clues that led us into endless culs-de-sac. Even my wife's irrepressible drive and her continuous investigations to find out something about my beginnings had come to very little.

But that one call and those few precious words, 'I think I'm related to you', sent a shockwave through us all and provided, at last, the key that helped me unlock the mystery of myself.

Even then, when we followed the trail, the tale we uncovered was an astonishing one. It was a story that was hiding in plain sight, a scandal that shocked society and made national headlines before I was born. Behind it all was an incredible drama filled with forbidden love, passion, heartache and betrayal.

I wasn't the only victim of the events that took place in my family in 1930s' Ireland. There were many of us who were shorn like leaves from the trees to be buffeted and whipped by every wind.

Meanwhile, the architects of our devastation slipped away and conspired to conceal their past. Maybe they hoped that the turbulent events of their lives would be forgotten behind the hazy veils of time. Yet, inadvertently, they had already sown the seeds of their exposure. Even back then, those seeds were sprouting into tender shoots and surviving, despite all the shame and darkness that was heaped on them.

Among them was a blond-haired baby, whose only defence was a hand-knitted blanket wrapped around him. This baby grew into a terrified boy, a small, wiry child with sandy curls, who is now so distant he's like a ghost who wanders faintly within me.

And then there are the teenager and the young man, other lives, other parts of me, whom I look back upon with compassion and remote fondness. But they're all separate from me now, shadows of the past. Yet those ghosts can still sometimes surprise me with their familiarity. Something random can trigger an emotion, a sight or a sound, that makes them reappear in sharp focus in my mind.

Like the day we received that phone call and the first secrets of my past began to be exposed one by one. It was then that the small boy with the straw-coloured curls stepped out from the shadows and, after a lifetime of hiding, refused to be forgotten any longer.

Part I

1

Orphan Boy

The boy lowered his head, stretched his arms to the top of the wheelchair, dug his heels firmly into the ground and heaved again. His bare, stick-thin legs strained in their hobnailed boots, and his hands were splayed taut at the back of the chair. His face turned tomato red with the effort, but the wheelchair wouldn't budge.

Old Mr Mulligan hunched forward, jerking wildly, as if his fury alone could move it. 'Push, you useless pup! Push harder!' he roared, now blindly swiping behind him with a cane. The boy scrambled away to avoid a blow, and the chair rolled several feet back down the incline.

The boy's eyes filled with tears. The obstacle, a knot of swollen tree roots, lifted the ground, like a miniature mountain range. The roots and the steep incline of the laneway were dreaded adversaries on this frequent journey.

'Guttersnipe. Useless guttersnipe!' squealed Mr Mulligan, his face now the complexion of beet.

The boy got back into position behind the wheelchair and braced himself again. He stretched his legs behind him, angling his shoulder and hands against the chair's oak frame. Then he lowered his head and, mustering all his strength, made another run at the jagged ground ahead of him.

This time the force lifted the chair over the hump, and for a half-second, Mr Mulligan was suspended in mid-air. Then the iron wheels clattered down, and the old man followed, smacking down heavily on the wooden seat. The boy gasped in relief, but Mr Mulligan shrieked in outrage. 'I'll kill you, boy! As true as God, I'll kill you!'

He tucked his cane back under his arm, smacked the arms of the chair in irritation and yelled for the child to move. The boy knew Mr Mulligan had a mind only for the creamy pints of porter awaiting him in Matt Smith's.

The sun was low in the sky when he got to the pub. He reached up for the doorknob, tugged, and a waft of stale beer escaped, with a cloud of smoke. He could see the glow of cigarette tips from the men hunched at the bar.

'Don't you budge from here!' the old man warned the boy, as he rolled over the threshold and eagerly vanished into the darkness.

The boy rubbed his aching arms, leaned against the pub wall and settled in for a long wait. He could already see his best friend's father approaching with another man he didn't recognise.

'Hello, Johnny boy!' Mr Kavanagh said, stopping outside the pub to ruffle the mop of curls on his head. 'Aren't you a great little lad helping Mr Mulligan all the way here? You must be nearly five now, are you?'

Johnny reddened, but his chest filled with pride at this rare praise, and he nodded shyly, even though he wasn't sure what age he was. Mr Kavanagh leaned down to him and whispered conspiratorially behind his hand, 'If Mrs Kavanagh asks, you never saw me. There's a good lad.'

'Who's the kid?' asked Mr Kavanagh's companion, as the two men entered the pub.

'One of the little fellas fostered by the Mulligans. A grand lad.'

There was that word again. 'Fostered'. Johnny wasn't sure what it meant.

Brian O'Connor said that the Mulligans weren't his real mam and dad, but Mam said that Brian O'Connor should mind his own bloody business.

Still, it made Johnny wonder about the hazy pictures in his mind from a time he couldn't quite remember. He had a memory of sitting up in a pram, covered with a plump white quilt, facing a window. Bright sunlight poured in on him, and he felt warm and safe. He tried, but he could never quite recall what lay beyond the window in that bright, sunshine world. But he knew everything was clean and cosy and happy. It was a different world from the home he knew now.

The air grew colder in Stepaside village and Johnny stamped his feet, pulled his jacket closer and tugged at his shorts in a vain attempt to shield his legs from the chill. His stomach rumbled, and he wished he'd had his tea before Mr Mulligan demanded that they leave for the pub.

The sky was studded with stars before the barman opened the door to let the old man out. Even under the street's dim gaslight, Johnny could see that Mr Mulligan's eyes were glazed and shiny.

'I haven't all night,' the old man barked, and the beer fumes lingered in the frosty air, as Johnny struggled to manoeuvre the wheelchair.

The mile-long journey home felt as if it would never end. The night was velvet black, and they met nothing on the winding country lane apart from swooping bats.

Mr Mulligan swore and grumbled as they made their way along the foothills of the Dublin mountains, but Johnny was scarcely listening. He felt dog tired, and his stomach ached with a familiar hollow feeling. He wondered if Mam would have kept tea for him, or if she'd accuse the old man of drinking all the housekeeping money.

When they reached home, Johnny dragged the old man through the squeaking gate right up to the foot of the cottage steps, where he called to Mrs Mulligan for help.

The old woman hobbled out, clutching a tattered cardigan over her nightshirt. The oil lamp in her other hand added a ghoulish glow to her face. Even in the flickering light, Johnny could see her resentful glare.

'Get out here, Gerald!' she yelled back into the cottage, in a weary tone.

She descended the steps, one stiff leg at a time, as another small boy appeared at the door in his shirt. Gerald's hair stood up on one side, and he rubbed the sleep from his eyes with his fists.

He stuck out his tongue at Johnny behind Mrs Mulligan's back, and Johnny scowled. He didn't like Gerald: he snatched food from Johnny's plate when Mrs Mulligan wasn't looking, and he never got the job of wheeling Mr Mulligan anywhere.

'Come on, you two, pull,' said Mrs Mulligan, her arthritic knuckles gripping the back of the chair. The two boys and she dragged the chair *thunk, thunk, thunk* up the steps, with Mr Mulligan roaring all the time.

'Shush, you oul sod! You'll wake Peter!' hissed Mrs Mulligan, but the old man only swore louder.

Inside, the smell of burned cabbage and the musty odour of damp assailed Johnny's nostrils. It must have been past midnight, but the old man demanded his tea. Johnny hovered hopefully as Mrs Mulligan raked the coals in the range, but she bristled when she saw the two boys watching her.

'Go to bed, you two!' she ordered, raising the poker and making a half-hearted swipe at them.

The boys retreated into the gaping darkness off the kitchen where their shelter lay. It was a shed of sorts, a lean-to, constructed of rusting corrugated iron and separated from the kitchen by an old timber door. Straw bedding and an assortment of empty flour sacks and old overcoats were strewn on the earthen floor inside.

Gerald arranged his makeshift blankets and wriggled underneath. Johnny fumbled with the knotted laces on his boots and undid his jacket buttons before following him under the covers. He could see the stars and a few scudding clouds through gaps in the metal sheeting. It didn't look like rain. When it rained, the boys were allowed to sleep on the kitchen floor.

Mrs Mulligan kept the light down low to save the paraffin, so Johnny could watch only shifting shapes and shadows through the gaps in the door panels. But he heard her crack an egg and, sitting upright under the flour sacks, he saw her silhouette, turning the bread on a toasting fork over the open coals.

The smoke-blackened kitchen, the only living area in the cottage, contained little furniture, other than a pine table and stools. A picture of the Sacred Heart, brown with nicotine stains and soot, hung on the wall above the range.

Off the kitchen were two bedrooms, their walls bulging with tumours of damp. The old couple occupied one, while their nine-year-old grandson, Peter, slept in the other. A short, narrow hallway, coated with a faded red wash, ran between the bedrooms to a peeling front door. The roof was badly patched, but Mr Mulligan said he wouldn't waste a penny more on it.

Johnny's senses were filled with the aroma of toasting bread, so he barely heard the old couple bickering. He jumped when Mr Mulligan's fist landed with a fierce clatter on the table.

'Is it too much to expect a bit of tea on the table when I get home?' the old man bellowed.

'Yer tea was on the table hours ago, so you can hold your whisht now,' Mrs Mulligan replied.

Gerald pulled the covers over his head, but Johnny continued to watch through the gaps in the door. He thought he could hear Mr Mulligan snoring now, but then Mrs Mulligan banged a tin plate on the table. Johnny leaned forward, and in the half-light saw Mr Mulligan's face twist in disgust.

'What in the name of Jaysus is this? Do you call this tea?' He was roaring thunderously now, and Gerald half-rose in fright from under the covers.

'If you didn't waste eleven whole pence on every pint of porter . . .' Mrs Mulligan began, but suddenly she shrieked.

The tin plate made a loud clang as it struck the wall behind her, its contents spilling into the darkness below.

Gerald sat bolt upright. The old man roared, and his wife screamed back. The sound of their grandchild dragging his bedroom door open, scraping it across the uneven clay floor, interrupted their argument.

Peter was a rangy boy, five years older than Johnny and Gerald. He appeared in the kitchen in his nightshirt. 'Nana, won't you give poor Granddad a bit of peace?' he admonished, but Johnny saw him give his grandmother a crafty wink. 'Come on, Granddad, let's get out of here. I'll help you to bed.'

The old man threw a few more oaths in his wife's direction, but he surrendered to his grandson's attentions. Peter could always mollify his grandparents. Johnny watched the boy wrestle control of the wheelchair as Mrs Mulligan dabbed her eyes, then blew her nose heartily into a tea-towel. He waited, hardly breathing, until all the Mulligans had disappeared, and their three creaky beds went silent. Then he pushed open the shed door and crept into the darkness of the kitchen.

He saw Gerald's shadow on his heels at the same time as he caught sight of the toast, which had fallen from the tin plate. He leaped for it before Gerald did. Gerald didn't give in and tried to wrestle it from Johnny's grip. They scuffled and thumped each other noiselessly until Gerald ripped off a corner of toast. Johnny stuffed the dry remainder into his mouth. His fingers rummaged for Mr Mulligan's scrambled egg amid the blanket of clock beetles scurrying on the dirt floor. He found only slivers, but he ate them nonetheless.

The boys crept back into the lean-to and tugged the door after them. Johnny dragged at the covers for warmth, and when Gerald elbowed him in the ribs, he punched him back. But he was exhausted by now, and Gerald was too, so they fell asleep.

In the 1930s and 1940s, local authorities and charities used a boarding-out system for those children in their care who were too old for nursery wards but too young for industrial schools.

We know now that the system was more about economics than children's welfare, but the policy was dressed up in well-meaning terms. I've read old documents about the benefits of having the children cared for in the families of 'the respectable poor'. They speak of placing children in homes in rural localities in 'healthy surroundings'.

The reality is that some foster families regarded those children as sources of monthly income and slave labour for their farms. The conditions in which institutions placed the children were often appalling.

Margaret and Thomas Mulligan were sick, poverty-stricken, and well into their sixties when I arrived there in 1938. I was less than three years old. A retired farm labourer, Mr Mulligan was wheelchair-bound and a violent drinker. Yet the authorities regarded him and his wife as suitable foster parents for two three-year-old boys.

They also raised their daughter's son while she worked in England. No father was ever mentioned, so I believe she was a single mother. In my records, held by the Christian Brothers, Peter is referred to as the son of Mr and Mrs Mulligan.

2

Childhood

Johnny awoke shivering in the frosty morning air. The tips of his fingers stung, and his nose felt icy, so he burrowed under the bedding until Gerald elbowed him.

As soon as Mrs Mulligan began to set the fire, Johnny knew it was time to pull on his short trousers and jacket, to wiggle his feet into his boots and to get to work.

His first job was to empty the Mulligans' chamber pots in the outhouse. Then Mrs Mulligan poured warm water into a basin. Johnny lathered up the soap and shaved the old man. Mr Mulligan was a powerful, squat man, with a pigeon chest, a bulbous purple nose and a black temper. Johnny had to be quick to avoid a cuff on the ear or a clatter across the head. But the morning after the row, the old man was sunk low in his wheelchair. He remained silent even when Mrs Mulligan slammed the kettle onto the range with a hard bang.

After shaving the old man, Johnny joined Gerald in the yard. They had to clean the henhouse, feed the pigs and clear the pen before school. The ground was still frozen, but soon they would start digging rows and planting the first potatoes of the season. In the summer, they tended the small orchard, and looked forward to the arrival of cooking apples in the autumn. Those Lord Derbys were hard and bitter, but the boys scoffed the windfalls at every opportunity when the Mulligans weren't looking.

When they finished their work in the yard, they knocked on the back door and waited until Mrs Mulligan let them in. She poured two mugs of tea and smacked down a slice of bread in front of each of them. Johnny thought the bread must be as hard as the Blarney Stone. The two boys eyed each other, then looked at Mrs Mulligan.

'None of yer nonsense. Dunk it in yer tea. There's nothing wrong with it!' she said. 'Then get to school, the both of ye.'

As Johnny left for school, he saw the Brennan twins skulking outside the gate, waiting for Gerald. They nudged each other, and one called Johnny an eejit, but they didn't touch him because they knew Georgie Kavanagh was waiting down the road.

Johnny called Georgie his 'best friend' but, in truth, he was his only friend. The local boys liked to pick on Johnny. He was smaller, more timid and notably shabbier than most boys his age. He was also 'fostered'. The kids didn't really know what that meant, but they knew it wasn't a good thing. The bullies backed away when Georgie was around. Everyone knew that Georgie trained in the boxing club with his father and was handy with his fists. With a shock of wiry chestnut hair and a healthy smattering of freckles, Georgie was a strong lad and fitter than most boys his age. He was also protective of his smaller friend.

'You touch Johnny Cameron, and I touch you,' he used to warn other lads.

They walked to Sandyford National School together, and they shared the same classroom, even though Georgie was a year ahead of Johnny. It was a long walk, and Johnny spent much of it tugging at his scratchy tweed shorts.

Johnny liked school, even though their teacher, Mr Shannon, was a fiery man with a ready cane. But school was a welcome relief: anything was better than having to be at home around old Mulligan.

Still, when the bell rang, Johnny ran out of the place as if Hell was roasting his heels. Georgie followed, and they dashed down Murphystown Road, their satchels flying behind them.

'Me mam says you have to collect a bucket of pig slops for your mam,' Georgie said, panting after their dash from school one day. 'And she says you're to stay for tea if you like.'

They both knew that Johnny liked nothing better than tea in his friend's house. His heart soared, and he salivated at the thought. He loved being in the Kavanaghs' house. Their kitchen was warm and clean, and the windows were draped with floral curtains. The flash of pink from the pot of geraniums on the sill added even more cheer.

'Sit up here, Johnny love,' said Mrs Kavanagh, pulling out a chair as soon as the boys arrived. 'Do your homework now, lads, until your dinner's ready.' She looked in exasperation at the rest of her brood as they milled around the small kitchen.

Georgie's younger sister scowled at Johnny. 'How come Georgie's friend is always allowed come to tea and not mine?'

Mrs Kavanagh glared at her. 'I decide who eats in this house, not you, madam,' she said.

Georgie grinned and stuck out his tongue at his sister, but Johnny flushed. He knew why Mrs Kavanagh invited him because he had overheard her talking to Georgie's aunt while he was sitting on the back step one day. 'It's not right, Mags. They leave that poor little stray half-starved over there, and another little fella the same.'

'Sure you're doing what you can. Isn't it hard enough to keep feeding our own?'

'I still feel bad,' she said. 'It's no place for children, poor lambs.'

Everyone had to wait for Mr Kavanagh to come in from work and to wash his hands and face over the kitchen sink before they could eat. As soon as he sat at the table, Georgie's mother set a big pot of vegetable and barley soup or a warming stew on the table.

Johnny basked in the glow of the cosy family atmosphere and he liked to make-believe he was one of them. He tried to imagine what it would be like to live with the Kavanaghs all the time – he envied and admired Georgie in equal measure.

'There's plenty more left in the pot, Johnny,' Mrs Kavanagh would always say, as soon as Johnny had bolted down his plateful.

Johnny hated leaving, but he had to get home or he'd be in trouble. He thanked Mrs Kavanagh for his tea and collected the slops from the kitchen step. The bucket was full to the brim with potato peelings, turnip and carrot tops, stale bread crusts, soured milk and table scraps.

Johnny needed his two hands to carry the bucket before him, and he staggered under the weight as he made his way down the road, occasionally stopping to rest his arms. He made sure to bring the bucket with him into the Mulligans' kitchen.

'Mrs Kavanagh asked me to wait for this, Mam,' he blurted, before she or Mr Mulligan clipped his ear for being late.

Before he could gauge their mood, he spotted a small boy who was not Gerald hovering in the gloom of the kitchen.

'Take that bucket outside, and show George how to sort out the sheds,' said Mrs Mulligan. 'And don't come back in until I tell you.'

Outside, Johnny stared at the new boy, and George glowered back with hostile eyes. He was slightly taller than Johnny, and under his unruly brown hair he had shrewd, narrow, red-rimmed eyes. 'Where's Gerald?' Johnny asked.

'Who's Gerald?'

'He lives here.'

George shrugged and affected a bored look.

'Where are you from?'

'What's it to you?' the boy replied sullenly.

It was Johnny's turn to shrug. He walked off to secure the henhouse, herd the pigs back into their shed and clean the pen. George leaned against the shed wall, out of view of the kitchen window, and did nothing to help.

When Johnny had finished, he sat on the doorstep and waited for Mrs Mulligan to give them tea. It was almost dark when she handed out a slice of bread and dripping to each of them. 'Stay out of my sight now until yer ready for bed,' she said.

As she slammed the door, George snatched the bread from Johnny's hand and ran to the fields with both slices. Johnny legged it after him, but George stuffed the food into him as he ran. He stopped halfway down the potato field when his cheeks were swollen with bread.

Johnny shoved him in the chest, and George staggered back two paces. He opened his mouth to show the half-eaten bread and managed a satisfied grin.

'Dirty thief!' Johnny yelled.

George's expression turned from exuberance to rage.

'Don't call *me* a dirty thief!' he said, through the mouthful of bread. His eyes were angry slits as he swung at Johnny, who took a blow to his chin. Stumbling back, he lost his balance and landed with a thud in the dirt. George flung himself on Johnny, his face red and twisted with fury, and pummelled him fiercely about the head. 'What did you call me?' he yelled, gripping Johnny's collar with both hands.

Johnny acknowledged defeat. 'Nothin'!'

'So who's the dirty thief then?'

'No one!' said Johnny, trying to stave off another blow with his arm.

'I'll kick the head offa you,' said George, clambering back to his feet.

As he turned to go, he booted Johnny hard in his stomach. Johnny lay winded, gasping for breath among the potato furrows. He could taste the warm, salty trickle of blood in his mouth.

His old nemesis Gerald was gone, but it seemed that his life with the new boy was going to be even worse.

The local authorities had responsibility for inspecting foster homes until the boarded-out child was nine years old. Dublin City Council, which was responsible for carrying out the inspections in our area, failed in that respect.

Any 'child at nurse' placed with the Mulligans seemed to fall through the cracks. I was aware of other boarded-out children in the Sandyford area, who seemed to have lovely homes. But the children sent to live with the Mulligans suffered years of neglect along with physical and emotional abuse. Food in the house was scarce and of poor quality. Stale bread, wiped with the fat of pork or beef, known as 'dripping', was our staple diet.

Gerald Kane, the first boy who was fostered alongside me, was there one day and gone the next. He disappeared from the Mulligans' house, and I never saw or heard of him again. The second, George Mackessy, who gave me the thumping on the day he arrived, remained with the Mulligans for many years. He died while he was still living there after a fall that left him impaled on a gate on the farm. He was taken to St Columcille's Hospital in Loughlinstown, where I remember hearing that he suffered for months. His death certificate states he eventually died, aged twelve, of tuberculous meningitis on 2 November 1948 and describes him as a 'nurse-child'.

I know that poor lad never experienced much nursing while he lived with the Mulligans.

3

Fairy Godmother

Mrs Mulligan squinted at the translucent sheet of airmail paper in her hand, and reread it to confirm the words she hadn't expected to see. She dropped the letter into her lap, and looked at Mr Mulligan in astonishment. 'Bridie's coming home!' she exclaimed, the onionskin paper crackling in her grip. She lived far away in England and didn't come very often. Her lined face lit up as she turned to Peter: 'Yer mammy's coming home for yer thirteenth birthday!'

Bridie's homecoming sent Mrs Mulligan into a frenzy of spring-cleaning. The boys were instructed to fill the washtub with well water, scrub the linens and old blankets with carbolic soap, then hang them on the washing line that stretched across the yard. Mrs Mulligan said Peter couldn't be disturbed to help them because he was studying, but Johnny saw him reading comics on his bed as he worked outside the older boy's bedroom window.

There was a flurry of activity on the day of Bridie's arrival. Mrs Mulligan wrung the neck of a brown hen and sent Johnny to the local shop to buy a half-pound of currants for a tea cake. Johnny remembered Aunt Bridie from the last time she came, and he wasn't looking forward to her return.

When Aunt Bridie's hackney car pulled up, everyone gathered on the front step, and Peter ran out to greet his mother. Her face was thin and pinched under her plain scarf, and her bony frame was discernible even under a buttoned tweed coat.

She held Peter a little away from her, looking him up and down with approval, then pecked him on the cheek. She and the driver lifted a new Raleigh bicycle from the car boot. It was shiny black with a red stripe and had a black carrier on the back. Johnny gasped as she gave it to Peter. He had never dreamed that such a treasure could be given to a boy.

He watched, sick with envy and longing, as Peter rode it up and down Murphystown Road all that day.

'Don't let those little hooligans on the road use that bike!' Bridie warned.

The bike was brought into the kitchen that night for safekeeping, and Johnny devoured it with his eyes. He had never wanted something so much in his life. He gazed at it in wonderment until a sharp whack across the legs from the old man's stick broke his reverie.

'You keep your dirty mitts off that!' Mr Mulligan snapped.

Johnny's face reddened as everyone glared at him accusingly, and George sniggered.

That night, Johnny lay beside George, too upset to sleep. He listened to the laughter of Peter and the adults in the kitchen. He wondered why his mam and dad didn't like him. What was he doing wrong? They kept telling him he was a bad boy, and that he was ungrateful, but he didn't mean to be. He resolved to try harder. He would be so good that they'd like him too, and he fell asleep dreaming of the day when he'd get his own shiny new Raleigh bicycle.

But the next morning Aunt Bridie raged at Johnny and George in the yard. 'You're a right pair of useless urchins! You've let the place go to rack and ruin. Neither of you is setting foot under this roof again until every weed in that field is cleared! Do you hear me? You'll sleep in that field until it's done!'

Johnny started by pulling up the weeds between the broken paving in the yard. George went to the far corner of the field, out of sight of the Mulligans' kitchen window, where he sat with his back against the beech tree, scraping the soil idly with a twig.

The cat appeared, hunching her back into a high arc, winding her way around Johnny's bare legs. The white and ginger creature often followed him as he worked around the smallholding. He loved Kitty and considered her his pet, and Mrs Mulligan sometimes let him bring her saucers of milk when Mr Mulligan wasn't looking.

Johnny laughed as Kitty chased after the trailing ivy

he pulled off the wall in the yard. When she tired of the game, she sprang onto the yard wall to clean her ears and whiskers.

Johnny had to work hard to finish cleaning the field. By late afternoon, he was very hungry and tired, but he looked with satisfaction at the vast pile of brambles and weeds for burning. He felt proud of his work. At teatime he turned back to the cottage. George scrambled to his feet and followed him.

Aunt Bridie opened the back door, but her lips were thin and puckered with disapproval. 'What did you do this morning?' she demanded, staring at Johnny.

Johnny was confused. 'I weeded the back, Aunt Bridie.'

'Liar!' she said, and slapped him across the face with the flat of her palm.

Johnny raised a hand in shock to his stinging face.

'What were you doing out here this morning?' she roared, her face now twisted with rage.

He was terrified and had no idea why she was attacking him. He could see George, shuffling backwards, retreating a safe distance.

'I weeded, like you told me!' Johnny wailed.

She clattered him hard across the head, leaving him staggering backwards with the blow.

Old Mulligan nodded appreciatively behind her. 'It's time someone put manners on those pups!' he said.

Bridie's eyes glittered with malice as she stared at Johnny. 'You are a bloody little liar, do you hear me? A bloody little liar!' she yelled, grabbing Johnny by the ear.

'I saw what you were doing. You were playing with that bloody cat instead of doing what you were told.'

She smacked him hard again and again on his head and across his face, but he twisted free of her clutches and fled, running for the road around the front of the house.

He was devastated. Like most children, he had a natural instinct for justice, and the unfairness of what had happened weighed heavily on him. He tried to earn the same love and attention that Peter got, but whatever he did, he was beaten. He wanted to run far away and never come back.

He tore down Murphystown Road until, blinded by tears, he tripped over the broken kerb around the bus stop. He landed heavily in the dirt, skinning his knees. He bawled even more then, but he didn't care any more. He continued to howl until a woman's voice spoke.

'Do you need help, little boy?' he heard her say.

He lifted his face from the ground, blinking hard to clear his vision. He recognised the woman as Miss Digby-French, the daughter of the local Church of Ireland clergyman. Old Mulligan used to say that she was 'very lah-di-dah for an oul spinster of thirty'.

Johnny felt ashamed then for lying on the ground like a baby, and he struggled to his feet, gulping down his sobs. He dragged the sleeve of his jumper across his wet face. He stole a timid glance at the lady's beige swing coat, her shiny chestnut curls and her blue hat before he lowered his lashes to stare at his boots.

She opened her handbag, took out a white handkerchief

and dabbed Johnny's wet cheeks. Then she licked a corner of the hanky and crouched down to wipe his scratched and bleeding knees. She smiled at him. 'Now, that's a bit better, isn't it?' she said. 'Do you want to tell me why you're crying?'

Even through his sobs, he could hear that she spoke differently from anyone else he knew.

'I played with the cat,' he blubbered.

'What's wrong with playing with the cat?'

'I was supposed to be weedin' the back.'

'I'm sure it's okay to play with the cat for a while,' she said. 'You did some weeding too, didn't you?'

He hiccuped and nodded, his tearful eyes still downcast.

'There, you see, you're a good boy really, aren't you?'

He nodded again, with another hiccup.

'Why don't you keep me company until the bus comes? My name is Miss French, and I live just over there.'

She indicated the pretty two-storey country house called Ashton Lodge just down the road. It had Georgian-paned windows and a well-tended rose garden in front. Johnny had been to the back door of Ashton Lodge many times collecting slops from the housekeeper.

'What's your name?' she asked.

'John Cameron, Miss.'

'I'm very pleased to meet you, John Cameron,' she said, standing up. Peeling off a white glove, she extended an elegant hand to shake his filthy one. 'Maybe you'll come to visit me some time, and we can be friends.'

He nodded shyly. He thought she was very pretty, and he

liked how she stroked his hair before boarding the bus. He touched his hair after the bus pulled away, and he hoped he'd see Miss French again.

He didn't go home again until after dark, when Aunt Bridie gave him another clatter across his head and sent him straight to bed.

It was later that week, as Johnny was collecting slops on the road, when he saw Miss French again, standing at her garden gate.

'Would you like to come in for tea, John?' she asked.

Johnny blushed fiercely, but he carefully placed the slops bucket inside the gate. He hoped Miss French wouldn't notice his dirty feet as he followed her into the house.

The boy glanced around at his surroundings. He saw gleaming dark wood floors and a graceful banister, which curved invitingly to the top of the stairs.

Johnny followed Miss French through an open door. A burnished mahogany piano stood close to flowing claret velvet curtains, which framed the windows. A log fire blazed in a white marble fireplace. An elderly man was sitting in a winged armchair, peering at them over a corner of his newspaper.

'Father, I'm pleased to introduce Mr John Cameron, who lives with the Mulligan family,' she said. She sounded, Johnny thought, as if she were introducing royalty.

'John, this is my father, the Reverend Arthur Digby-French, but you can call him Mr French.'

'Very pleased to meet you, young man,' said the minister, then turned to his daughter. 'Eleanor, darling, please forgive me if I don't join you both for tea, but I'm feeling the cold in my bones today. I'm going to stay by the fire until your mother comes home.'

The old man seemed pleasant enough, but Johnny was still glad that he was staying where he was.

Miss French led him along a hall lined with gilt-framed paintings, then down a few steps into a large kitchen with a flagstone floor. A fire burned in an open grate, and the dressers were full of pretty china. A long kitchen table and a dozen lath-back chairs dominated the room.

She indicated for Johnny to sit at the table. As she filled the kettle and rinsed the teapot, she enquired after the health of the Mulligans and asked him about school. She sawed off two thick slabs of warm bread from a loaf that was cooling on a rack and plastered them with butter and jam. Johnny was so distracted by the aroma of home-made bread and the sight of the strawberry jam that he found it difficult to answer her questions.

The combination of warm, fresh bread, creamy butter and sweet strawberry jam was like nothing he had tasted before. He didn't remember ever having such a treat.

He was also in awe of the elegant lady sitting across the table from him, leaning in, smiling, as he tried to steal a glance under his lowered lashes. No adult had ever spent so much time talking to him, and no one had spoken as kindly to him before. Johnny thought it must be the best day of his life.

As he left, Miss French insisted that he must call again, and Johnny smiled with shy delight.

After that day, he dawdled every time he passed her gate in the hope she might invite him in, and he ran to her every time he saw her. The weeks turned into months and Miss French never seemed to grow tired of him. He marvelled that she never scolded or hit him.

'That's my John!' she'd say in delight if he did anything at all, like clear his plate from the table. 'You're such a smart boy,' she'd tell him.

Until then, he'd believed he was stupid because that was what everyone told him.

She gave him the only present he had ever received in his young life: a small stainless-steel harmonica. He treasured that harmonica, which he kept buried deep in his pocket. He took it out only to play when he was sure that no one who might take it from him was around.

Being with Miss French made Johnny feel like he could be somebody. He was too shy to say so, but he thought she was like a magical princess or someone from the stories that the master sometimes read to them at school.

She was like his own fairy godmother, living across the road.

I dread to think what my life would have been like if Miss French hadn't taken me under her wing. My very survival might have depended on her. Apart from Mr and Mrs Kavanagh, she was the only adult to show me kindness as a child and the only one to lavish attention on me.

A cursory background check would have told the authorities that the Mulligans were eminently unsuitable foster parents. Mr Mulligan was fined several times in the Petty Sessions Courts, at least once for assault on a neighbour, and another for drunkenness or 'riotous drinking'. He was also taken to court several times for the non-attendance of his children at school for up to forty-one days at a time. The 1911 census lists Thomas Mulligan as illiterate, so he probably hadn't had much of a childhood himself, but he could never have been described as decent foster-father material.

I think his wife, Margaret Mulligan, was a kinder person. I didn't live in fear of her, but she didn't intervene when her husband beat us. In hindsight, she had had a tough life too and was a victim of her husband's foul temper as much as we were. Whatever few shillings she made taking in foster children old Mulligan squandered on drink, so she must have struggled to keep any food on the table.

I have one vivid recollection of her holding my hand as we were going to Mass on a Christmas morning. That this sticks in my mind suggests that such demonstrations of affection were rare.

4

Artane

Johnny suspected that something was afoot on the morning he was told to stay home from school. It was a grey, overcast Wednesday, and he knew it was odd that George was sent to school and he wasn't. He thought, at first, that they were keeping him home to work in the fields, but Mrs Mulligan insisted that he stay in the house. He knew he'd get a clatter if he asked why, so he shelled the peas, scrubbed the potatoes, washed dishes and said nothing.

Around midday Johnny heard the rumble of a car on the road and ran to the front door to see it go by. It was unusual to see a car at all, so his heart raced with excitement when the big, shiny vehicle stopped outside the cottage. He watched, enthralled, as two tall men in dark coats emerged from it.

The neighbours were already peering out of their doors along the country road, watching the strangers and their grand motor outside the Mulligans' place. As the men approached the front door, Johnny ran back to Mrs Mulligan as she hurriedly stripped off her dirty apron. 'There's visitors in a big car!' he said, breathless, and with eyes wide with amazement.

He followed Mrs Mulligan as she opened the door, and when he saw the white collar, he realised that one man was a priest. Johnny felt alarm when Mrs Mulligan suddenly caught him by his sleeve and dragged him in front of her. He looked up at the two men towering above him.

'He's all ready for you, Brother,' said Mrs Mulligan, addressing the priest.

'We'll look after him from here. Thank you, Mrs Mulligan.'

The man in the collar placed two firm gloved hands on Johnny's shoulders and steered him down the narrow clay path behind the other man. Johnny looked back over his shoulder to see Mrs Mulligan standing at the open door.

'Mam! Mam!' he called, stricken with terror.

He struggled to look around again and pleaded to Mrs Mulligan with frantic eyes, but she stood there, expressionless.

'No nonsense now, boy. Get in and sit quiet,' the priest said, as he bundled Johnny into the red leather seat behind the driver.

Johnny's heart hammered in his chest when the man slammed the car door behind him. A wave of nausea rose in his stomach. As the motor pulled off, Johnny strained his neck around in time to see Mrs Mulligan disappear into the cottage. She hadn't looked back.

Johnny slid down into the furthest corner of the red leather seats. He didn't know where he was going, and he didn't dare ask. He had never been in a car before, so it should have been a thrill, but a ball of fear was lodged in his throat, so big and hard that it threatened to choke him.

The men talked between themselves in the front seat, but neither of them addressed Johnny. Everything passed in a blur, and the boy absorbed none of the sights or sounds of the long journey. Who were these strange men, and where were they taking him?

They drove for a long time before the car came to a stop outside a pair of enormous iron gates. The driver blew the horn. A man appeared, squinted through the window and saluted the men with a wave of recognition. He drew open the gates, and the car proceeded down a long drive before it stopped in front of the largest building Johnny had ever seen. With its towering four-storey façade, it looked grim and forbidding. Straight away, Johnny was even more fearful than before.

The priest left the car, walked up a flight of steps to the main door, and the imposing building swallowed him into its darkness. The driver got out then too, and opened the door beside Johnny.

'Here we are, son. This is your stop.'

Johnny cowered in the seat. He didn't want to get out, but the driver held out an insistent hand. Johnny slid out of the car, holding it.

The man led him through a tall gate, and Johnny was stunned by the wall of sound that greeted him. Hordes of children milled around a vast concrete yard. The shrieks and shouts bounced off the walls, and Johnny was riveted to the spot in shock. Hundreds of children sprinted, ambled and idled everywhere in that huge pen. He had never seen so many people in one space before.

Almost all the boys had identical crew-cuts with fringes, and they wore the same rust-brown jackets and short trousers, with long black socks and hobnailed boots. He saw priests, so many priests, in black cassocks standing like sentries around the walls.

Johnny's knees trembled when a knot of smaller kids noticed him. They nudged each other and pointed in his direction. The ringleader picked up their football and, tucking it under his arm, he and his playmates approached. Johnny looked over his shoulder. The driver was gone, and the gate was shut. He had never felt so alone, even though he was surrounded by a circle of curious eyes.

'Wheraya from?' the ringleader demanded suspiciously.

'Murphystown.'

'Where's that?'

'Dunno.'

'Are ya a bogtrotter?'

'What's a bogtrotter?'

'Jayz, he doesn't know what a bogtrotter is! He must be one so!'

The little gang brayed with laughter before the interrogation continued.

'D'ya have a ma?'

'Yeh.'

'Did she give you any sweets?'

'No.'

'Whass in yer pockets?'

Johnny's hand moved protectively towards the harmonica. It was his only possession in the world.

But then a bigger boy barged through the knot of boys surrounding him and shoved aside the ringleader. 'Beat it, you lot!' he said. 'Tommo, get lost, or you'll find yourself on another charge.'

The lads sloped away, glancing back darkly at the older boy. He had a crew-cut, like the others, and a thin face, a narrow, pointed nose and blue shadows under his eyes. He wore the same shorts, jacket and grey shirt as every other boy.

'Okay, your name's Cameron, right?' he said, his nose lifting slightly, as he officiously checked a sheet of paper in his hand. Johnny nodded in silent assent.

'You're to come with me. My name's Tinny, and I'm a monitor. The Brothers said to get you registered and bring you around. I need a slash, so I'll show you the jacks first.'

He led Johnny around the high concrete wall of the handball alley where about thirty buckets stood in a line. It was a cold afternoon, but the buckets were nearly all full, and the stench was overpowering. Tinny saw Johnny's face wrinkle. 'You think it's bad now, wait till the summer.' He snorted.

Johnny had so many questions, but he didn't dare ask any. He mutely followed Tinny into the forbidding building.

He felt small that day, but the immense space inside made him feel even smaller. The ceilings towered far above his head, and the sound of Tinny's boots striking the brown tiles vibrated around them.

The grey light outside streamed through tall paned windows, yet there was a distinct chill in the air. Johnny was wearing his grey school jumper, but he could feel goose bumps on his arms, and he could hear the hollow sounds of distant voices echoing like ghosts through the place.

Tinny led him to an open door and presented his sheet of paper to the man seated at a desk inside. 'Right, let's get you registered, son,' the man said, opening a leather-bound book and drawing his finger down the lines in it. 'You are, let's see . . . John Cameron,' he said. 'Do you know your date of birth, son?'

'September the ninth, 1935,' Johnny replied. He'd learned it from the master at school.

'That's right. Here you are. Your number is one-one-nine-six-three. Now repeat that after me and memorise it. It's important to know your number. They'll get very angry with you here if you don't know it.'

'One-one-nine-six-three, sir,' Johnny parroted.

'Good lad, keep saying it to yourself, so you don't forget it.'

The man handed Tinny a note. 'Take him to the storeroom

first, and then show him his bed,' he said. 'Make sure you get him to the infirmary before the doctor leaves at four. Tell the doctor we need his medical report.'

Johnny muttered 11963 over and over to himself as Tinny led him down a warren of corridors to the storeroom, which was lined with shelves piled high with clothes.

A small grey man in black robes sat inside the door at a big oak desk, which bore a stack of ledgers, a jam-jar of pens and several orderly piles of papers. He scrutinised Johnny. 'Number, please.'

'One-one-nine-six-three, Father.'

'There are no "fathers" here, little boy. You address us as "Brother" or "sir",' he said, sternly.

He turned to an open ledger on his desk, and began taking notes. 'Name, please?'

'John Cameron.'

'Age?'

'Eight, sir.'

He looked at Johnny. 'You're a small lad for your age, aren't you?' He moved around different shelves, collecting a pile of brown garments and topping them with a pair of hobnailed black boots. 'Hand over the clothes you're wearing and get dressed in these,' he said. Johnny wondered why he had to change his clothes, but he did as he was told. The new shorts felt as bristly as his old ones.

He followed the older boy up endless flights of stairs, and finally blurted out the question that was screaming in his head. 'Tinny, where am I? When can I go home?'

The older boy turned to him, his expression twisted in scorn. 'You don't even know where you are? This is Artane Industrial School.'

Johnny gasped in confusion. 'But I have a school.'

'This is your school now.'

Johnny was still bewildered, and his sense of panic grew. 'What time do I go home?'

'What are you on about, eejit? You don't go home. No one goes home.'

Tears welled in Johnny's eyes, and his stomach lurched. He felt sick, but he had nothing to vomit, only that empty feeling in his gut.

He didn't understand, but he didn't trust himself to ask another question without crying. Why had Mam let the men take him away? He knew he must have done something really bad this time.

For many decades, as soon as children turned eight, they were eligible to be sent to any of the dozens of industrial schools around Ireland.

By law, a dependant of the state had to be accused of an offence before he or she could be detained in one of these child prisons. The process of detaining a child began with a court application made by the gardaí or a charity, like the National Society for the Prevention of Cruelty to Children (NSPCC).

In my case, the applicant was a Rose Clancy of 52 Southern Cross Avenue in Inchicore. To this day, I have no idea who she was, but she presumably worked for one of the so-called children's 'protection' societies.

By law, the child was also supposed to be brought before the court and a judge. I have a vivid recollection of the day I was taken from my foster home, so I know I never went to court. The paperwork says that by order of Justice McCarthy of the Children's Court in Dublin, I was detained in Artane on 29 March 1944, until I reached my sixteenth birthday.

The system of detention suited the government and the Christian Brothers. The more children the Brothers had in their care, the more payment they received from the government. For the Christian Brothers, every boy detained in their institutions meant another 'headage payment' – a grant from the Department of Education and from the relevant Health Board. For the government, industrial schools were an efficient and cheap way to wash their hands of unwanted children or children whose parents struggled to feed or care for them.

It was a common belief that the children in industrial schools were juvenile delinquents and troublemakers. Yet, according to the Ryan Report, only 8 per cent of the 3,685 children sent to Artane between 1940 and 1969 were there for any 'criminal' offences. The vast majority were sent away for 'improper guardianship', which mostly meant that their families were too poor to keep them. The rest of the time, they were children like me, imprisoned for the crime of having no family at all.

5

Trapped

The Brother stared down his nose at Johnny. He had thick brown hair, a long face, and his belly protruded from under his black cassock. Johnny eyed the long leather strap hanging from his waistband.

'So what have we here? A new recruit?'

'Yes, sir.'

'Do you play any music or sport, little man?'

'Football, sir.'

'Football, is it? Not soccer, I hope.'

Johnny shook his head in earnest, even though he didn't know why.

'Good, because we don't have any foreign sports here.'

The Brother looked at Johnny more intently then, his

eyes boring into him. 'Have you anybody out there, boy?' he asked, tilting his head to one side.

Johnny was confused. 'Anybody out there?'

'Yes. A mother or a father,' the Brother replied testily. 'Family who'll be visiting.'

'My mammy and daddy are in Murphystown, and so is Miss French.'

The Brother stared hard at him, so Johnny lowered his eyes to meet that leather strap. 'Don't let me keep you, boys,' the Brother drawled, then clasped his hands behind his back and sashayed down the corridor.

Tinny waited till he was well out of earshot. 'That's Joe Boy, Brother Joseph. Better stay out of his way.'

Tinny led Johnny to a vast room filled with more beds than Johnny had ever thought possible in one place. There must have been ten long straight lines of dozens of beds running through the room. Each iron footboard was lined up against the next bed's head-post.

'This is Dormo Five,' said Tinny, consulting the scribbled note from the clerk. He went down through the rows of beds. 'Your bed is row three, twenty-three down. Here you are. This is the way it must be left every morning. And don't be a baby and wet it. They'll kill you for that here.'

The taut white sheet and the rigid grey wool blanket tucked over it was grander than he was used to, but Johnny yearned to get back to his old straw bed with sack covers. Everything about this place seemed terrifyingly enormous after years living in a tumbledown two-bedroom cottage.

Tinny led the way through a warren of corridors until

they reached a long bright room lined on both sides by beds filled with boys. Their heads popped up as they craned to see who was at the door.

'The infirmary,' whispered Tinny.

A man in a thick wool suit was rummaging distractedly among a stack of papers at his desk, but a nurse in a starched white uniform paused as she folded a pile of laundered sheets. 'What is it?' she sighed.

'The office has sent a new boy,' said Tinny, hurriedly handing over his sheet of paper. 'They need his medical report.'

'Another one?' groaned the doctor, throwing a disinterested glance over his spectacles at Johnny.

The nurse steered Johnny to the wall against a measuring stick. 'Three foot, ten and a half inches,' she intoned, as the doctor began jotting notes. 'Step on the scales,' she said, prodding a finger in Johnny's back. 'Let's see . . . Three stone, thirteen pounds, Doctor.'

'Come over here to me, John Cameron,' said the doctor, a heavy-set man with receding black hair. He looked Johnny up and down. 'Hmm, slight frame, blue eyes and light hair,' he said, as he scribbled in his book.

He pinched Johnny's nose between his forefingers. 'Dry nose,' he said, noting it down. 'What age are you, John, and where are you from?'

'I'm eight, and I'm from Murphystown, sir.'

'Slight lisp,' said the doctor, scribbling again. 'Open your mouth like a good boy.' He looked inside. 'Your tonsils look fine, but your teeth need seeing to. Make a note for him to see the dentist, Nurse.'

The doctor looked into Johnny's ears and listened to his chest with a stethoscope. 'All done. You can go now,' he said, and the nurse ushered Johnny out the door.

In the hall they saw a Brother, arm outstretched, gripping a boy by the throat. The little lad's legs were thrashing mid-air, and his hands were twisting ineffectively at the Brother's hand, trying to free his neck.

The man flung the child to the wall, and he fell, coughing and gasping for breath. The Brother stormed down the hall in Johnny and Tinny's direction. The boys kept their heads down as he passed, cassock billowing, hard-soled brogues cracking off the tiles. Johnny looked at Tinny in fear, but Tinny just told him to hurry.

'It's almost time for yard assembly,' he said. 'You're in Division Sixteen. Stay at the back and do what everyone else does. Lift your knees, stamp your feet and march.'

They arrived in the yard as hundreds of boys hurriedly arranged themselves in lines.

Tinny hissed: 'Don't mess it up. Driller the Killer goes mental if you don't stay in line.'

The Brothers roared and shouted as the boys ran in every direction.

'Fall in, fall in or face the wall!' bellowed a Brother, as another blew an ear-piercing whistle.

Tinny shoved Johnny into a line.

'Starting Divisions Fifteen, Sixteen, forward march! Left, left, left, right, left . . .' bawled a drill sergeant, in a soutane. As soon as the boy in front of him moved, Johnny followed.

'Lift your boots, swing your arms,' urged Tinny, out of

the corner of his mouth as he marched in step beside the pint-sized army.

'Divisions Thirteen, Fourteen, forward march! Left, left, left, right, left . . .'

The Brothers stood around, cuffing and whipping boys who were out of step, and Johnny's heart began to race.

When the marching stopped, Johnny realised he was in a chapel. It took twenty minutes of evening prayers and a decade of the rosary before his pounding heart began to slow. Then the marching began again.

'It's teatime,' said Tinny, and Johnny's spirits lifted unexpectedly. Tea. He hadn't eaten all day.

Johnny was overwhelmed by the vastness of the hall he entered. More than sixty metres long, its high truss roof accentuated its enormity. It was filled with more than forty tables, each accommodating twenty boys. The refectory of Artane Industrial School was designed to feed all 830 inmates in one sitting.

Tinny shoved Johnny into a line of boys standing in silence at the table. Once the sound of marching boots stopped, the Brother at the top of the room led the grace.

'Amen,' the boys replied in unison, blessing themselves.

'Fall out!' the Brother ordered.

A noise bomb exploded as all 830 boys talked and yelled at once, tugged and dragged benches and tables, which scraped noisily across the wooden floor. Everyone clambered to get a seat and grab a tin plate on the table.

There was shoving and fooling as kitchen hands moved up the tables pouring sweetened milky tea from big kettles into mugs. Other kitchen hands, boys in their apprentice year, doled out a single bread loaf and a dish of warm dripping between every four boys.

The lad opposite Johnny grabbed the loaf first and hacked off almost half with a serrated knife. He held his hunk in a vice-like grip before passing the rest of the loaf to his friend, who tore off a big slice too.

'Hey, gimme the yang, you greedy hoor,' yelled the boy beside Johnny, wrestling the bread from the second boy's hand. He took most of the last piece, leaving a thin crust on the table. 'That's for you, new boy!' he said, laughing before he eyed the mug of tea in Johnny's hand. 'Gis your slash if you're not drinkin' it.'

Johnny gripped the mug of lukewarm tea, mopped up the last of the dripping in the bowl with his bread and stuffed it into his mouth in one go. He would soon learn that gnawing hunger was part of the regime at Artane. Every day at midday, the boys were served two ladles of potatoes and vegetables in a gravy they called 'slurry'. They got meat on Sundays, usually a slice of corned beef, with a piece of bread. Mostly it was a diet of bread and dripping for breakfast and tea.

Everyone complained about the hunger and the terrible food, but Johnny knew what it was like to go without anything and not to know when he'd eat again. The food was tasteless, nutritionally poor, and there was never enough of it, but they were fed three times a day. After the years of starvation with the Mulligans, Johnny never complained about the food at Artane.

Sometimes he even appreciated the Artane regimentation and military-style routine. It barely changed, and there was a certain comfort in knowing what to expect all the time.

Dinner that first night was filled with boys bickering and fighting over the bread. Then they began wandering in and out of the hall, playing marbles or cards and using the latrines behind the handball alley. But at 8.30 p.m., the sound of a bugle told them it was time to fall into line again. The sound of boots marching in unison on the tiles filled the air as they moved in military formation to the dormitories.

Johnny reached his bed, his heart banging with the effort of keeping up with the boys around him. He eyed a tall, lean Brother with oiled black hair standing by the altar in the room.

'Oh, Jayz,' a boy behind him muttered under his breath. 'Not bloody Bones again.'

The Brother's chin jerked up, and his dark eyes settled on the boy who had spoken. 'Face the wall, O'Dwyer!'

O'Dwyer grimaced as he joined two other boys facing the wall, their arms extended high and straight over their heads.

Following the other boys' lead, Johnny changed into the nightshirt stored under his pillow. He folded his clothes, placing them neatly by his boots under the head of his bed. All this was done in complete silence. Everyone knelt by their beds, and all 150 boys in the room recited their night prayers along with Brother Kevin.

'Lights out!' ordered the Brother, and someone flicked a switch that plunged the dormitory into darkness. When his eyes adjusted, Johnny saw the glow of a light from the stairwell. He got in under the blanket, curled into a tight ball and did his best not to cry.

What was he doing here? How long was he here for? Where were Mam and Dad, and why did they let them take him away? Did he do something bold? Would anyone tell Georgie and Miss French that he was here? Fear and homesickness stuck in his throat.

Johnny felt, rather than saw, a Brother's shadow in the instant before he was violently yanked from his bed. He found himself dangling in mid-air with the Brother who had led the prayers gripping him by the collar of his nightshirt.

'What are you doing, you little piece of filth?' he roared into Johnny's petrified face. Johnny could see the hair tufts in his nostrils as the man's face loomed into his.

He tried to jerk free, but the man had him tightly, and he clattered Johnny across the head with his free hand.

The boy cried out in wild-eyed terror.

The Brother's eyes were black in the darkness and Johnny was close enough to smell stale tobacco on his breath.

A voice called in the darkness: 'He's a new boy, Brother Kevin. He only just got here.'

'Shut your mouth!' the Brother barked, his head jerking from Johnny to stare into the darkness. He scrutinised

Johnny's face once more before he dropped him to the floor. 'I'm feeling generous, boy,' he said. 'You get one chance. You lie with your arms crossed over the blankets, like you're supposed to. I'll be watching you.'

Trembling with shock, Johnny scrambled back under the blankets and, glancing at his neighbour, crossed his arms over the bedclothes. He had been in the place only a few hours, but he knew he wanted to get out of it.

That night he heard the crack of leather on naked skin and listened to the screams of O'Dwyer and the other boys being lashed in the hall. Other strange cries and sounds rang out through the place. He slid down as far under the bedclothes as his folded arms allowed.

Despite the lump in his throat, he swallowed his sobs, but nothing could stop the tears from rolling down his face.

For a long time, I dreamed of getting away from the Mulligans, and then, when I was eight, my dream came true, and strangers took me away in a big black car. Well, they always tell you to be careful what you wish for, don't they? I wasn't to know as the car wound down Murphystown Road that I was on my way to one of the most feared and reviled institutions in the country. Nor did I know that it would be nearly half a century before I saw my best friend again.

It happened at a twenty-fifth wedding anniversary party at the old Mountain View House in Stepaside, County Dublin. As I watched the band perform, I thought I saw a familiar face. I looked once, and I looked again. The face reminded me of him. I stared hard. Could anyone recognise a childhood pal after fifty years? But the more I looked, the more I was convinced. The man on the drums was my old best friend, Georgie Kavanagh, from down the road in Murphystown.

'You remember I told you about my best friend as a kid in Murphystown?' I said to my wife. 'I think that's him playing the drums.'

'Really? Why don't you go over and say hello?'

'Sure, he wouldn't know who the hell I am.'

'You remember him, why wouldn't he remember you? Go over and say hello.'

I know my wife well enough to recognise she doesn't give up. So, during a break in the music, I approached one of the few pleasant memories from my childhood.

'Hello again, Georgie Kavanagh,' I said. 'You probably won't remember me.'

Georgie stared wide-eyed at the ghost from his past. 'Oh, my God!' he said. 'Johnny Cameron. I thought you were dead!'

6

First Days in Artane

Johnny woke with a fright to the loud clanging of a bell. The raucous clash of metal on metal triggered a flurry of panicked activity in the dormitory. Boys scrambled from their beds and started tugging, then tucking the bedclothes into taut lines as the Brothers raised the urgency levels of the morning call by howling orders through the halls.

'Six o'clock, rise and shine. Last out faces the wall!'

'Time to start scrubbing, ye dirty pups.'

Johnny followed the bare-legged stampede to the washroom at the end of the corridor and joined in the frenzy. Boys snatched toothbrushes from the next boys' mouths, and carbolic soap flew down a line of washbasins.

They splashed ice-cold water over their faces and fought tugs-of-war over wet towels.

Yelps and screams followed the progress of Brother Kevin and another Brother as they moved down the aisles of basins, idly lashing boys with their leathers as they went.

'Move it! Move it, or by God, I'll thrash the life outta ye!' Brother Kevin yelled.

Johnny's pulse raced as he tried to keep up with the alarming furore around him. The boys had only minutes to scrub themselves before they charged back to the dormitory where, frantically, they dressed and finished making their beds. Then they stood to attention as Brother Kevin thundered down the dormitory at speed, inspecting the boys' work and clattering the occasional child as he went.

'Straighten that sheet, *amadán*!'

'Pull up those socks, O'Neill. You must enjoy getting the back of my hand.'

Then the boys marched out again to the parade ground in a confusion of shrill whistles, a bugle, and Brothers roaring in the darkness.

Johnny fixed his eyes on a boy – a pale, freckled fellow – and did exactly as he did. The division marched around the high concrete wall of the handball alley where the combination of the pungent smell and his anxiety made him feel like retching.

The toilet visit was brief and frenzied, like everything that morning, and the Brothers barked at everyone to get back into their divisions.

'LET'S HEAR THOSE FEET . . . QUICK MARCH . . . SWING THOSE ARMS . . . LEFT, LEFT, LEFT, RIGHT, LEFT . . .

BOWYER, CORCORAN, I SEE YOU! YOU TWO PUPS, FACE THE WALL. I'LL PUT THE SMILE ON THE OTHER SIDE OF YOUR FACES LATER . . . SWING THOSE ARMS HIGH! . . . LEFT, LEFT, LEFT, RIGHT, LEFT . . .'

Johnny was disoriented, his limbs almost rigid with fear as he marched into yet another building. It was only when he stumbled into a pew and glanced around in the flickering candlelight that he realised they were in the chapel again.

Morning Mass began, and the steam of 830 boys' breath rose into the high, vaulted roof above them. The priest droned his way through the Latin Mass, and the chapel seemed a sanctuary of calm, compared to the terror Johnny had felt since they'd woken that morning.

Chapel services became a welcome break in the eternal scramble to meet the Brothers' exacting timetable. For those reasons alone, Johnny learned to cherish the twice-daily half-hour visits there. That morning, when the boys filed out in their divisions, the first rosy fingers of dawn streaked across the sky.

Breakfast was more bread and dripping, but this time, Johnny was faster and snatched his share of the loaf before the fellow beside him.

Then Tinny came for him again and led him to his classroom for his first day at school in Artane. Framed pictures of the Sacred Heart and the Virgin Mary, hanging from the picture rails, dominated the room; a map of the world peeled off one wall, and a blackboard stood on an easel inside the door.

Johnny tried to slide into one bench and then another, but none of the boys would make space. He glanced around, flustered and desperate, but then Brother McCarthy strolled in. The boys called him Snake because they said he was quiet but deadly when he struck. He was a small, lean man with tightly shorn grey hair over pale darting eyes and thin lips.

'What have we here, then?' he said, peering at Johnny. 'A new boy, is it?'

All the boys turned to Johnny, who blushed furiously. 'Yes, sir,' he said, in a low voice.

'Well, where are you from, boy?'

'Murphystown, sir.'

'Murphystown? A lovely little country boy we have here so! What's your name, boy?'

'John Cameron, sir.'

'Little Johnny from the country!' He smiled. 'Isn't that nice, everyone?'

The boys tittered.

'We have a tradition here with new boys, you know,' said the Brother, 'that they must get up and sing a song for the whole class.'

Johnny was a shy child, so the prospect of performing before a classroom full of strangers was almost as terrifying as Brother McCarthy. 'I don't know any songs, sir,' he said, in a barely audible whisper.

'Of course you do, boy!' said the Brother. 'Everyone knows a song. Now, what song are you going to sing for us?'

Johnny stared down at his shabby new boots.

'Hurry up, boy! We don't have all day. What are you going to sing for us?'

'I can sing "Hey Little Hen", sir,' Johnny volunteered at last.

'That's wonderful! Little Johnny from the country is going to sing a song about a chicken! How about that, class?'

The boys roared with appreciative laughter at the Brother's wit.

'Okay, little Johnny, hop up here,' the man instructed, patting his desk, 'and begin your performance.'

Johnny's cheeks burned red as he clambered onto the desk and stood up to sing in his reed-thin voice.

Hey little hen, when, when, when,
Will you lay me an egg for my tea?

He could see the boys in the class gleefully pointing at him and laughing; he gulped, trying to swallow the rising panic he felt. His tremulous voice was nearly a squeak now, as he stammered:

H-h-hey little hen, when, when, when
W-w-w-will you try to supply one for me?

Brother McCarthy's leather hit the desk with a loud wallop, and Johnny leaped with fright, causing the boys to laugh even more heartily.

'Sing up, boy. We can't hear you!' the Brother barked.

Tears welled in Johnny's eyes and he croaked louder, faster, stumbling through the words, desperate to reach the end of the verse and his humiliation.

G-g-g-get into your nest,
Do your little best,
Get it off your chest,
I can do the rest.
Hey little hen, when, when, when
W-w-w-will you lay me an egg for my tea?

Brother McCarthy gave a thin smile of satisfaction and a slow clap as Johnny stared down at the desk in shame.

'Oh, now, wasn't that marvellous, boys?' he said. 'Big *bualadh bos* for our chicken boy, Johnny! Move over there, lads, for our chicken boy. I think there's a roost for you down at the back of the class.'

For weeks afterwards, the boys taunted Johnny, flapping their elbows and chanting, 'Bok-bok-bok-baaaak!'

At eleven o'clock the bell rang, and the boys marched in silence to the parade ground where they stood still until they heard the roar 'FALL OUT!' The lines crumpled and the boys milled around, finding their friends, teams and cliques in the concrete square.

Johnny stood in the yard alone. He didn't know a soul except Tinny, who was with the other monitors. He felt sick with nerves and ached to escape this place and go home.

Instead, he moved to a quiet corner of the yard and tried to calm himself with his harmonica.

He had taught himself to play it, encouraged by Miss French's constant praise. He grew uneasy as the freckled boy he'd followed all that morning approached him. He was small and slight, with light eyelashes and eyebrows and translucent skin. He stood in front of Johnny, staring. 'What's that?' he asked.

Johnny lowered it from his lips and held it protectively behind his back. 'A harmonica.'

'Can I have a go?'

Johnny looked at him suspiciously.

'I won't take it or anything, I promise. I just want a go.'

Johnny reluctantly handed it to him.

The boy blew into it, and when the sound poured out, he beamed with delight. 'Teach me how to play!' he said.

Johnny showed him a few notes, and then, emboldened, asked the boy the question that was foremost on his mind. 'How long do we have to stay here?'

The boy shrugged. 'Dunno. Ages. Until we're big.'

Johnny's stomach swooped and sank. It was true, so. He wasn't going home. How long would it be until he was big?

'You can get out on visiting Sunday if you have a ma or da or a granny who comes for you,' the boy said. 'Do you have anyone?'

Johnny's hopes lifted. 'Yeah, I've got Mam and Dad, and I've got Miss French too.'

'You're lucky,' said the boy sadly.

Mam would visit him this Sunday, Johnny thought. Maybe she'd take him back if he promised her he'd be really good.

Johnny's new friend was called Noel Fish, and they met in the yard every break. Noel had another quiet friend, a loner named Patsy Flanagan. Taller than Johnny and Noel, he had dark eyes and hair.

Sometimes they played handball, or a game with pebbles called Jackstones. But mostly they played the harmonica and tried to avoid the attentions of the older bullies and the Brothers.

Within days, Johnny discovered that some of the children were gentle, soft-eyed, silent and lost. But others were hard, with a steely glint in their eyes, and hands that were quick to curl into fists. The hard lads, especially those from inner-city Dublin, were as much part of the reign of terror in Artane as the Brothers.

On most days, the Artane boys were left pretty much to their own devices on the parade ground, but if a full-scale fight broke out, the Brothers blew their whistles, and ran from every direction to weigh in with their boots and fists.

Despite the constant threat of violence, Johnny looked forward to getting into the parade ground. It was the nearest thing to freedom that the boys had, even though they were confined to a concrete yard. It was a break from the monotony and the incessant marching, silence and lessons.

In the classroom, Brother McCarthy seemed to vent much of his explosive temper on a boy in the second row. Green squinted a lot. His hair sat like a brown pudding bowl around his head, and he had a gap between his two front teeth that made him look villainous. But he was harmless, a dunce when it came to lessons, and McCarthy picked on the boy mercilessly. Maths class was always a trigger for his unpredictable violence.

'Come on, Green, you big thick. Stand up. Now answer me. What's seven times twelve? We've been through this before!' he yelled.

Brother McCarthy stood in front of Green, arms behind his back, rocking on his heels and looking up at the ceiling.

'Green, I've all day to wait for your answer. We're not moving on from this. So, come on now, you great big gobshite, what's seven times twelve?'

Green stood quivering in frozen silence. Brother McCarthy rocked on his heels. It was difficult to breathe in that room, it was so thick with tension. It was almost a relief when McCarthy's big hand swung out and smacked Green's head with a force that sent him tumbling on top of the boy beside him.

'Eighty-four, you great big thick, you! What is it, Green? Eighty-four!'

McCarthy started thrashing Green furiously, while the boy scrambled around the floor trying to escape the flailing leather.

'Repeat after me: seven times twelve is eighty-four. Repeat after me, eighty-four!'

But Green was too busy screaming from blow after blow.

Only when McCarthy was red in the face from exertion did he stop.

Later in the yard, the boys crowded around Green to inspect his injuries up close. His lip was swollen, and his left eye was closed with the battering. His nose was still bloody.

'I'm going to tell me da,' he said. 'Me da will visit next Sunday, and he'll kill McCarthy. He'll batter him, so he will. Me da says the Christian Brothers are nothin' but a shower of dirty feckin' bogtrotters.'

But Green's da didn't visit the next Sunday, and the boy was beaten by McCarthy many times more before his da came again.

Johnny, like Green, waited in the yard every visiting Sunday for weeks in the hope that his mother or Miss French would come and get him. He remained in the parade ground, hoping this would be the week that he was called to the gate. But no one ever came for him.

It's strange the things that stick in a person's mind. Performing 'Hey Little Hen' on my first day in Artane School is seared into my memory. The song is a cheery 1941 ditty, a British wartime classic made popular by Joe Loss and his Orchestra. Yet I have only to hear the opening bars of that song and my heart pounds with the same terror it did on that day nearly eighty years ago.

It sounds like such a minor event in the context of the brutality of Artane, but that childhood trauma remains as clear as yesterday to me. The cold eyes of the Brother, the scorn and laughter of the boys still haunt me to this day.

It was hard to make friends with the other boys in Artane.

There wasn't any bonding or camaraderie that I remember. Noel and Patsy were the closest to friends I had.

The Brothers' 'divide and conquer' methods worked, and we were all trying to survive. Anyone would 'rat out' another boy to a Brother or a monitor if they thought they could avoid a beating. When we saw a boy being beaten into the ground by a Christian Brother, all we felt was relief that it wasn't us.

The Brothers used an assortment of implements to torture and beat the boys. They had giant rulers, and wooden blackboard dusters that flew across the classrooms; they used fists, boots and hurling sticks in the parade ground. But their preferred instrument of torture was the leather strap that hung from each Brother's waistband. A trader from the bootmakers' shop in Artane said they made them to order. They used a filling of nails, keys, old coins, rusty washers or whatever took the Brothers' fancy. The metal was sandwiched between two lengths of black leather, which were then stitched roughly together. They were designed to rip open the skin and inflict as much pain as possible.

Those Christian Brothers never saw any incongruity between holding a Bible in one hand and a torture strap in the other.

7

The Good, the Bad and the Ugly

Johnny saw dozens of naked boys run as a herd into the shower block and, seconds later, heard a chorus of screams.

'The water's freezin' again,' a little lad whispered dolefully, his breath hanging on the icy air.

Johnny stood naked on the tiled floor, but he shook more from terror than from the cold. It was Saturday, 1 April 1944, three days after he had arrived, and he was having his first experience of Artane's 'shower day'.

The division ahead tumbled out of the showers into the hall. They scrambled into their clothes, with the Brothers still lashing at their nakedness.

Brother Moran, known as 'Ming', short for Ming the Merciless from the 'Flash Gordon' comic strip, ordered

Johnny's division forward. 'Move it! Last two of ye in gets six of the best on yeer backsides!'

Johnny joined the scramble through the doors to the showers. He did what everyone else did and snatched a sliver of carbolic soap from a shelf and a scrubbing brush off a hook and ran to an empty shower cubicle. He stood shivering, waiting for what was about to happen next.

An invisible hand turned on the water, and there was a collective screech as the burn of the icy water hit everyone. Any boy who instinctively leaped out of the shower jumped straight back in when he felt the lash of a Brother's leather. There was nothing so painful as a whipping on wet flesh.

'Scrub! Scrub! Scrub yeerselves clean, ye filthy yokes, or I'll use the leather to take the skin off ye meself,' roared Ming.

The icy water stung like needles, and Johnny had never felt so cold in his life. The muscles in his neck and shoulders contracted, and his arms stood out like rigid poles. There were so many goose pimples on his skin that he looked like a badly plucked fowl.

When they turned off the water, the race began again, and Johnny fumbled his buttons as he tried to dress and flee the floggings in the long hall. He came to dread Saturdays because of the showers.

As the weeks continued, and no one came, Johnny resigned himself to staying in Artane for a long time. He stopped waiting to be called to the gate on visiting Sundays. It was not a calm acceptance of his situation: it was more like losing all hope. After the shock of being taken from the only home he had ever known and those initial brutal days in Artane, he shut down, mentally and emotionally, and became more withdrawn. He was on his own, and no one was coming to help him.

The first few days in Artane were indelibly imprinted on his mind's eye but, after a while, the years stretched into a long, dark blur punctuated only by memories of the most violent events, which surpassed the normal, everyday brutality of the place. In a place where terror and violence were the fabric of life, only the worst episodes of savagery stuck in his mind.

Johnny learned that the dentist was another occasion of terror in Artane. Even the hard boys looked scared when they heard of his arrival in the school.

'What does the dentist do?' he asked one boy.

'He yanks out yer teeth with the pliers!' the boy replied with relish. 'There does be blood gushing out your mouth and all down your face.'

The boys queuing outside the infirmary visibly trembled as they listened to the agonised cries of those inside. Only a handful of lads swaggered out with beaming smiles after receiving a clean bill of health. Most staggered, marble-white with shock, trickles of blood running down either side of their mouths.

Johnny thought he was going to faint when the Brother called his name and shoved him through the infirmary door. He began sobbing when he was told to get into the high chair in the room.

'Open wide and none of your nonsense,' the supervising Brother ordered.

The dentist, a stern-faced man in a white coat, peered into his mouth and tapped his teeth with a metal implement. 'Three extractions here,' he said, turning to add a note into the ledger on his desk.

Johnny didn't know what 'extractions' meant, but he knew it wasn't good when the Brother got a firm hold of his shoulders.

Suddenly the dentist's hairy knuckles filled his mouth. He felt unbearable pain and immense pressure as the man's fist turned one way, then twisted the other. Johnny howled and kicked into fresh air. His heart hammered in his chest as he heard mechanical sounds of grinding and cracking in his head.

Then there was a 'pop', and a sudden release, and the dentist's fist left his mouth. The iron taste of blood filled his mouth instead. His lower jaw throbbed with pain, his throat watered, and he thought he was going to vomit.

'There now. Hardly worth all that fuss, was it?' said a nurse. She made him rinse with something that tasted like soap and spit it into a kidney-shaped metal dish.

But then they pushed him back into the chair, and the dentist's hairy arm loomed into his face, and he tasted his big knuckles again.

After the dentist had pulled out all three teeth, the Brother released Johnny. The boy's head spun, and his legs felt like jelly. He gripped the door jamb to stop himself sliding to the floor, and saw a sea of wide eyes and scared faces swimming around him. In a stupor of shock and pain, he tottered into the hallway, not knowing what he was doing.

'Less of the amateur dramatics, boy,' barked a Brother, who brought him to his senses with a smack to his head. 'Get back to your classroom!'

Even in the midst of Artane's monotonous brutality, there were rare days when joy could be found in the place, such as when the Brothers screened a film.

The first time he marched to the theatre room in the school, Johnny didn't know what to expect. From the reaction of the other boys, he knew this was a great treat, but he'd never seen a film before. As the Brothers set up the projector and the screen, the boys chattered with excitement. Everyone cheered and whooped when they switched off the lights, and the opening credits to the movie began.

And then, like magic, he saw the moving pictures and lost himself in the make-believe of Tinseltown. The world on the screen was rendered in black and white, but those films contained more colour, warmth and emotion than Johnny had ever experienced.

The films the Brothers screened were always a few years old, but that didn't matter to the boys. They watched westerns, like *Stagecoach* and *Billy the Kid*, and adventure films, like *The Mark of Zorro*.

On the days when his mind rode across the Wild West or flew on a rocket ship to Mars, he forgot the misery of Artane. Movies helped him imagine the possibilities that lay beyond the walls of the place and enabled him to dream.

Johnny also loved Sundays when the sky was clear, and the Brothers brought them for walks around the neighbourhood. They walked two by two, lines of boys snaking down the road, their hobnailed boots crunching on the concrete.

The boys were objects of curiosity and pity and sometimes even hostility as they made their way through Artane's countryside up to Coolock Village and back again in their poorhouse tweeds.

'Me feet are crucifyin' me,' Noel grumbled, as his ill-fitting boots clopped up and down, irritating his chilblains.

But Johnny loved those Sunday walks, mostly because they took him outside the walls of Artane.

The numbers in the school dwindled in August, when children with parents or guardians were allowed home for three weeks. Many Brothers took turns to return to their hometowns during that summer month. The first fine day they had in August, the Brothers marched several hundred boys to the wooden platform at Killester railway station where they caught the steam train to the beach.

Arriving at Portmarnock in their institutional tweeds, the boys would enjoy an annual treat of lemonade and buns. They would paddle in the sea, build sandcastles, fill moats, collect shells and torture crabs. Johnny loved it.

Shortly after entering the school, the Brothers had made him join the Artane Boys Choir. He was suspicious in the beginning, but soon he began to look forward to the rehearsals. The choir was led by an amiable man called George Quinn, whose gentle enthusiasm for the job made his class a pleasure.

But these highlights were rare. Mostly, Artane was, at best, cheerless and dreary, at worst brutal and terrifying. Johnny lived in a climate of fear where physical, mental and emotional abuse was an everyday occurrence.

'Facing the wall' was one of the Brothers' favourite forms of torture and psychological warfare. They left small offenders standing for hours, toes and nose tipping the wall, hands stretched straight over their heads, arm muscles cramping, hearts hammering in fear of the beating that was coming.

When Ming took over Johnny's classroom during his first year in Artane, Johnny endured one of his worst ever hidings. Ming wielded the leg of a chair as a weapon in the classroom. He liked to bang it on the narrow trestle desks or slap it menacingly into the palm of his hand as he sprang questions on his trembling pupils.

Johnny's stomach flipped one day when Ming jabbed him with the chair leg during an English lesson.

'What's your number, boy?' Ming demanded, out of the blue.

Johnny's mind turned blank with fear.

BANG! Johnny leaped as Ming whacked the desk in front of him.

'One-one—'

BANG! The brother's mad eyes narrowed in his meaty face, and Johnny saw his teeth visibly grinding.

'One-one-nine—'

This time, there was no warning. Ming lunged at Johnny,

dragging him over the desk by the hair and flinging him to the floor. He struck him again and again with the chair leg.

'No, sir! Stop, sir!' Johnny screamed, but Ming's inner psycho was released and couldn't be quelled.

Johnny curled into a tight ball to save himself, but this infuriated the Brother more, and the clubbing became even more violent. Johnny thought he was going to be killed. Beads of perspiration rolled down Ming's forehead, and his breath was ragged with the exertion before finally, exhausted, he lowered the chair leg.

A nail or splinter in the weapon had gouged flesh from Johnny's neck and back, and blood covered the floor. He was sent to the infirmary, where they bandaged up his wounds. Within days a septic tennis-ball-sized lump had appeared on the back of his neck, and Johnny was sent back to the infirmary. The nurse held him in a headlock as the doctor examined the wound.

'It'll have to be lanced,' he heard the doctor say.

They stripped him and plunged him into a tin bathtub filled with cold water. While the nurse pinned down his arms, the doctor cut open the wound with a knife.

Johnny screamed and struggled to break free of his torturers while the boys in the infirmary ward watched the gruesome procedure with open mouths. Johnny screamed again when the nurse poured the burning disinfectant, horse iodine, into the wound, and the doctor stitched up the opening with the help of her fierce grip.

The physical pain he endured in Artane was often almost unbearable, but Johnny soon learned that the Brothers could inflict other forms of pain that were far worse.

When I entered Artane in 1944, the Second World War was still raging across Europe. Meanwhile, the religious orders waged another kind of brutal warfare against the thousands of children in their care.

The medical records note that I was three foot ten and a half inches tall and spoke with a lisp when I arrived at the school. Yet within months a grown man, who carried the leg of a chair to beat children, had left me in a puddle of blood. It seems incredible, but it's true.

When I look back, I see that many of the Christian Brothers nurtured a complete disgust for the children in their care. To them, we were repellent creatures and they treated us little better than they would disease-ridden rats.

I recall two of the congregation who were different. Both were retired, and they were holy men, very good people. But they were an anomaly. The rest looked for any excuse to give us a battering.

My memories of that infirmary lancing were confirmed when, recently, my daughter Aileen applied for and received my medical files from the school. The event is recorded in a single line that reads 'Abscess in neck opened by Dr Masterson 21-8-44'.

The primary function of Artane infirmary was to avoid bringing boys to hospital and any intrusive questioning from the authorities. The Brothers didn't want word to spread about what was really happening in the place.

The dentist's arrival twice a year was another day of horrors for the children. The records show that on 2 May 1944, the dentist performed seventy-eight extractions, including three of my teeth. Some boys had five removed in one sitting without any anaesthetic or pain relief.

It was little wonder that some made a break for it during the Sunday walks. A few got away over the years, but most were brought back by the gardaí, and God help them when the Brothers got hold of them again.

The scars of the beating I received at the age of eight are still with me in my eighties. Each time I meet new home care nurses, they ask about the scar on my back. The once lurid red gash on my neck has faded to pink in recent decades, but its jagged ridges are still there today as a lasting memento of Artane. Yet the invisible scars the school inflicted run far deeper.

8

A Lifeline

'Cameron! Cameron! Letter for John Cameron!'

Johnny gawped at the monitor calling his name and waving the cream envelope in the air. He didn't quite believe it. He looked around the refectory as if expecting some other John Cameron to stake a claim to the letter.

'It's for you, dummy,' said Noel, giving him a shove.

Johnny scrambled to his feet, cheeks burning as he walked to the top of the hall to collect the only letter he had ever received in the year he'd been at Artane.

He checked the cream envelope, still suspecting a mistake, but it was addressed in an elegant looped hand to Mr John Cameron c/o The Christian Brothers School,

Artane. The Brothers monitored all correspondence to and from the boys, so the envelope was already open.

His hand shook as he pulled out and unfolded a crisp sheet of paper, but his heart lifted as his eyes scanned Miss French's address in the top right corner.

Greeting him as 'My dearest John', her brief letter told him that she was sorry she hadn't been able to contact him sooner, but she and her mother would call to visit him the following Sunday. 'We are so looking forward to seeing you again after all this time,' she wrote.

Johnny blinked to squeeze the tears from his eyes, so he could read that letter again and again. 'My dearest John.' Dearest. No one had ever called him that before.

In his early days at Artane Johnny had despaired when no one came to see him. He experienced an ache in his gut when he saw other boys being hugged by their parents and grandparents on visiting Sunday. He obsessed about all the reasons why the Mulligans and Miss French might have abandoned him. Maybe Mrs Mulligan had seen him fighting with the other foster boy, George. Maybe Miss French had got tired of him. He wished he could see them and ask them both for a second chance. If he could only see them again, he'd beg them to take him back, and he would never give them a reason to put him in this place again.

But as the weeks turned into months, all hope wilted. No one cared for him outside, and no one cared for him at Artane. He felt worthless. He had almost forgotten what happiness felt like when he received the letter from Miss French.

As he waited in the yard on visiting Sunday, he tried to smooth his hair and straighten his jacket. He peered through the gate, hoping to catch a glimpse of Mrs and Miss French as they came up the drive.

He was taken by surprise when Brother Doody collared him with his brown-stained fingers, then bent down so that his grizzled face was almost up against Johnny's. He could smell the Woodbines off the Brother's breath.

'You mind your manners around them fine ladies coming to see you, you hear me?' he warned in a low growl. 'And if I hear one word from them of you complaining about anything around here, I'll give you a hiding you won't forget. Are we clear on that, you little pup?'

Johnny nodded furiously.

All the boys knew they were never to complain about their treatment in Artane, and few ever did. The boys knew there would be terrible repercussions if the Brothers heard about such disloyalty, but they also suspected that no one would believe them. They were the dregs of society. People would always take the word of the men of God over that of 'delinquents' and 'bastards'.

Miss Eleanor French and her mother, Mrs Synolda French, arrived with big smiles, ham sandwiches and a quarter-pound bag of bullseyes. Johnny laughed and cried at the same time – he was so happy.

'My poor John,' said Miss French, clutching one of his hands in both of hers. She realised he was near hysterical. 'We're here now, but we would have been here months ago if we could,' she explained. 'We had to apply for permission to visit you because we're not related. It took much longer than we expected, and they wouldn't even deliver a letter to you in the meantime.'

After that first visit, Miss French returned every month or two. He knew he had to be patient because she lived a long way away. Besides, she ran the shop in Dublin Zoo and her busiest day was Sunday, which clashed with visiting Sundays.

Johnny didn't have to tell Miss French that he was desperately unhappy at Artane, but once he knew she was coming to visit, his spirits rose. He was too young to fully articulate it, but her visits were vital to him. She gave him a sense of hope in that place of despair. The Brothers' treatment of the boys told him that, to them, the children meant less than nothing, but Miss French's visits made him feel that he mattered. He knew she liked him, and for a child who felt unloved and unlovable, that meant a lot.

One day Miss French brought Johnny to Dublin Zoo on an outing, and paid a photographer to take his picture at the gates. Johnny marvelled at his tiny black-and-white likeness. Miss French got permission to take Johnny and Noel to the zoo another day and paid for a stamp-sized photograph of them riding a giant Indian elephant.

Sometimes Miss French couldn't take time off from her job in the shop at Dublin Zoo, so she brought Johnny along as her assistant. She didn't even mind when he ate more sweets than he sold.

He never received the food parcels she tried to send to him because the monitors who were supposed to deliver the post stole the contents. Everyone was starving in there, and no one could resist the temptation of a food parcel.

Every year she brought him a small gift for his birthday, usually a ball, a book, a toy gun or a cowboy hat. Then Johnny saw roller skates in an advert in an English comic, and became obsessed with them. They weren't an ordinary pair of skates: the advert said they were 'double ball-bearing roller skates'. He asked for them for his birthday.

Miss French was doubtful and said she didn't even know if they were sold in Dublin. Still, he begged her to find them for him. There was nothing more important in the world to him for his eleventh birthday.

On the visiting Sunday before his birthday, Miss French arrived at Artane carrying a big brown-paper parcel.

'You got them?' Johnny asked, his eyes wary as he stared at the package.

'Open it and see,' she said.

His hands shook as he untied the twine and carefully peeled off the brown paper. He gasped when he saw the box bearing an image of the skates on the front. 'Oh, Miss French, you got them! You got them for me!' he breathed, and she twinkled with delight.

In his heart, he hadn't believed she would buy the skates for him. He knew they must be expensive and hard to find, but she did. Those skates meant so much to him: they represented an adult who had finally come through for him.

They were a huge boost to his self-esteem. When he wore those skates, the message was clear: 'Look at me!

Look at the wonderful present someone gave me! I'm not worthless!' All that day, Johnny rolled around Artane feeling prouder and happier than he had in his entire life.

No one ever spoke about depression in those days. There were people who 'took to their beds' but 'depression' was never mentioned. The really broken people were incarcerated in one of the district lunatic asylums. Those who weren't bad enough to be committed were just considered 'odd', and those who killed themselves were never spoken about at all.

No one ever considered that a child could be depressed, but in my first year at Artane I felt so alone and isolated that I didn't care if I lived or died. But that was what the school was designed to do. The rigid discipline and constant brutalisation were intended to break us, to deprive us of hope or spirit, to make us malleable, meek and servile.

So, I am eternally grateful to Miss French, who gave me hope again. She even enquired about the possibility of fostering me, but the authorities never entertained the idea. She was a single woman with little income but, most of all, she was a Protestant.

When I was an adult, she unearthed one of the handwritten notes I had sent her from Artane. It is dated the month before my thirteenth birthday in 1948 when I was in my fourth year there.

Christian Brothers School Artane
August 4, 48

Dear Miss French,

I have settled down all right now, but I am still thinking of the day you brought me to the zoo. You were so kind to me.

I hope that you will soon be able to get my photograph. Tell my mother that my birthday will be at the ninth of next month.

Hoping all at home is well.
Your fond friend,
John

I don't recall what had happened previously for me to say that I had 'settled down all right now', but I was surprised to see that I was still referring to Mrs Mulligan as 'my mother'. By then I had become aware that she wasn't a blood relative, but I guess she was the only mother I ever knew.

Miss French wasn't a big hugger or kisser or affectionate in a tactile sense. She was a product of her upbringing and era as much as most of us are. But she was someone on the outside who came to see me. People who have families, no matter how bad they are, will never understand the loneliness of having no one at all. Knowing that I mattered to someone was the lifeline I needed to survive in that place.

Not everyone was as lucky as I was. I found a reason to live, a chink of light in the dark, thanks to Miss French. Patsy Flanagan had no one to save him.

9

Dark Nights

The hair on the back of Johnny's neck rose, and he shivered uncontrollably. He could see Brother Joseph at the top of the dormitory, sitting on a wooden chair in the flickering half-light. A rictus grin stretched across his face, and a naked boy lay across his bared lap. An eerie smile played on the Brother's features. He watched the reaction of the boys, as he alternated between fondling the boy and masturbating his own exposed flesh. The boy, whose anguished cry had torn Johnny from his sleep, was frozen with terror. His black eyes stared out at them and into the darkness.

Johnny glanced around to see other boys blinking in drowsy confusion or staring in shock at the unfolding horror. But no one dared utter a word, and one by one they slithered back under the blankets, burrowing down as far as they could and uttering silent prayers that they wouldn't be next to be dragged out of their beds.

In the morning, Johnny wondered if he had imagined it but, after one glance at the red-rimmed eyes of the boy who had been in the Brother's grip, he knew he hadn't.

Johnny felt a deep sense of revulsion at what he had seen, but it took him a long time to understand what had happened. He never forgot the scene, or the fear he felt. Neither did he ever come to understand the darkness that filled Brother Joseph's twisted mind.

The terrors of Artane continued as much after dark as they did during daylight hours. There was no respite. The boys sometimes referred to a Brother as a 'filthy oul feck', but no one spoke about the monsters of the dark. Yet as soon as the lights went out, strange cries reverberated all around the building.

He heard pleas of 'Don't, sir!' and 'No, sir!', the crack of leathers lashing on naked skin, and howls of boys trying to escape whatever hell they had been dragged into.

The Brothers accused the boys of 'doing badness' if they didn't cross their arms over their bedclothes. But Johnny, like many of his age group, had no idea what they meant. Only the boys who were taken away at night knew what happened, and they never spoke about it.

Johnny knew for sure that something terrible went on only because he heard them sobbing as they returned to their beds in the dead of night. It felt as if the whole building was haunted with pain, and he went to bed with the constant fear that he'd be next.

His worst fears were realised when he was woken one night by a sense of unusual lightness. His bed covers had been lifted. A cold chill ran down the back of his neck, and he could hardly breathe as he saw the outline of a Brother looming over him.

But the instant he felt the grasping hand wrestling to get between his legs, it was like an electric shock. He screamed and scrambled bolt upright in the bed. The heads that popped up around him in the dormitory saw Johnny being struck hard across the face.

'Shut your mouth, you pup. I'm checking for bed-wetters,' growled the Brother.

Johnny watched shadows dancing on the ceiling for hours afterwards. Every time he heard heavy-shod feet approaching, he squeezed shut his eyes and uttered silent prayers that the Brother wasn't coming back for him. He knew no one would help him if someone came for him in the dark.

He was almost grateful when he heard anguished cries because whatever was happening was happening to someone else. The bogeyman was real, and Johnny feared him every night of his life in Artane.

The boys responded to the reign of terror in different ways. Johnny reacted by trying to make himself invisible. He shrank from the Brothers, flinched at any touch. He ached to escape from the place, physically longing for an end to it all.

One night he watched a spider creeping slowly, picking its way across the cracked plasterwork of the ceiling. When it reached the flaking window frame, he saw it slip into a black shadow and vanish. Johnny lay there with envy in his heart. He wanted to be something so small that he could disappear from this hellhole. There were many times when he wished he'd never wake up in the morning.

But he knew that even if he could have told Miss French, it would be worse for him. He felt powerless to do anything in the face of abuse. The boys didn't believe anyone would protect them.

Johnny heard rumours that Patsy Flanagan was being taken from the dormitory at night. Patsy was in the year behind and in a different room from him, but they met up every day in the yard. Patsy never said anything, but he leaped at any loud noise. Johnny could see that things weren't right but he didn't know how to talk to him. All he knew was that his friend was very afraid.

After eight o'clock one night in February 1951, the Brothers began herding the boys up the stairs towards the dormitories. By now Johnny was fifteen years old, in his final year at Artane. Patsy, who was a step in front of Johnny on the staircase, had another full year at the school.

Johnny trudged mechanically up the stairs, eyes fixed on the back of Patsy's jacket. Threats were the soundtrack to the boys' every move, so he barely heard the Brothers' casual abuse now.

As Patsy reached the top, in one swift movement, he

sprang over the banister and was gone. He did it so lightly that he might have been leaping over a turnstile into a meadow. It was that fast, that easy.

The hollow thud was followed by a communal gasp, and suddenly cries of horror and confusion resounded through the stairwell. Amid all the tumult Patsy lay silent and still, face down on the hall floor below. Johnny stared in horror at Patsy's crumpled form. Then he saw him disappear under a flurry of darkness as the Brothers swarmed over him.

The others began driving the boys to the dormitories, lashing out at them with their leathers. Johnny's head was reeling, and his legs felt like liquid under him.

'What happened?' the boys asked him, and he shook his head in disbelief.

'He was in front of me one minute, and then he wasn't.'

'Did he fall? Was he pushed?'

'No, no. He was there in front of me one minute, and then he wasn't.'

He knew that Patsy had gone over the banister deliberately, but he couldn't say the words. It would be a terrible thing to say that Patsy had jumped, that Patsy had wanted to die. Johnny lay awake that night, wondering if his friend would be okay. It wasn't until the next morning, when the priest offered up a prayer for the soul of Patsy Flanagan at Mass, that Johnny realised he would never see him again.

In those days, the term 'sexual abuse' wasn't in our lexicon. Most of the boys were young, naive and sexually unaware. There was no sex education, and nobody talked about the depredations of the Brothers at Artane. The sexual abuse that went on there remained a shameful secret for forty or more years after I left.

I admitted that I had been touched inappropriately and groped by Brothers when I was sent to a psychiatrist as part of the process for the Residential Institutions Redress Board in 2005. When I told them I was never severely sexually abused, like some boys, the psychiatrist suggested I might have repressed such memories. I don't know. It's possible. A child living in constant trauma has to adopt strategies such as denial for their own self-preservation. But if I have buried memories, they're buried for a good reason, and I'm happy to leave them there.

I know I was a prime target for Brothers who were sexual predators. I was quiet, shy and a loner, especially vulnerable because I was an orphan, who had no visitors for at least a year. However, I may have had one sliver of good fortune by arriving at Artane in 1944. According to the Ryan Report, at least five sexual predators, a whole nest of vipers, were removed from the institution in that year. I seem to have arrived just as investigations swept through the school, and maybe there was a hiatus in the levels of abuse.

In another stroke of luck, Miss French began visiting me at some point in 1945, and any Brother with evil intentions would have thought twice about abusing a child who had access to the well-spoken daughter of a Protestant cleric.

Patsy Flanagan's death hardly merited a mention in the newspapers of the day. I know now that he died within hours of the incident on the stairs. The Irish Press *published a single paragraph in its News in Brief section on page five, three days after his death, saying: 'A verdict of accidental death was recorded at the inquest in the Mater Hospital Dublin on Patrick Flanagan (14) who fell 14 feet from the banister of a stairs in the school on February 18. The Coroner, Dr MacErlean, said he was satisfied that adequate supervision was exercised by the school authorities.'*

According to the school records, the Brothers brought Patsy to their own infirmary for at least an hour before they took him to the Mater Hospital. He underwent an operation under general anaesthetic to repair 'lacerations in his mouth', according to medical evidence, but his condition deteriorated and his short life ended on Sunday, 18 February 1951.

At the post-mortem, the pathologist's verdict was that the boy had died of 'cardiac and respiratory failure, secondary to acute congestion of the lungs'.

At the inquest, a monitor claimed that Patsy had gone upstairs to the dormitory but had returned to do a 'circus trick' on the banisters. 'He seemed to overbalance and fell face downward to the floor below,' the monitor testified. The Brothers described a similar version of events, adding that Patsy was in high spirits following a visit to the circus. But there was no circus, and Patsy wasn't doing 'circus tricks'. Yet the authorities interviewed no one except the Brothers and their trusty monitors.

Some Artane boys have since claimed that Patsy fell because he was being chased by one of the Brothers, so the Ryan Report investigated the death as part of their remit. An unnamed Brother, who was on duty on the first-floor landing that night, said that Patsy 'just accidentally fell over the staircase'.

But Patsy Flanagan didn't accidentally fall. He was right in front of me on those stairs, and he deliberately flung himself over the banister. He wanted to die. He couldn't bear another night in that place. I have no doubt about it.

The Ryan Report said that the evidence 'does not support a conclusion that the Christian Brothers were at fault for the boy's death'. But I'll always believe that Patsy's blood is on their hands. Thanks to their barbaric treatment, they might as well have flung him over the banister themselves.

Eighteen former industrial schoolboys, who testified for the Ryan Report, said they attempted to commit suicide and actively harmed themselves during their years of detention. All of them alleged they were being sexually or consistently physically abused at the time. Some were admitted to hospital but, still, no one asked any questions. Patsy was the boy who succeeded in killing himself.

I couldn't deal with the intrusive nature of the questioning of the Redress Board. In the end, I felt I didn't need to put myself through another ordeal at the hands of the state, and I quit the process.

The Redress Board's job was to decide the severity of abuse that each of the former residents had suffered. Those who stuck it out were compensated according to a scale of abuse that was scored by the board. Afterwards, I learned that they rated the brutality I suffered as twelve out of a possible twenty-five. I know what I endured at Artane, so all I can say is, God help all those who scored higher.

10

Leaving Artane

Brother Doody appeared at the workshop door. His eagle eyes scanned the room before locking on John's.

'Cameron, report to the Brother Superior's office!'

The other boys stared as John dropped his tools on the workbench and hurried out, his heart racing. What had he done? he wondered. It was serious when an inmate was called to the office.

As he knocked on the Brother Superior's door, the familiar ball of fear in his throat threatened to choke him.

'Enter!' said the voice inside.

John saw the bald pate of a man scribbling furiously into a ledger on a mahogany desk. A wooden mantel clock ticked heavily over the slate fireplace beside him.

'Now . . . Cameron,' he said, at last focusing on him. He searched through the papers on his desk and waved one triumphantly. 'So, you're leaving us tomorrow.'

John had known his days as little Johnny Cameron would be over when he turned sixteen. He was now an adult whose departure from Artane was inevitable. But it came as a shock to be faced with the prospect of leaving the penal institution that had been his home for eight years. 'I'm leaving, sir? Tomorrow?'

'Yes, young man. And I'm sure you'll give glowing reports of your time here when you leave.'

'Yes, sir.'

'You're a very fortunate boy. You've been taught a valuable trade, so you'll have gainful employment.'

John had spent the previous two years working from morning to night in the carpentry workshop. All the boys in Artane finished their formal schooling at fourteen to begin tuition in a trade.

Matty Doran, who worked in the bakery, took it on himself to advise the younger boys on the apprenticeships. He always ended with the dire warning: 'Whatever yis do, don't yis get sent to the farm!'

John didn't need Matty to tell him that the farm was the worst apprenticeship of all. The farm traders rose before dawn and had a half-day's work done before the bell rang for breakfast. John saw those boys dragging their boots as they came in for supper every evening, dog-tired and caked in mud. Nevertheless, the majority were sent to the farm, even though most were from Dublin and had no interest in agriculture. John heard all the stories about the boys who were worked almost to death for little or no pay.

When he turned fourteen, John spoke up for the first time in his life. He approached the Brother in charge of appointments to the workshops and asked to go to the carpentry shop. Brother Flynn lowered his spectacles to the bridge of his nose and stared hard at John. 'You'll go where you're told, young man!' he growled.

John knew what he had to do. He told Miss French that it was his heart's desire to do carpentry, and within the week, she and her formidable mother arrived at Artane for an appointment with the Brother Superior.

John smiled to himself as he watched the two women advance upon the Brother's office, handbags clutched determinedly to their middles, heels clacking resolutely. He knew they were an implacable force once they made up their minds. As he expected, they emerged victorious from the meeting.

'That's all decided now, Johnny. You're going to the carpentry shop,' said Miss French, with the air of someone who had just ticked off an item on her 'to do' list.

Like most of the workshops, the carpentry shop was run by a lay instructor from the outside. Unfortunately, this instructor was as big an advocate of corporal punishment as the Brothers. Mr Mellon was a short fellow with an even shorter fuse. He kept a stout wooden stick within arm's length and didn't need much of an excuse to use it.

Despite the brutal working conditions, John discovered that he had a natural skill for working with wood. His hands were deft and dexterous, and he had a meticulous eye for detail. The hours he spent in the carpentry shop slipped by pleasurably if Mr Mellon managed to hold his violent temper. Woodworking felt so natural to John that he wondered if he might have inherited the skills. His obsession with his past began very early on in Artane. Many of the boys had family outside, and he longed to find someone belonging to him.

What started as a nagging need became a burning desire as he grew older. Some people believe that orphaned children carry the trauma of separation from their biological parents even when they are parted very young. By now John knew that he had been handed to an orphanage in Dublin when he was five months old, after he would have bonded with his mother. He felt, deeply, the anguish of abandonment.

Like a salmon struggling to return to its spawning grounds, the yearning to find his home overwhelmed him at times. He had so many questions about his past, and not a single person could answer them. He fantasised about what his mother was like. At Artane, he had memorised a sentimental rhyme called 'Orphan Child', a rose-tinted story about a woman who, through no fault of her own, was taken to Heaven and had to leave her child behind. That mother became John's mother because he never wanted to believe he had been an unwanted child.

John Cameron

Orphan Child

I have no mother for she died
When I was very young;
Yet still her memory round my heart
Like morning mists have clung.

They tell me of an angel form
That watched me while I slept;
And of a soft and gentle hand,
That wiped the tears I wept.

And that same hand that held my own,
When I began to walk;
The joy that sparkled in her eyes
When first I tried to talk.

For they say the mother's heart is pleased
When infants' charms expand.
I wonder if she thinks of me
In that bright, happy land.

I know she is in heaven now;
That holy place of rest.
For she was always good to me.
The good alone are blest.

I remember too when I was ill,
She kissed my burning brow.

The tears that fell upon my cheek,
I think I feel them now.

The day the Brother Superior told John he was free to leave Artane should have been the best day of his life. John had always believed that, once he was free, he would hare down the long driveway and run gleefully into the arms of the outside world.

So his initial reaction to the Brother's words confused him. He felt oddly numb, and a new sense of dread replaced the old. The Brother continued fumbling among documents on his desk. 'We got a letter last week . . .' he said '. . . from Miss French, who has secured you a position in a carpentry shop in Sandyford for thirty shillings a week.'

John was standing in silent shock.

'And this morning we got good news from Mr Peter Mulligan, who has agreed to provide you with your old lodgings back in Murphystown. You'll pay Mr Mulligan out of your thirty shillings.'

The Brother looked up at John with an air of triumph, as if he had done it all himself, even though they both knew that Miss French had organised everything. 'Isn't that great news?' He beamed.

'Yes, sir. Thank you, sir,' said John.

Yet John wasn't sure. Artane was a brutal home, but it was the only home he knew. When he left the Brother Superior's office, instead of feeling joy, he felt bereft, as if he was being abandoned all over again.

He made his way to the chapel, compelled for some

reason to tell the choirmaster, Mr Quinn, why he could no longer attend practice. He was grateful when Mr Quinn reflected some of the shock he felt.

'Really? They're sending you out?' Mr Quinn gasped. 'I wouldn't have guessed you were sixteen already.' He rummaged through his pockets and pressed a sixpence into John's palm. There were tears in the man's eyes as he held the boy's hand. 'Good luck, son. You're a good lad. I know you'll do well for yourself.'

John wished he was as confident as Mr Quinn, but he was touched by the kind gesture. He had experienced very few in his life, and he knew he would never forget it.

John left on the morning of Wednesday, 26 September 1951, with his first pair of long trousers, a sixpenny piece and a basic trade in carpentry. He didn't say goodbye to anyone: he didn't know how to do so without dissolving into tears.

That day should have been an indelible memory, an event seared into his mind's eye for ever. Instead, his departure from Artane is a complete blank, and, to this day, John has no idea how he got to Sandyford. His first memory after leaving Artane has always been of standing on the Murphystown road looking at the Mulligan cottage, holding a small brown paper bag of his possessions.

He never saw any of the Christian Brothers again or, indeed, any of the other boys from Artane. And if he had, he would have crossed to the other side of the street. He swore he never wanted to see anything that reminded him of that place.

The dread I experienced standing outside the Brother Superior's office in Artane has never left me. My whole life I've felt fear at the prospect of interacting with authority figures. I can't pick up the phone to enquire about car insurance without feeling as if I'm back outside the office door of the Brother Superior.

My official discharge date from Artane was the day before my sixteenth birthday on 8 September 1951. However, the records state that I was 'detained' for an extra eighteen days, presumably to sort out my future accommodation and employment.

When I left Artane, I believed that the Brothers had trained me in a useful trade. The records there say that I was a 'good carpenter, neat, accurate, dependable'. I didn't know that the trade unions held a vice-grip on the apprenticeship system, which meant that most of the training in Artane was useless.

In reality, we were trained to provide everything that was required inside the walls of the institution. At best, we were trained to be the labourers and servants of the respectable middle classes of Ireland. The boys' schools, in particular, provided farmers with the cheap, uneducated labour they needed. The girls' reformatory schools provided household skivvies.

What I recall most about our education in Artane was the brutality. It's something to this day that I have never understood. They say that children exposed to constant abuse and violence are likely to develop similar behaviours, but in all the decades I've spent dealing with young people, I have never raised a hand to a child or ever felt any desire to.

11

Alone

The front door of the Mulligan cottage was on the latch, so John had only to apply a light shove to the door with his shoulder and step back into the home of his childhood.

By now only the ghosts of Mr and Mrs Mulligan remained in the shadows of the gloomy cottage. They had both died during the eight years when John was in Artane, so their grandson Peter lived there alone.

The place was still mostly as John had left it, although now linoleum concealed the earthen floor. John could still see the oppressive figure of old Mulligan lurking in the corner in his wheelchair, and his stomach churned.

He knew this should have been his first taste of freedom but, instead of relief, he felt only gnawing anxiety and fear. The silence in the cottage was unnerving after years of doors slamming, Brothers yelling, boots marching and instructions being barked.

He was jittery, scared even. Instead of feeling elation that he had escaped the institution, he had a troubled sense that Artane had abandoned him. The day he left was one of the loneliest days of his life.

What do I do? he wondered, his mind and pulse racing.

Artane had had rules and a timetable that occupied every moment of his day. He hadn't realised that he would miss that. He didn't know what was wrong, but he felt lost, totally adrift, without the rigid structures he was used to. He needed someone to tell him what to do, but there was no one.

He was hungry, but there was no refectory or mealtimes any more. The cottage felt claustrophobic after the vast rooms and high ceilings of Artane, so he sat on the doorstep and waited for hours until Peter came home from work.

Peter arrived in his old Ford Anglia on that Indian-summer evening. He waved as he opened the passenger door for a beautiful girl, with a mane of glossy curls, to get out.

'Hello, hello, Johnny Boy! Welcome back!' he said cheerily, as if John had been away on a weekend break.

He introduced him to his fiancée, Angela, but John was so shy that he could barely lift his eyes to meet her curious gaze. Peter flung open the door to the second bedroom. 'Throw your stuff in there,' he said. 'It's not the Ritz, Johnny Boy, but it'll have to do.'

As Peter exchanged easy smiles with Angela, the old familiar feeling of envy swept over John. Peter had had a mother, grandparents and even a bicycle when he was a boy. Now he had a girlfriend, a car, charm and even his own house. He had a normal life. John yearned for a life like his.

Watching Peter that evening, it came to John that he wanted a girlfriend who would become his wife so that they could make a family of their own. He was tired of feeling alone.

Within days, he had started work in a small carpentry company in Piper Hill in Sandyford, owned by the appropriately named Mr Wood. He was a friend of Miss French's family and a kind soul.

'Lad, I can only give you temporary work doing odd shifts at nights and weekends because you don't have a union card,' he explained. 'I can only give you the work the others don't want to do, or the men will object.'

John couldn't work without a union card and the proper certificates. Membership of the Amalgamated Society of Woodworkers (ASW) was virtually closed, except to the sons of members. It was the same in Britain.

Miss French met with politicians, besieged priests and harangued the ASW in her mission to get John a union card. 'How fair is it that a talented young boy can't use his God-given skills in carpentry because he doesn't have a father?' she demanded. She persuaded another family friend, who owned a big construction firm, Collen Brothers, to offer John a full-time job. The firm's headquarters in East Wall was a sixteen-mile round-trip from Murphystown.

John needed a bike, and there was no way he could raise the five pounds to buy one.

'I can help you with a loan,' Miss French told him, pressing the money into his hand. It was a vast sum to her, but she gave it to John, and he was always grateful for her trust.

'I promise I'll pay you back every week, Miss French,' he told her.

On his first morning in East Wall, the gateman directed John to the yard foreman's office. It was a prefabricated building with a glass hatch at one end.

'So, my new assistant has arrived!' said the burly foreman, who appraised John with a look that stretched from his straw-coloured curls to his worn boots. Frank Quirke was young but had a voluminous mane of silver hair that made him look older. 'Your job pays thirty-five shillings a week, lad,' he said. 'And you help us record everything that leaves and returns to this place. Nothing comes in or out without a docket, and every docket has its place.'

Mr Quirke led him into the yard where dozens of drivers were milling as they awaited their loads and instructions. 'Lads, this is my new assistant, John Cameron,' he bellowed. 'And yis all better be on yizzer best behaviour because he's the boss's pet, so he is!'

John blushed a shade of beetroot as all eyes swivelled in his direction, and Mr Quirke laughed uproariously.

John spent most of his first day in the office with the elderly secretary, Mrs Burgess, while she taught him their filing system. She was a plump woman with thick spectacles, and grey hair pulled severely into a bun. She didn't try to hide her disapproval at John's presence in the office. 'I don't know what young Mr Collen was thinking, foisting a whippersnapper like you on us here,' she said, shaking her head in sad bewilderment at Mr Collen's lapse in judgement.

Mr Quirke arrived back to the office mid-morning and slumped into the seat behind his desk. 'So how do you know Lyle Collen?' he asked John.

Mrs Burgess looked up from her desk, pushed her horn-rimmed spectacles down her nose and fixed John with her beady eye.

'I don't know him at all,' Johnny admitted.

Mr Quirke glanced at Mrs Burgess. He seemed suspicious. 'So why would Lyle Collen come down here and ask me to look after you?'

John was relieved that they seemed to know nothing about him. Now that he was out in the real world, he realised he wanted to hide his origins. He was deeply ashamed of his background. 'A neighbour of mine called Miss French is a friend of Mr Collen's,' he explained. 'She asked for a position for me, so he's given me a job as a favour to her.'

Mr Quirke regarded him carefully. 'So, you're not a left-footer then?'

'A left-footer?'

'Like Mr Collen – a Protestant.'

'No. I'm Catholic.'

'It's good to have Protestant friends like Miss French,' he

said. 'Mr Collen never came down here before and asked for special treatment for a new boy with no office training.'

'I'm not looking for special treatment, honestly, Mr Quirke,' said John. 'I just need a job until I get my card and can join the carpentry shop here.'

The yard office boss seemed satisfied with Johnny's explanation. 'Well, Mr Collen said he'd come by this week so you'd better look busy when he does,' he said.

'What's he like, so I'll see him coming?'

'He'll be the only one pulling into the yard in a red Jaguar convertible.' Mr Quirke snorted. 'You'll spot him easily enough. Our Mr Collen is the original Playboy of the Western World.'

John was spellbound when he heard that Mr Collen was a racing driver, who took part in the Monte Carlo rallies. He was flushed with shyness and nerves when his boss arrived at the yard foreman's office days later. Lyle Collen was a lithe and handsome man in his thirties. His hair was slicked back in an elegant quiff, and he wore the smartest pinstripe suit John had ever seen.

'Pleased to meet you, John Cameron,' Mr Collen said, extending his hand, and John noted his immaculate nails, his gold wristwatch and the scent of soap and jasmine about him.

John had been schooled by Miss French, and he parroted her words dutifully. 'Thank you so much, sir, for this opportunity,' he said. 'I really appreciate your kindness, and I won't let you down.'

Lyle Collen smiled broadly and slapped John on the back.

'I'm sure you won't, my good man,' he said. 'The French family are old friends of ours, and we value Miss French's recommendations highly, so we're delighted to have you on board.'

John's ambition was still to join the carpenters' shop at Collen Brothers, so he enrolled to get his certification in Bolton Street at night. He felt an incessant need to prove his worth and saw education as a way to show that he was as good as everyone else.

Mr Collen expressed reservations about combining work, studies and thirty miles of cycling between Murphystown and the city twice every day, but John needed a rigid schedule that took him from early morning to late at night. He was used to the controls of Artane, so it anchored him. He was saddle-sore and whippet-thin, but he had a routine.

While he enjoyed his work and studies, his home life deteriorated after he found Aunt Bridie sitting by the range one evening. She glared at him with the same fondness he recalled from years earlier.

'Look at you, like the bad penny, always turning up.' She eyed him through a plume of cigarette smoke.

He felt he could have said the same about her, but he didn't dare.

'I don't know how you got back in here again, but you know Peter's getting married soon, and his wife doesn't want your sort hanging around,' she said, with a scowl that conveyed immense distaste.

Aunt Bridie moved into the room that John was paying

for, and Peter didn't utter a word about his tenant sharing the room with his mother.

Days after Bridie's return, Lyle Collen offered John a lift home in his curvy red convertible. John knew no one had seen the likes of the Jaguar Roadster in Murphystown, and he hoped that Peter might be home in time to see him arrive. The car roared up outside the cottage, and Mr Collen sprang out of the vehicle to help remove the bicycle they had managed to wedge into the boot.

John's heart sank when he saw Aunt Bridie storming up to the garden gate, her mouth a grim line. She glanced from the well-dressed gentleman to the flash motor, then folded her arms and stared with undisguised disgust at John.

'So what trouble is he in now?' she demanded.

John's cheeks burned with humiliation, and he was so embarrassed that he didn't even hear Mr Collen's reply. John could never shed the shame he carried for being an ex-Artane boy.

Not long afterwards, John arrived home one evening and found his scant belongings scattered on the front step. The sight sent terror pulsing through his veins. He realised with horror that they were throwing him out.

He froze in the small front garden, the colour draining from his face. He felt blind panic. Aunt Bridie sauntered out, one arm folded across her chest, the other brandishing a cigarette. She eyed him coolly. 'I've told you before we don't want your sort here,' she said. 'You're not coming back in, so take your stuff and get lost.'

He gathered up his few things, his hands trembling, and

tied his bundle to the back of his bike. Bridie leaned in the doorway, smoking and smirking as she watched.

John didn't understand the violence of the emotional response he was experiencing, but he felt as if his gut had received a blow from a heavyweight boxer. The prospect of homelessness sent his anxiety spiralling to new levels.

As soon as he began wheeling his bicycle down Murphystown Road, tears rolled down his face and his shoulders heaved with sobs. He knew his response was not rational. The cottage was miserable for him, harbouring memories of a wretched childhood. Since Bridie's return from England, living there had been even more depressing.

Yet he was in turmoil. It seemed to him that this was another rejection. And it was piled upon a sense of abandonment at his recent ousting from Artane. It was more than he could cope with. He felt sick and truly broken.

He had no one in the world to turn to except Miss French, and he wondered if she would want to see him now. Hadn't he already imposed enough on her kindness? There was only so much anyone could tolerate of him.

After the death of the Reverend Arthur Digby-French in 1950, Miss French and her elderly mother had moved out of Murphystown Road. They were now living with Miss French's brother, Bob, who lived in a country house in Kilternan. Too distressed to cycle, John walked his bike all the way there.

When he reached the winding lane that led to Miss French's house, he stopped and tried to pull himself together. Grateful at least that he was now beyond the gaze of curious passers-by, he sat on the ground, and pulled his knees into himself. The only sounds were of the leaves rustling in the wind and the birds settling for the night in the boughs and hedgerows.

Then something strange happened. John's mind cleared, the sense of devastation lifted, and a call of the void filled his head instead. With tremendous relief he realised there was a way out. He didn't have to go to Miss French's house; he didn't have to risk more rejection; he didn't have to go on at all. He was calm and felt in charge of his life again.

The plan was clear to him. He would get back on his bicycle, and he would reach Dún Laoghaire by nightfall. Then he would walk to the end of the pier and throw himself into the rolling black waves.

Looking back, I was institutionalised in an era when no one even heard of the term. The military life of Artane was normal for me; having to make my own choices was alien. When they let me out, I'd never cooked anything for myself in my life, and I had never shopped for anything for myself. I was a pathologically shy and socially inept teenager, feeling alone and scared.

I never understood Bridie Mulligan's aversion to the boys her parents had fostered. As a single mother, who had had to surrender her own child to her parents, she might have been expected to feel more sympathy for motherless children. When she threw me out, I still hadn't adjusted to the idea of living outside Artane. Everything was new and frightening and, having no social skills, I couldn't connect with people. I needed shelter, no matter how bad it was. Looking back on that night, I was in the throes of a mental breakdown. It wouldn't be my last.

Below is a letter from Lyle Collen to Miss French, written twenty days after I left Artane.

*

Collen Brothers (Dublin) Ltd,
Building and Civil Engineering Contractors,
East Wall,
Dublin NE 6

16 October 1951

Dear Miss French,
John Cameron has started this morning, and I sincerely hope he will make a success of his career. He is at present in the yard foreman's office doing clerical work and other odds and ends.

His wages will be 35/- per week, and in a few weeks' time, when I know more about him, it will be possible to say what work he is really suited for.

In the meantime, we will make various enquiries about technical schools with a view to sending him to the one more suited and most convenient. Personally, I feel that Bolton Street will also be too far for him. It will be expecting too much of the youth to do a day's work and then travel in and out to Bolton Street in the evenings. I understand there is some sort of a school in Dundrum, and I have asked John to enquire of same.

I will let you know at a later date how he is progressing.

Yours sincerely,
Lyle Collen

12

The Search

'John? John? My God, are you all right?'

John jolted awake, lifted his face from the cool stone wall and unfurled himself from a tight ball. The light was almost gone, and he was still lying in the laneway to Miss French's house.

Miss French leaned over him, peering anxiously into his tear-streaked face. 'Oh, John!' she cried. 'Whatever has got into you? I came down here looking for one of the hens. You could have been out here all night!' She helped him to his feet and steered him towards the house. Registering his bloodshot eyes, she said no more until John was sitting at the kitchen table, and she had the kettle boiling on the range.

The turmoil of emotions John had experienced earlier had taken its toll. His will to live was sapped but so, too, was his energy to do anything about it. He sat despondent, barely registering Miss French's presence until her slender hands reached across the table for his. 'Right, John. Tell me the worst. What's happened?'

He could see his reflection in her light blue eyes, and she seemed almost to hold her breath. That was when his face crumpled, and the tears flowed again. He could hardly utter the words.

'They've thrown me out!' he sobbed. 'Aunt Bridie threw me out. I'm homeless.'

'They've thrown you out? Of the cottage?'

He nodded miserably.

'Hah!' she said, startling him. 'Is that it? Oh, my goodness, I thought it was something serious.'

She laughed while John stared in disbelief.

'Good Lord, Johnny, that dreadful woman did you a favour! I'm glad you're out of that terrible house. I said it to Mother from the start: they should never have put you back in there.'

Miss French's response to his predicament made his earlier reaction feel hysterical, unhinged even. John felt foolish. Miss French made homelessness sound like the best thing that had ever happened to him. She had always been able to turn his world around. She promised to find him far better lodgings than he'd had in the Mulligan cottage.

'Meanwhile, you'll stay here tonight, and let's hope the

Christian Brothers don't hear about it or they'll lock you up again!' she said.

The next morning, he freewheeled down the rocky laneway from her home, knowing he was in good hands. He wondered what had come over him the day before. It wasn't hard to love life when surrounded by the leafy loveliness of Miss French's home on a spring morning.

The old country house was called Newtown Verney, and it had two acres of gardens in the heart of Kilternan's countryside. It was an impractical home for an infirm widow, with her ageing unmarried son and daughter. Yet the modest manor seemed a perfect match for Miss French: she and the house were like relics from another era, genteel and elegant, but both had seen grander days.

The views, which swung from the highs of the Wicklow mountains down to the Irish Sea, never grew old. On sunny days, the scent from Miss French's sweet peas, rose bushes and lavender filled the air. It was a rural haven not far from Dublin but another world from the grey smog and concrete of the city.

As promised, Miss French found lodgings for John with a middle-aged couple in Jamestown, only a five-minute cycle from her house. Relieved to have a roof over his head again, John slaved for his landlords. He dug the garden, cleaned the dry toilets and did every dirty job around the house.

A fellow lodger, Kevin Casey, shook his head, as he watched John dig rows for seed potatoes one bitterly cold weekend. 'Cameron, stop being the resident dogsbody and get out of here!' he said. 'For Jaysus' sake, son, you're young, you're supposed to be enjoying yourself.'

Kevin was a few years older than John and was going out with the landlord's daughter, so he kept a watchful eye over his shoulder as he issued this advice. 'Get some digs in town and go out and enjoy yourself, man,' he urged, in a low voice.

But it wasn't easy to find digs on an office assistant's salary of thirty-five shillings a week.

The shackles of Artane were hard to shake off, and when John fell asleep, the Christian Brothers resurfaced like monsters from the deep. It wasn't unusual for him to be shaken awake by Kevin or one of the two other lodgers who shared the room. John would find himself covered with a lather of sweat, facing shocked roommates who had been rudely roused.

'Jayz, lad, you put the heart across me sideways with yer screaming!'

The scars of the institution didn't fade, and he felt as if the stench of the place still lingered on him. There were many dark days when he felt life wasn't worth living, and times when he considered ending it all. He felt a terrible loneliness a lot of the time. It was like there was some impenetrable barrier between himself and everyone else. He wanted to be normal, but he didn't fit in. He had no sense of belonging, no sense of where his place was in the world.

The primal need to find his tribe grew stronger. He tried to plaster over the cracks, but barely below the surface a black hole sometimes threatened to swallow him. John became more and more obsessed with finding out who he was and where he had come from.

The only biographical information he had was a single line from the Christian Brothers. He was born in Enniscorthy, County Wexford, on 9 September 1935, and his file said he was 'delivered' to St Brigid's Orphanage on Eccles Street in Dublin when he was five months old.

As soon as he had his first day off at Collen Brothers, he rose before dawn, and cycled for nearly six hours to the town of his birth. He was determined to get a copy of his birth certificate and uncover the first clues to his family background. He submitted his name and date of birth at the local health board office and nervously waited for the first official document of his life.

His anxiety grew when he noticed that people who had arrived after him were collecting their certificates and leaving before him. The worst was confirmed when the registrar returned, shaking his head. 'I've gone through everything, son, but there's no John Cameron registered for that date or at any time around that date. Are you sure they gave you the right details?'

John wasn't sure about anything except the crushing disappointment and despair in his gut. It seemed like the worst kind of betrayal. By not registering his birth, it was as if no one had wanted to acknowledge his existence. He really was a nobody: officially he didn't exist. Yet he still couldn't extinguish that burning desire to find his family. So, he travelled around Wexford on his bicycle, weekend after weekend, but didn't find a single lead.

On Miss French's advice, he wrote to St Brigid's Orphanage in Dublin, but no one replied to his letter. Officialdom slammed down the shutters on any enquiry he made. Concealment and shame were the climate of the time, and most people believed that the past should be forgotten. His fellow lodger, Kevin, at first attributed the younger man's disappearance every weekend to a secret girlfriend. He was aghast when John confided that he was looking for his parents. 'There's me thinking you were a sly old dog and instead you're off digging for trouble,' he said. 'Put the past behind you, son, and get on with your own life.'

John wished he could, but he lived with that disquieting loneliness. It never left him, and it plagued him with questions to which he didn't have the answers. The only good news came when John was issued with his union card. He raced straight to Miss French's home to tell her.

'Miss French, you did it!' he said, waving the precious card before her. Miss French dropped down onto a kitchen chair, as if taking a well-earned rest, and clapped her hands with delight.

John moved into the carpentry shop and his wages improved incrementally every six months. With each pay rise, he sought better lodgings. Kevin was ecstatic when John moved into new digs near Sandyford church.

'Fair play to you, boy. You got out!' He pumped John's hand.

John didn't have the heart to tell him that he regretted the move because his new place was even worse than the last.

When John finished his five-year apprenticeship, he received an offer of double his pay from a company called Artel Displays. He felt a debt of gratitude to Lyle Collen, and it seemed like a betrayal of sorts to hand in his notice, but John's boss was generous to the last: 'If it doesn't work out, don't be afraid to come back to us,' he said.

Even five years after leaving Artane, John felt lonely. He watched as newfound friends and roommates got engaged and married, and he was envious. A succession of girlfriends passed through his life during these years but, even though he enjoyed their company, he didn't fall in love.

He didn't demand much from life, but he wanted a partner and a family of his own. In the absence of blood relatives, he wanted to create his own family around him. Now, in his early twenties, he thought it was time he settled down.

Miss French wasn't exaggerating when she said that the Christian Brothers would yank me back to Artane if they discovered I was living under the roof of a Protestant.

The Brothers kept a proprietary eye on the boys after Artane, even though we weren't always aware of it. They believed they had a 'duty of care' that allowed them to extend their control beyond the school. I found records that showed they were still making enquiries with Collen Brothers about me in 1954 when I was nearly nineteen. In a 'Report of Conduct and Character in School', they described me as 'honest, obedient, respectful, a boy of excellent promise and good quality'.

The elitist tones of 'good quality' aside, I have to say the Brothers kept their high opinion of me quiet. It had been well hidden when I was at Artane.

13

Falling in Love

John sat at the dining-room table in his Churchtown lodgings, idly leafing through the *Sunday Press*. A cosy fire crackled in the hearth beside him while the winds howled outside the window. His eye was drawn to a Department of Education advertisement offering scholarships for teacher training. When he saw those with woodwork skills were invited to apply, his heart skipped a beat. In his mind's eye, he saw himself at the top of a classroom, and he liked that image. John had a constant need to prove and improve himself, and the scholarship presented him with an opportunity that had seemed beyond his reach.

The prospect of becoming a schoolteacher was attractive not only because it came with security and long holidays. It also represented the possibility of a respectable position in society and a rise in his social status: he would no longer be a tradesman but a professional.

Learning a profession seemed an impossible dream for a boy from Artane. He read every word of the advert before carefully folding the newspaper and bringing it to his room.

In his heart, he didn't believe he stood a chance of getting a place on the course so he didn't even tell Miss French when he sent off a stamped addressed envelope to the Department of Education requesting an application form.

Even when he applied for the scholarship it seemed as though he had notions well above his station, but he filled out the form and sent it back. Months later, he had almost forgotten about his application when he found a brown envelope addressed to him on the hall stand.

The harp postmark indicated that it was from a government department. He slipped the letter into his pocket, hoping the landlady wouldn't enquire about its contents. He didn't dare open it until he was alone in his room.

Later, he smoothed it out on the chair beside his bed and read and reread the letter until he was sure he understood it correctly. He had to be sure. It was so incredible that he couldn't believe it.

The letter said he had been successful in his application and advised him that he would attend Coláiste Garman Teacher Training College, near Gorey in County Wexford, at the start of the new term in September. The Department of

Education would provide full bed and board for the three years' training and one pound a week spending money. It all seemed too good to be true. Fortune had just smiled on him, and he wasn't used to it. He needed to share the news to make it real, and the only person he could think to share it with was Miss French. He pedalled all the way to her home.

'I think I'm going to be a teacher,' he said, giving her the life-changing letter. 'Can you believe it? It's a Department of Education course, and it says I'll be living in a college near Gorey. Miss French, I can't believe they've offered me a place.'

As she scanned the information in the letter, a smile spread across Miss French's face. She shook her head in awe. 'I think I need to sit down now.' She laughed, and John felt a glow of achievement.

'I always said you were such a smart boy,' she said proudly, but he still felt he had exceeded both their expectations.

His work colleagues declared he was crazy to throw away a well-paid job, but John wasn't swayed. He sold his bicycle, bought a second-hand motorcycle and headed for Gorey that September. When he looked up at the imposing country pile that was to be his home for the next three years, he wondered if he'd done the right thing.

Coláiste Garman occupied the grand old Ramsfort House, a rambling manor, which boasted three distinct wings built across different ages. Students and lecturers filled the place during the week, but during weekends and the holidays everyone went home except John, and the house fell silent.

It was lonely to amble around and see no one for days, apart from the caretaker. Accommodation in the old house was basic and draughty, but he had free meals and the luxury of a single room, so despite some misgivings, he was determined to push on and become a teacher.

One afternoon, John was heading for nearby Gorey town when he saw a figure slumped on the road just outside the college. He leaped off his motorbike and knelt over the crumpled shape of a girl. 'Are you okay?' he gasped, relieved when he saw her stir. Her bike lay several yards away, a gnarled mudguard poking out from the twisted wheel spokes.

'You must have been thrown over the handlebars,' he said, as she tried to get to her feet. Her legs folded under her, and he had to support her around the waist to stop her sliding to the ground. 'Where do you live?' he asked.

'My parents are in the college,' the girl replied shakily, and held a bleeding arm across the front of her mud-spattered cardigan. She was small and light, so John picked her up in his arms and carried her back to the college.

As he reached the steps into the Coláiste, the school's caretaker came running towards them. 'Treasa!' he yelled, scooping the girl from John's arms and raking her with frantic eyes.

'*Cad a tharla*?' he demanded.

John had a good grasp of Irish from Artane, and he honed it in the Connemara Gaeltacht, where the Department sent him for teacher training during the summer holidays.

'*Caitheadh í as a rothar*,' he replied.

The girl tried to reassure the man. *'Níl mé gortaithe, Daidí,'* she said. *'Níl ann ach beagán fola, rud ar bith tromchúiseach.'* I'm not hurt, Daddy. It's only a little blood, nothing serious.

From that day on, the caretaker, Martin Walsh, greeted John in Irish. Originally from the Gaeltacht area of Ring in County Waterford, Martin was delighted for any opportunity to converse in his native language. A sturdy, dark-haired man, who was methodical in his work, Martin had a musical soul, and he taught music to students every summer. His wife Annie, a small, tidy woman, was the college cook, and they raised their family of ten in a house they had built on the estate grounds.

When they discovered that John played the harmonica, they invited him to their house sessions, and the family became a big part of his life. He realised that family can be anyone who welcomes you into their lives. Like Miss French, they never asked any questions – they didn't care who he was or where he came from. The Walsh family just accepted him into their home.

Treasa became increasingly important to him too. He guessed that she was nineteen or twenty years old, but he knew very little else about her except that she was passionate about Irish music. She was a beautiful fiddle player and, more to the point, she was a beautiful girl. With a mutual love of Irish music, John and she had plenty to talk about. Treasa also liked to show him the impressive scar on her arm from the accident and joke that he was her knight in shining armour.

John knew he shouldn't be thinking about her. He was already going out with a young local woman named Carmel, whom everyone called Carmelito for her dark good looks. However, for months now, Treasa was foremost in his mind. She had a silky mane of light golden-brown hair and brown eyes that were unnervingly steady. She also had the shapeliest legs he had ever seen. John's favourite nights were when he got to talk to Treasa on his own or when she played the fiddle during sessions in the house. He loved how she closed those beautiful eyes and lost herself in the music. As a young man riddled with insecurities and anxieties, John envied Treasa's self-containment and her air of quiet calm. She seemed to face everything with serenity and a smile, and her bright spirit was like a comforting salve to him.

Sometimes, when he stole a glance at her, he met her dark eyes returning his gaze. Other times, though, she didn't seem to be aware that he existed. She was the youngest of Martin and Annie's ten children, and she always seemed to be running around doing something for her six brothers or for one of her parents' guests. Treasa always left his company too soon.

'I could chat about music all day,' she admitted, one evening, as she got up to go. 'But I've got to clean the boys' boots and get my homework done for the morning.'

He was glad she didn't notice his face fall. *Homework? Did she say homework?* he asked himself. The news that Treasa was still at school came as a bombshell because he had never thought for a moment that she was so young.

Well, if she's in her final year, it means she's eighteen or near it, he reasoned. He fretted about it for days before he had the opportunity to ask her.

'Me? I'm sixteen. Why?' she said.

'Oh, just wondering,' he replied, his heart sinking to the depths of his boots. The realisation that he was nine years older than her came as a terrible blow.

The madness of this attraction became more apparent when John began practical teaching in Gorey Tech, and he found Treasa looking up at him from the front row of his class.

After that he put her out of his head. It was the sensible thing to do. John loved Treasa's family, and the last thing he wanted was to jeopardise his friendship with her parents. For the first time in his life, he had started to feel he belonged somewhere.

How would they have taken it if he'd started dating their teenage daughter? He knew they would see it as a huge betrayal of their trust. Now that he was exposed to the magical alchemy of real family life, he wanted to remain part of it.

John felt awkward with Treasa, but she continued to chat to him as if he was a peer. Conscious of the age difference, he tried to keep a distance. Despite his best efforts, though, he still found himself drawn to her. He tried not to be. But when he daydreamed, it was Treasa's image that floated into his mind and, try as he might, he couldn't replace it with Carmelito's.

They were foolish dreams anyway, John admitted. The

attraction was one-sided because Treasa never gave any indication that she was interested in him. And as close as he felt to the Walsh family, he couldn't bring himself to admit to his past. He wanted them never to find out that he had been at an industrial school. He feared that even the kindly Walsh family might reject him if they knew the sordid truth.

On the odd occasion that Annie Walsh enquired about his family or his past, he was always vague in response. He was grateful that she didn't probe further. However, Treasa, with her natural directness and curiosity, wasn't so easy to fob off.

'How come you never see your family?' she asked John one day.

John's heart beat faster, but he spun her his standard yarn, the one he used whenever anyone got too inquisitive. 'My mother died giving birth to me,' he said. 'Then my father went to America and was killed in a car crash, so I was raised in foster homes.'

It didn't feel like too much of a lie. For all he knew, John reasoned, some of it might be true.

He could see from Treasa's expression that she doubted the story, but he was relieved when she made it clear that she didn't care about his past: 'What does it matter how anyone is born or raised?' she said. 'All that matters is what they do afterwards. Some people from the most privileged backgrounds are wasters their entire lives, and look at you. You had the worst start in life with no parents and see what you've achieved.'

Treasa always saw the best side of him, and it made him smile. His confidence grew, along with his feelings for her but, even after she finished school, he was too insecure to try to forge a romantic relationship.

More than anything, he dreaded misinterpreting the situation between them. He didn't trust his own instincts. What if she didn't fancy him? What if the chemistry he felt between them was all in his own head? He wished he could be sure how he stood with her because he didn't think he could handle it if she were to reject him.

Sometimes their eyes met and held across a room, and at others, when he sought her eyes, she looked to be miles away. Treasa could seem quite aloof and standoffish. She was impossible to read.

Even as his three years of teacher training came to an end, he couldn't pluck up the courage to make his feelings known. His relationship with Carmelito wasn't going anywhere, but he hadn't the courage to break up with her either. She was a lovely girl, but she wasn't the girl for him. He would be leaving Gorey soon, though, and that would bring a natural conclusion to the Carmelito romance without the need for confrontation or awkwardness.

In May 1960, during his final weeks in Coláiste Garman, John accompanied Carmelito to a local dance hall. They were dancing to the band's version of 'Volare', when John spotted someone out of the corner of his eye, and his heart began to race. He wasn't sure at first, but then, yes, he saw Treasa across the smoke-filled room. He had never seen her there before.

He craned his head to watch her as she walked around the edge of the hall. Her silky hair was held back with a broad blue band, and she wore a pale blue dress with a crinoline swing skirt. She looked unusually shy, uncertain and unbearably sweet.

Then her eyes swung around the room and fixed on his, and suddenly no one else existed. John's response was knee-jerk as he took Carmelito by the elbow and steered her off the dance floor.

'What are you doing?' she said, irritated to be swept away during one of her favourite songs.

He stood staring at her, dumbfounded. *What was he doing?* He cleared his throat and said the first thing that entered his head: 'Sorry, Carmelito. I forgot something. I'll be right back.'

He had to reach Treasa before someone else did. He tore a straight line through the heaving bodies in the hall, like a ship's bow breaking through the surf. There were beads of sweat on his brow. *Was he imagining it or had her eyes really lit up when she'd seen him approach?* He asked her to dance, and she placed her cool hand in his clammy one as the band began to play the Everly Brothers' hit, 'All I Have To Do Is Dream'.

Her brilliant smile never faded as they waltzed, so he allowed himself a little surge of hope. *Okay, maybe she's not just being polite. She seems to be enjoying herself.*

Then came the big test. John hardly dared meet her eyes as he casually invited her to the bar with him for 'a mineral'. She looked into his eyes, and it seemed to him that she could see straight through him. He held his breath, knowing this was her opportunity to make her excuses and leave.

'I'd love to,' she said simply.

This time he got the message, and his heart swelled with happiness. Treasa liked him, and not just as her parents' friend.

The dance hall was wedged full of people, and the air was thick with smoke, so he easily managed to dodge Carmelito. He felt relief when he caught a glimpse of her on the dance floor with another admirer.

The evening passed like a dream, until Carmelito's sister spotted him in a huddle with Treasa over their bottles of Nash's Red Lemonade.

'Where's Carmel?' the sister asked, suspicion glinting in her eyes. John blushed crimson, and he stammered something about losing her in the crowd. She stormed off to report on his treachery.

John looked shamefaced. He didn't want Treasa to know that he had arrived with Carmelito, then dumped her.

'Be straight with her, John,' said Treasa. 'If you're not taking her home, at least go and tell her.'

Experience had told John that avoiding an unpleasant situation was always the more sensible course of action. 'Ah, sure,' he said, twirling the straw in his lemonade bottle. 'Wouldn't it be better if she found out in her own time?'

He didn't spare a thought for Carmelito as he emerged from the dance hall with Treasa on his arm. He felt like a prince leaving with the fairy-tale princess after the ball.

John didn't know a lot about the world, but he knew that Treasa meant more to him than any other woman he had met.

At the same time, he fretted about her parents and their reaction when they discovered he was courting their daughter. He was relieved when Treasa suggested that they keep their new relationship to themselves for a while. 'It's not like we have to sneak around or anything. Everyone is used to seeing us together anyway,' she said.

Their first official date took place in the seaside village of Riverchapel that weekend. John parked by the beach, and Treasa sat side-saddle on his motorbike, watching the waves rolling in.

As they talked, he watched her tanned legs swinging and saw her dark eyes sparkle in the sunlight. The sea breeze tossed the golden highlights in her hair, and he couldn't resist her. His lips swooped in for their first kiss, and when she kissed him back, his heart soared.

They never told anyone about their burgeoning romance, but everyone knew. Whenever they saw each other, the air between them was heavy with meaningful looks and unsaid sweet nothings.

He had nothing to worry about where Martin and Annie were concerned: they were not surprised by this turn of events.

'We're only surprised that it took you so long!' laughed Annie, scrubbing potatoes in the sink. 'Haven't we seen you mooning over each other for years?'

From the very start, John and Treasa's relationship

was uncomplicated. They adored each other, and neither wanted to spend any time apart. John was insecure about many things, but not about Treasa. She ignited a new love, joy and sense of security that he had never experienced before.

She was loving, and her every gesture was affectionate and encouraging. John didn't find it easy to be demonstrative and, at times, felt emotionally stunted compared to Treasa. But she wasn't a clinging or needy type of girl, and she never demanded more than he could give.

For the first time, he had a true sense of belonging. Home for John was being with Treasa. That summer, John stayed in Gorey and they spent fine evenings sitting together on Tilly's milk stand, opposite the college, where the farmer left his churns each morning.

John knew exactly what Treasa meant when she said it felt as if they had known each other for ever. From the beginning, he wanted to tell her that he loved her, but he never dared say it. He tried to summon the courage to let the words leave his lips, but it always failed him.

It was six months after they started going out together that Treasa looked into his eyes and declared that she loved him.

He was startled. She stood in the fading light, gazing at him with her solemn eyes, expressing the sentiments he most wanted to hear in the world and the words he had wanted to say for so long.

The depth of his emotional response took him by surprise. He meant to respond that he loved her too, but the lump in his throat obstructed the words and tears flowed down his face instead. Treasa gazed at him in shock. 'What's wrong, John?'

The walls around his emotions collapsed, and everything poured out at once. Overwhelmed by a colossal wave of joy, relief and anguish, it was a while before he could pull himself together and explain.

He was twenty-six years old, and no one had ever uttered those words to him before. Treasa's declaration of love touched John to his soul.

Treasa is the woman who brought my world to life, and I still feel her love and devotion every day. For a long time, I expected very little out of life. I didn't think I deserved happiness. Today, I like to refer to Charles Dickens' wise words: 'Happiness is a gift and the trick is not to expect it, but to delight in it when it comes.'

So, I delight in my good fortune to have found the perfect partner in life and to have the best family a man could hope for. Even though our age difference seemed a lot back then, Treasa insists that we were always the perfect age for each other because she was more mature for her years, and I was entirely immature for mine.

14

The Proposal

Despite wrapping their arms around each other, John and Treasa shivered in the damp, cold night. Bundled up in tweed coats and wool scarves, their apparel was no match for the easterly wind that blew through the half-built toilet block in the backyard of Coláiste Garman.

It was one of the few places where they could find shelter from the driving rain and spend a few precious moments alone.

So John was immediately alert when Treasa pulled away from his embrace, and announced, 'We need to talk.' Her tone was urgent and serious. His insecurities rose to the surface, and his mind began to run.

What could be wrong? What have I done?

He blew warm air into his cupped mittens and stamped his feet on the concrete ground, more to reduce his anxiety than to banish the cold. But Treasa took a firm hold of his arms and fixed him with her unwavering gaze. A few tendrils of hair had escaped her tightly tied scarf and quivered around her head, but her eyes were liquid black and focused in the darkness.

He couldn't stop himself fearing the worst and hardly breathed in case his world was about to implode. *What if Treasa isn't as happy as I am?*

Her question was direct and straight to the point. 'Are we going to make it official?'

John let the meaning of her words sink in. Here she was, taking him by surprise again. She needed to know if they were going to make their commitment public.

'Oh, God, yes!' he said, breaking into a relieved smile and pulling her to him again. 'Yes, let's make it official!'

They selected 19 August 1963 for their wedding day. As per the legal requirement, the banns were read in church on three successive Sundays in Gorey to let everyone know of their intention to marry.

Meanwhile, John discovered he had a natural vocation for teaching, and he enjoyed engaging with young people. He worked for three days a week at a school in Enniscorthy and the other two days at another in Gorey. However, he also learned that a teaching vocation didn't pay well and that he could earn far more on the building sites than in the classroom. Every holiday, weekend and evening was filled with roofing and building nixers.

One weekend, he took a rare day off to make another attempt to find a family connection.

'Let's try looking for your birth cert again,' Treasa suggested. 'Maybe the fellow who looked the last time didn't look properly. Perhaps someone else will find it.'

By now, John was almost resigned to never unravelling his past. He didn't hold out much hope that he'd find a birth certificate, but Treasa was determined that they try again. John filled out another application at the registrar's office in Enniscorthy and sat in the waiting room, head down, studying the palms of his hands.

'Look, it's worth another try,' Treasa insisted.

John nodded, but he braced himself for the inevitable disappointment. After ten minutes, the registrar returned with a certificate in his hand. John and Treasa looked at each other in astonishment.

'You found his birth cert?' Treasa asked.

The man squinted at them through his spectacles and wiggled the certificate at them. 'It's what you came here for, right? That'll be sixpence, please.'

Their eyes scoured every detail. His full name was John Daniel Cameron, and his mother was Elizabeth Cameron, her maiden name Maguire. His father was recorded as William Donald Cameron, whose profession was 'clerk'. This was incredible! For the first time in his twenty-seven years, John held an official document that confirmed who he was and who his parents were.

'My mother and father were married?' John said, looking at Treasa in amazement. He wasn't expecting that.

The birth certificate also listed Mary Walsh as 'present at birth'. Her address was recorded as Lymington Road in Enniscorthy, and she was named on the certificate as the 'informant'.

It was then they noticed that John's birth had been registered on 12 October 1959, just three years earlier.

'No wonder you never could find your birth cert before!' said Treasa.

Treasa had the presence of mind to ask the registrar if he had ever heard of Mary Walsh.

'She was the midwife around here for years, and she's still on Lymington Road.'

John and Treasa knew precisely where they were going next. They found Mrs Walsh's cottage at the edge of town and were relieved that the woman, who answered the door, wore a welcoming smile. Her eyes were bright and enquiring, and her permed hair was lightly flecked with grey.

John was a maelstrom of emotion, hardly trusting himself to talk, so Treasa instinctively took over. 'Mrs Walsh, I hope you don't mind us calling to your door like this, but you delivered my fiancé, John, here in 1935,' she explained. 'He never knew his parents, and we were wondering if you'd give us a few minutes of your time to answer some questions.'

The woman raised her eyebrows, but she pulled open the door and beckoned them in with a smile. 'Come in, come in. You're welcome as long as you don't mind the mess,' she said. 'Sure, I love catching up with any of my babies.'

Mary Walsh led them to her immaculate kitchen and settled them at the table, then put the kettle on the range. 'Haven't you done well for yourself with your lovely fiancée?' she said, smiling at John. 'Now, what's your full name, dear, and the names of your parents? I'll do my best to help.'

As John uttered his surname, Cameron, he was sure he saw a shadow pass over her face and a flicker of recognition in her eyes. Or was it a look of alarm?

Mrs Walsh turned at that minute to rinse the teapot in the sink, but when she faced them again, her expression was a friendly smile. He couldn't discern anything amiss. 'I love to meet my babies, but I delivered an awful lot of them,' she said. 'I can't remember anything specific about your mother, although I don't think she was from around here. I can't put a face on her at all. It's very hazy now, I'm afraid.'

'Can you tell us why you registered his birth only three years ago?' asked Treasa. 'You're on the birth certificate as the informant.'

'That wasn't me personally, dear,' she explained. 'Part of every midwife's job is to notify the Registrar's Office about a baby's birth. By law, the parents are supposed to register the birth, but sometimes, if the parents don't do it, the registrar has to check the midwife's details to do it.' Mrs Walsh shook her head, and turned to John. 'It shouldn't have taken over twenty years, but mistakes do happen. Your registration must have got overlooked.'

The former nurse apologised that she didn't have more

information for them. 'It was nearly thirty years ago, you must understand, and I sometimes delivered several babies a day.'

John left Mrs Walsh's home feeling unsettled. There was something about her that he couldn't put his finger on. Treasa was also suspicious. 'She seems like such a nice lady, but why do I get the feeling she knows something she's not telling us?' Treasa said. 'As soon as you said your name, she remembered you, I'm sure she did, but why would she hide something all these years later?'

John put their meeting with the midwife behind him. He had his birth certificate at last, and this was the breakthrough he had been looking for. 'I know my mother's and father's names. It can't be that hard to find them now, can it?' he asked, his eyes bright and cheeks flushed with the excitement of this unexpected good fortune.

He could hardly wait to start thumbing through the phone directory to start the hunt, and felt he was finally on the road to uncovering his past.

15

Just Married

John couldn't resist turning to look back as the organist struck the first keys of the processional music. As the strains of 'Ave Maria' filled the church, he saw the silhouettes of Treasa and her father, Martin, at the open door. They were backlit by the golden rays of August sunshine outside.

The tears welled in his eyes, so he could see only a blur as Treasa came along the aisle towards him. John took a steadying breath. His heart was beating so hard, he thought it might break out of his chest. But as soon as Treasa's cool fingers reached for his, John felt calm. They beamed at one another in giddy disbelief that this day had arrived at last, and John marvelled at Treasa's transformation into the radiant and happy bride before him.

Her white gown had a raised boat-neck collar and a full short skirt that reached just below the knee. She wore a tiara and a short veil, and her bouquet was a mother-of-pearl-covered missal draped with flowers. The look was romantic and traditional with a 1960s' twist.

That she had created the dress herself made her appearance even more special. They had no money for extravagances, like a store-bought wedding gown, so Treasa and a nimble-fingered neighbour had fashioned her dress from fabric bought in Hickeys.

The day Treasa completed her gown, the postman had delivered the couple's first wedding gift. Treasa had waited until John came home from work to open it.

'It's addressed to both of us, but the postmark says Enniscorthy,' she explained.

John noted the neat ink-pen writing but didn't recognise it. 'Go ahead, open it,' he said.

Treasa cut the string and peeled away the brown paper to find an envelope taped to a slim white box. 'It's from your midwife, Mary Walsh!' she exclaimed, reading the card. She slipped the lid off the box; a white linen tablecloth lay inside. 'Our first wedding present!' she said, holding it up to the light excitedly. 'And it's from the woman who delivered you into the world.'

It was the other woman who had delivered him who came to mind as he emerged a married man from St Michael's Church in Gorey. *My mother should be here*, he thought, as he and Treasa held hands in the bright summer sunshine.

He looked into Treasa's sparkling eyes and didn't think he'd ever seen her happier. His own mouth was stretched into a smile he couldn't contain. He was always uncomfortable when he was the centre of attention, but with Treasa by his side he felt invincible.

Yet he still felt the hollow ache of longing within him. Today was a day for family, and he had none.

The rain was teeming as they travelled in their beribboned Ford Zephyr to the Woodenbridge Hotel in Avoca, but nothing, not even summer showers, could dampen Treasa's spirits that day. 'Happy is the bride that rain falls on!' She laughed.

Later, there was a bittersweet tinge to John's happiness as he looked out at the assembled guests at his wedding breakfast. He yearned to see a face out there that looked like his or belonged to him, but he didn't have a single blood relative in the room. Miss French was there for him, of course, looking so elegant in a fitted navy suit and a jaunty pillbox hat. Her mother Synolda had died by now, and Miss French lived with her brother alone in the big house in Kilternan. Her gift to the couple, the exquisite three-tier wedding cake she had made, was proudly displayed in the centre of the room.

Miss French sat at a table with John's old boss, Lyle Collen, and his wife, Ethel, and Lyle gave a sentimental wedding speech about love and marriage that had Miss French dabbing her eyes furiously.

John's former roommates, Eddie and Andy O'Connor, and their father, Hugh, were also in the room, along with his old landlord Peter Mulligan and his wife, Angela. The vast majority of guests, however, were made up of Treasa's family and friends.

Martin and Annie had invited their musician friends, which ensured great music and dancing. So, Treasa and John danced to the strains of Bridie Gallagher's 'I'll Always Be With You'. Treasa's sister Nessa, the bridesmaid, joined them on the dance floor with her husband, Sean Looby, who was John's best man.

John and Treasa spent the first night of their marriage in a room over the Ardmore in Bray, a pub owned by John's former roommate Eddie and his wife, Margaret.

The next day, the newlyweds clasped hands tightly as the Aer Lingus Viscount accelerated for take-off to Wales. This was their first time on a plane, and they were exhilarated by the experience. Once airborne, the white-gloved air hostess proffered a tray containing coupes of champagne.

'I feel so glamorous!' Treasa said, clinking her glass with John's and hardly hearing herself over the roar of the engines. John was stunned by the technological wizardry that propelled them at speed through the sky. He was mesmerised by the other-worldly sight of clouds through the small aeroplane window.

'We're like kings of the world up here!' he said, in wonderment.

The couple were met at Cardiff airport by Treasa's older sister Maura and her husband, Alf Crowther. They flapped around the young couple like mother hens, even though they had a brood of young children to mind. Alf, whose cheery laugh boomed through the modest terraced house, insisted that John borrow his car for their holiday.

'Sure, it's no honeymoon if you can't get off alone together,' he said, struggling to unravel the spaghetti arms of his youngest from around his leg. 'Get out of this madhouse and enjoy a bit of peace while you can.'

The honeymooners set off idly exploring the verdant valleys of Wales in perfect summer sunshine for two idyllic weeks. John and Treasa were overwhelmed by Maura and Alf's kindness. John hugged his brother-in-law and squeezed his hand the day they left for home.

After the honeymoon, the couple moved in with Treasa's parents in Gorey. It wasn't an ideal start to married life, but Martin and Annie's generosity allowed the young couple to save money that would otherwise have been spent on rent.

They weren't long home when two grim-faced gardaí arrived at the Walshes' door. It was never good news when the gardaí came. The local garda station had the only telephone for miles, so they were the bearers of all calamitous news.

They were sorry, the gardaí said, but they'd received a call to say that Alf Crowther was dead after a freak conveyor-belt accident at his workplace. John sat with his head in his hands for a long time that evening pondering on the unfairness of life. 'But Alf was such a decent man,' he said over and over to himself in bewilderment.

Treasa wrapped a comforting arm around him. 'You of all people should know that bad things happen to good people,' she said.

Alf's death made John even more aware of the fragility of life. He needed to find his mother and father before time ran out and, for all he knew, maybe it already had. Perhaps the only thing that remained of his parents was a gravestone in a lonely country churchyard.

Life took over, though, and six months after their wedding Treasa came down with a cough she couldn't shake off. It kept her awake at night, and she looked so tired that John persuaded her to see the doctor.

'Did he give you penicillin?' he asked, as he sat on their bed pulling off his muddy work boots that evening. By now he had given up teaching. His salary as a married teacher was thirty-two pounds a month, almost double his earnings as an unmarried teacher but a pittance compared to the hundred a month that he and Treasa's brother Ray each earned on the building sites around the country. It was tough work, but John knew it was his only chance of making enough money to afford a roof of his own.

'No, he didn't,' Treasa replied.

She seemed a bit preoccupied.

'So, what did he say?' John said, rubbing the soles of his aching feet.

Treasa sat on the bed beside him and took his hands in hers. 'He said we're expecting our first child,' she said, eyeing him carefully.

John's pulse rate quickened as he tried to absorb this news. The wind gusted outside, and he could hear Annie running water in the kitchen sink. 'You're having a baby?'

'*We*'re having a baby.'

Seconds ticked by, and John's mind raced. A range of emotions coursed through him: hope, dread, fear and then, finally, a surge of joy. 'Oh, my God, we're having a baby!' he said, a smile spreading across his face. Tears stung his eyes as he hugged Treasa, but then his fears returned, and he held her from him so he could look into her eyes.

'Did the doctor say you're all right?' He could see that Treasa was half-dazed too.

'I'm fine,' she said, 'except that I went in there with a cough and came out pregnant.'

We look so happy in the photos of our wedding day, and we're still happy today, thank God. Our kids always say we're perfect for each other because Treasa needed to mother, and I needed mothering. People find it difficult to believe, but the truth is that Treasa and I have never had a serious row in over fifty years together. Our daughters also say that Treasa is the only woman in Ireland who is proud to say she delivered breakfast in bed to her husband every day of her marriage. It was only for the first twenty-seven years. She slacked off after that, claiming she was afraid of carrying a tray on the stairs!

But I'm the first to admit that I've been spoiled throughout my marriage. I have the best partner in life, and all through the decades we've had the happiest of unions.

16

Babies and Midwives

John sat hunched, elbows on his knees, running one hand distractedly through his hair and holding a cigarette in the other. He'd been waiting in Gorey District Hospital for hours. Lengths of coloured tinsel hung along the corridor, adding a little festive cheer to the institutional gloom. A Virgin Mary statue, standing in a recess opposite him, had sprigs of holly scattered at her feet.

The packet of cigarettes he'd opened after they had taken Treasa to the labour ward was now almost empty.

He looked at his watch for the umpteenth time, his stomach flipping with nerves and lack of food. Two nurses bustled towards him, and he looked up in hope, but they didn't even glance in his direction as they hurried past.

A doctor emerged from the labour ward, peeling off a surgical gown as he strode straight past John.

It was 29 December, the heart of winter, and yet John felt the prickle of sweat on his forehead. *This length of time couldn't be normal, could it?* They had taken Treasa into the labour ward hours ago.

As he smoked his last cigarette, he spotted the nurse from earlier, her arms filled with blankets. He leaped to his feet and, with a jerk of her head, she beckoned for him to follow her. 'Mrs Cameron is back in the ward, and mother and baby are fine!' she said.

Treasa was propped up against plump pillows, her flushed cheeks the only evidence of labour. She looked up from the swathe of blankets in her arms to flash a reassuring smile at John. 'Isn't she beautiful?' she said softly, gazing again at the miraculous bundle in her arms.

John peered in, and it took only a glimpse of the perfect snub nose and those rosebud lips for his tears to fall. A wave of emotion washed over him as Treasa handed him their swaddled child.

'Look at those tiny fingernails. She's perfect, just perfect,' John said in awe.

'How do you feel about Fiona as a name?' Treasa asked, monitoring every jerk of the baby in John's arms. 'It means "fair and beautiful".'

But John couldn't repeat the name without crying.

'It's just . . . she's so perfect,' he said, his face crumpling again.

Martin and Annie arrived that evening, eager to see

their grandchild. They found their daughter taking the momentous occasion in her stride, but their son-in-law was still overwrought.

'I expected to find Treasa crying buckets, not you!' Annie laughed.

Now that he was a father, it was even more difficult to understand his own childhood. When he looked at Fiona, he felt a surge of love and protectiveness, as if he wanted to keep her safe in his arms always. He needed to know more than ever what had happened to make his parents part with him.

John and Treasa made a return visit to his birthplace in Enniscorthy to find a baptism certificate. They didn't know if he had been baptised in the town, but St Senan's seemed like a good place to start. John's heart lifted when Treasa suddenly jabbed her finger excitedly at a page in one of the registers.

'You're here!' she exclaimed. 'This is you!'

In faded ink, they again saw his parents' names, Elizabeth and William Cameron, and they read that Mr and Mrs Kinsella of Market Square, Enniscorthy, were his godparents.

'Maybe the registrar has heard of them,' said Treasa, her eyes gleaming with determination as she darted off down the church. *She's like a hound who caught a scent*, John thought as he followed her. He was astonished when the registrar nodded in recognition at the name.

'The Kinsellas are still on Market Square. They own the butcher's shop,' he said. 'Everyone knows Tom and Sheila.'

The lad at the butcher's counter directed them to the door with a glass fanlight around the corner. A bright-eyed woman answered, her hair tied in a loose knot at the nape of her neck, looking expectantly from John to Treasa.

'Sorry to disturb you, but we wonder if you can help,' said Treasa. 'You see, we found your name on my husband's baptismal certificate. We believe you're his godmother.'

The woman clapped her hands over her mouth in surprise. 'Oh, my goodness, I wasn't expecting this!' she said at last. 'I'm delighted to meet you, John Cameron. You're so like your father. I should have recognised you straight away.'

John felt a sudden unexpected surge of pride at discovering that he resembled his father, William.

'Please come in, come in,' Mrs Kinsella said.

'Tom!' she called ahead of her. 'Tom, put away that newspaper and come and meet your godchild!'

John sat on the edge of his seat, biting back endless questions as Mrs Kinsella instead peppered him and Treasa with questions. She asked where they were living, when they had met and married, and she asked her husband if he remembered the day they went to the church and became John's godparents.

Tom gave a noncommittal nod. When at last Sheila Kinsella settled down to sip a cup of tea, John was bursting with impatience. 'How do you know my parents?' he asked.

'Oh, you don't know?' she said, surprised. 'Mr and Mrs Cameron were our lodgers. We used to keep lodgers when we were first married. They rented the room at the top of the house where you were born. Your dad worked in the solicitors' office across the square here,' she added, indicating the direction with a nod.

John leaned in, desperate for answers. 'Do you know where they are now?'

Mrs Kinsella looked startled at the question. 'I was just going to ask *you*,' she said, clearly confused. 'The last I saw of them was when you were a few months old. You were in your father's arms on the railway-station platform. I still have that picture in my mind. I don't recall Elizabeth being there, but maybe she was. They were moving to Dublin.'

'And that was it?'

'That was it. I never heard from them again.'

Treasa saw the disappointment in John's face. He had been so sure that his godparents would lead him to his parents. She sat forward, earnestly searching the other woman's eyes. 'Mrs Kinsella, John has been searching for his mother and father all his life. He was put in an orphanage in Dublin when he was a baby, and he has never had any contact with them.'

Mrs Kinsella's eyes widened at this information. 'I'm so sorry,' she said. 'I never dreamed that would happen. Your father only said they were going to Dublin.'

Treasa interjected: 'So, if you can tell us anything about them, anything you can remember, we'd be very grateful. Even the smallest amount of information would help at this stage.'

Mrs Kinsella offered her visitors more tea, then topped up her own cup, but she seemed reluctant to say more.

'Anything at all, Mrs Kinsella,' Treasa prodded gently. 'Do you know what age Elizabeth Cameron was?'

'I was only a young married girl myself,' she said, 'so I hope you don't mind me saying but I remember thinking Mrs Cameron was quite old to be having a baby.' She hesitated, then added, 'But what did I know? She may have only been in her early thirties. Everyone over twenty-five seems old to you at that age.'

'Why did she ask you to be godparents?' Treasa asked.

'Oh, I was surprised myself,' said Mrs Kinsella. 'I suppose Elizabeth and I were close then, and they didn't know many other people in the town.' She lifted her cup and saucer and took another sip of tea before thoughtfully placing them on the table.

'I do remember something. At this stage, I suppose it won't hurt you to know it,' she said. 'We thought they were a married couple at first, but then your mother confided that she wasn't married to your dad. She had left her own husband to be with your father.'

John's eyebrows rose at this revelation.

'That news was shocking enough, it really was in those days,' Mrs Kinsella added. 'Then she told me your father was a Protestant, and he had left his wife too.' She slapped the palm of a hand on her chest. 'I could hardly believe it. We'd had no idea what was going on under our own roof until then.'

Treasa squeezed John's hand in support under the table but, riveted by the unfolding tale, he hardly noticed.

'To me, it was all very romantic, really,' Mrs Kinsella

said wistfully. 'They were like fugitives on the run, risking everything to be together.'

Then she seemed mentally to shake herself.

'After you were born,' she said to John, 'I think she got depressed. Looking back, it may have been the baby blues, but no one talked about that kind of thing then. Things weren't sitting well with her anymore.'

John's godmother paused as she tried to recall the sequence of events.

'I remember her telling me one day that she had a lot on her conscience and that she wanted to have her confession heard,' she said. 'She was afraid of a scene in the church, so she asked me to go to a priest to tell him about her situation.'

Mrs Kinsella stopped to stir her tea, and John barely resisted urging her on.

'She knew that the old parish priest, Father Foley, would have dragged her out of the church by the hair. He was a right oul divil, that fella. I did go to a priest on her behalf, a young fella – he wasn't long out of the seminary. He was a kinder man. I can't remember his name now, but I arranged for him to meet Elizabeth. But when she came back, she was in tears, very upset, she was. I don't remember your dad around. Maybe he was at work.'

'Why was she crying?' Treasa asked.

'The priest told her that if she wanted absolution, she'd have to give up both you and your father,' she said, looking at John now. 'He told her she was a married woman living in sin, with a child born out of wedlock. The only way she could get absolution for her sins was to give up her baby and her Protestant man and go back to her husband. Then, the next thing, they left. I don't know how long after, but it was out of the blue. They just said they were going to Dublin. Elizabeth said she'd write when she had a new address, but she never did. You were just a few months old then.'

She added: 'Like I said, I remember you in your father's arms at the station. It was you and Mr Cameron getting on that train.'

They tried to draw out Mrs Kinsella more, but her memories of his parents remained vague. She remembered his mother as 'quite a tall, thin, attractive woman', who dressed very smartly. John's resemblance to his father helped Mrs Kinsella recall him better. 'You look like Mr Cameron,' she said. 'I remember he was always very well turned out. He had a smart coat and a good hat. They were both very stylish to me then.'

But she couldn't remember where in Ireland they came from and didn't know where they went to, apart from Dublin. 'I'm sure I must have known where they were from, but it's all gone now,' she said, tapping her head. 'It's nearly thirty years ago.'

John left the house dazed and troubled. What had seemed like a promising breakthrough had led him straight into another dead end.

17

A Million Pieces

'JC! JC!'

John looked back to see his teaching colleague, Tim Keane, chasing after him. Tim's raincoat flapped behind him, and he had a pile of copybooks and folders under his arm.

'What's your hurry?' Tim panted, bending over to catch his breath, several copybooks tumbling out from under his arm. 'You're legging it out of here faster than the students!' he added, gasping as he gathered up his bundle.

John glanced at his watch and continued striding towards his car. 'I've to get some work done on a site before the light goes.'

Tim snorted impatiently, running to keep up with

him. 'It's Friday, for God's sake!' he said. 'We're going to Fowler's for a pint or six. Leave the work go to Hell and let your hair down for once.'

The thought of sinking a few cold pints sounded like Heaven, but John had promised his brother-in-law, Ray, that he would help him after school. They were building the roof on a house in Cherry Orchard. 'We're not all men of leisure like you.' John sighed. 'Some of us have second jobs to get to.'

Tim stopped in his tracks, and called after him: 'You know, the one good thing about you, JC, is that you're a stark reminder of why no man should get married!'

John gave him a wave and kept walking.

He'd returned to teaching in 1965 after the Department of Education sent letters threatening to sue him for five thousand pounds. They said he was in breach of the conditions of his scholarship, which included a commitment to teach for five years.

He began work in the newly opened Kylemore College in Ballyfermot, where he found that he related well to the children, many of whom came from underprivileged backgrounds. If only teaching paid better money, the job would be perfect, he thought.

Driving out of the school grounds, he caught sight of a lad from his class whom he hadn't seen in a week, sitting on a garden wall, legs swinging. John managed to pull in. Ray and the job could wait for a few minutes, he thought.

'Hey, Don!' he called, getting out of the car.

The youth looked startled. He was waiting for his

schoolmates and hadn't anticipated being cornered by one of his teachers. 'Hey, Mr C,' he said, with little enthusiasm.

Most people in John's life now referred to him as JC or Mr C. It started with the students, who nicknamed him JC or addressed him as Mr C because he signed their homework with his initials. His fellow teachers and friends had followed suit.

'I'm glad I bumped into you, Don,' said John. 'I was going to call out to your house this week anyway.'

Don couldn't conceal his alarm.

'Well, you're not sick anyway,' John continued, without missing a beat. 'That's a good thing.'

'I'm finished with school,' said Don, examining his scuffed brown brogues.

'Finished? So what do your parents have to say about that?'

'They can't make me go,' he said, with an air of defiance.

'So, what are you doing instead?'

'Nothin' yet. I'm lookin' for a job.'

'What kind of a job?'

'I'm on the list for H. Williams.'

'Doing what? Stacking shelves?'

The boy shrugged.

'Is that what you want to do with your life?'

Don's legs swung in and out, his heels kicking the wall in a desultory fashion.

'You're bored with school and all its restrictions, aren't you?' said John. 'But believe me, leave school now and you'll end up being bored and restricted for the rest of your life.'

Don kept his head down, and John knew that the boy wished he would go away. John felt he had to get through to him before it was too late.

'Do you really want to be stuck in a dead-end job stacking shelves in Ballyfermot all your life? Don, believe me, education is the key. You can get anywhere in life that you want with education. It's your ticket to adventure and choices.'

Frustration rose in John. He hated to see a kid throw his opportunities away. 'Sitting at home looks like the easy way out now, but if you don't get an education, you'll regret it for the rest of your life.'

Don's eyes remained down, his expression sullen.

'Why don't you come back to school while you're on the waiting list for H. Williams?'

'Mr C, it's a waste,' the boy said, exasperated now. 'I fail everything. I'm too thick to learn.'

'Look, come back to school tomorrow,' John said. 'I promise I'll help you through it, whatever it is. I'll get you help with any subject you want, I promise you.'

Don concentrated on his shoes, but John could feel that he was wavering. He added: 'And just think, it will get your mam and dad off your back.'

Don sighed, and John sensed victory.

'I'll see you at the staffroom lunchtime tomorrow, then?'

The boy shrugged. 'Okay, Mr C.'

'Don't make me call out to your house!' John warned the lad, as he ran for his car again.

There weren't enough hours in the day since he and

Treasa had started to build their house. The couple shared a dream of having a home in the country, so they were overjoyed when they found an affordable acre site in rural north-west County Dublin.

Farmland, Friesian cows and bird-filled hedgerows surrounded the site on Blakestown Road, Mulhuddart. They knew it was perfect for them the first time they laid eyes on it. There was no money to spare, so John designed the house, and he managed to make part of it habitable by the time their second child, Aileen, arrived on 2 September 1966.

'It may be only half-built, but the kingdom is all ours,' he said proudly, showing the building site to his new Sleeping Beauty. Treasa sighed with relief to be back in familiar surroundings after the drab confinement of the hospital.

'Bring the child inside out of the cold.' She smiled. 'And is there any chance of getting a proper bedroom built in this kingdom?'

Treasa picked her way around timber, bricks, cement and tarpaulins, and said a silent prayer that normality would come soon. She waged a constant battle to wrestle back control of the kitchen table, which doubled as John's workbench.

The kitchen sink was suspended on cement blocks, and machinery lay everywhere. However, the arrival of their second baby changed little in the house. As Aileen grew bigger, she learned to negotiate her walker around the colossal bandsaw in the middle of the kitchen. Treasa still didn't get her bedroom. The only thing that divided the house into living areas and bedrooms was the bright floral curtains dangling on a string.

The problem wasn't helped by John taking on more commitments. Once he discovered that he was the only teacher in the school without a bachelor's degree, his inferiority complex couldn't be quelled. He embarked on a degree course in UCD to prove that he was as good as everyone else, even though no one doubted it but himself.

John started his studies in September 1967, just before Treasa gave birth to their son Shane, on 17 October. Home life was hectic. They now had Fiona, a wilful toddler of just over two, Aileen a lively crawler of thirteen months and newborn Shane, all being raised in a house that was still under construction.

John looked around at his three children, and his heart swelled with love. He knew it would have torn his soul apart to lose any of them. The mystery of his childhood was even more difficult to comprehend, as his own family grew.

But neither he nor Treasa had the time or energy to go searching for his origins now. John's priority was to earn extra money. His teaching salary didn't stretch far enough to raise a family and buy building supplies to finish their house.

It was madness. He had a full-time teaching job and also had to attend lectures and study for his degree. Meanwhile, he worked on the building sites at night and every weekend, and he also had to try to complete the construction of his own home.

Shane wasn't out of nappies when Niamh, their fourth

child, arrived on 11 November 1969, after a traumatic breech birth. John felt pressure building inside him. He knew he wasn't himself.

It was only to be expected, he thought. Everyone warned him that the first years were the hardest. The children were a joy, but they were also hard work. However, even with the best of intentions, he couldn't describe himself as a hands-on dad. He worked long hours, and he felt guilty because, even when he was at home, he was too exhausted to engage with the children as much as he thought he should. He sometimes felt like an intimate stranger in the house. Family life went on without him more than it did around him.

He marvelled at Treasa, who appeared to thrive in the madness at home. She was a natural mother and homemaker, and she managed it all with cheerfulness even in the surroundings of their half-built home.

As a couple, they were blissfully happy, and the only source of conflict between them was John's secrecy about his childhood. He never talked about his past. He wanted no one to find out that he had been raised in an industrial school, and his heart would beat faster when anyone discussed their school experiences. But Treasa didn't understand his sense of shame and didn't see why they had to conceal his background.

The subject of the industrial schools arose one evening while John and Treasa were socialising with friends. It wasn't long after the closure of Artane in 1969 that Treasa broke their unwritten pact when she talked openly about John's time there. Their friends were sympathetic, of course, because everyone had heard stories about the brutality of Artane. Still, John saw their eyes swivelling towards him, and he felt they were reassessing him. Most people believed respectable families didn't have kids who ended up in industrial schools. He burned with humiliation.

'What are you trying to do – ruin me?' he said, through gritted teeth, as he and Treasa drove home that night. 'Why on earth would you tell anyone that I was in Artane?'

She shook her head and sighed in exasperation. 'Really, John, you'd feel a lot better if you talked about it and weren't always trying to hide it.'

There's no point arguing with her, he thought. Treasa would never understand the shame of being in Artane.

John continued to feel unwell, but he didn't know how to explain it because the symptoms were vague and shifting. It usually began with a tightening of the chest. It was happening a lot to him now. He got up in the morning, feeling as if his muscles were constricting, not allowing him to breathe.

When he tried to study, he couldn't concentrate, and that wasn't helping his state of mind. He panicked at the prospect of the end-of-year exams at UCD. How would he face anyone at the school if he failed them?

He felt anxious much of the time. Sometimes saliva pooled at the back of his throat in the classroom, and he felt as if he might be sick. He occasionally wondered if the other teachers in the staffroom were staring at him. At times he felt manic, as if he was overreacting. *Calm down*

. . . calm down . . . look normal, played on a loop in his head.

Then one Monday morning he woke to feel his heart pounding like a bass drum in his chest. His mind was a mess of static. Something heavy was weighing on his chest again, making it difficult to catch his breath. His limbs seemed unwilling to work, and getting dressed seemed like an overwhelming task. A terrible sense of foreboding was building in him, strangling him. Impending doom filled every jangling nerve in his body. He realised Treasa was looking at him in consternation.

'What is it, John? Are you sick?'

Her voice sounded very far away, and John didn't know how to answer. He couldn't form the words to tell her. There was a relentless buzzing in his head that made him want to run away, but he was paralysed, crushed by wave after wave of terror.

He saw the black robes of Christian Brothers flitting through cracks in his mind. He was rigid with fear, and yet he shook so hard, it hurt. He tried to explain but was shocked by the sounds that escaped from deep within him. A keening, a screaming of the soul.

Some door to his dark subconscious had opened, and everything poured out at once and threatened to drown him in pain. Hysterical sobs racked his body. Treasa held him, hushed the children, hushed him. She was the balm to his troubled soul, promising him that everything would be all right.

Shadows flitted around him, and the doctor came and went. Treasa fed him sips of water and pink pills that soothed away the buzzing in his head, eased the pounding in his heart and made him float into a serene void. Physically, mentally, emotionally, he had stretched himself too far and had shattered into a million pieces.

Treasa's cool, soft hands gathered up the pieces, put them all back together gently and dragged him away from the brink. The doctors signed him off work, and little by little, the darkness retreated. He was able to shut the door once more on the horrors of the past.

There was a slight tremor in his hands, a sign that his nerves were still frayed around the edges, but he could function again. He could smile, even if it didn't always mask the pain in his eyes.

Treasa despaired when John still refused to talk to a doctor about his troubled past. The nightmares and flashbacks about Artane had returned, but he wouldn't consider professional help. 'No, I don't want to talk about it to anyone. The anti-depressants are working. I'm fine again. Really.'

Determined to delay her husband's return to work, Treasa organised a family holiday. They caught the ferry to France where they stayed with their good friends Liam and Marie-France Healy. The healing powers of sunshine, friendship, good food and laughter made John feel whole again.

Soon after, he got back to his studies and graduated from UCD in 1971 with a degree in history and economics and a higher diploma in adult education.

In the years after his breakdown, Treasa did her best

to make John slow down. There was no more working on building sites at weekends. Every Sunday morning, she ushered him out the door and insisted that he enjoy a few hours of quiet to himself. If it was too wet to hoe his vegetable plot, John sat in the car and listened to the radio. And the kids watched him from the house and wondered why Mammy wouldn't let them outside to play with Daddy.

There was a new addition to our growing family on Christmas Day 1976, when our son Brian was born – coincidentally on the same day and in the same hospital as the daughter, Patricia, of dear friends of ours, Tim and Vivien.

In the end, I spent thirty-six years, from 1965 to 2001, teaching in Kylemore College, Ballyfermot, and the only reason I left was because I had no choice in the matter: I had reached retirement age. I left with a bundle of written tributes and letters from pupils, as well as many fond memories, all of which I still have.

I was only just out the door when they invited me back again – this time for adult education classes in home repairs and general maintenance. So, for three or four more years, I worked in adult education for twelve hours a week. It was a lovely way to ease into retirement, which finally happened in 2005.

18

Nell

John sat ramrod straight on his chair, struggling to keep his voice neutral. He had been trembling with anger since he had received the board letter that morning, which started, 'We regret to inform you . . .'

'This has become a bit of a pattern, Bob,' said John, tightly. 'Seán is a fine young teacher, but he's not qualified for the job, and I am. He doesn't even meet the basic criteria, and he got the job over me.'

John had always been ambitious, so after completing his degree, he attended many extra-curricular courses. He applied for promotion after promotion in Ballyfermot, but on each occasion he was turned down. In the early years, he attributed this failure to his lack of experience but, as time progressed, it became evident that he was being passed over for less qualified teachers.

Bob leaned back in his chair and shifted uncomfortably. John had always got on well with the school principal, but now the man couldn't even meet his eyes.

'Seriously, what's going on, Bob?'

Bob rubbed his temples with both hands. He wore an air of defeat. 'Look, JC, you know if it were anything to do with me, you'd have the job,' he said. 'I did recommend you, but the board decided otherwise.'

John shook his head in frustration. 'Why do they always do that? Please, just tell me why.'

Bob rested his clenched hands on his desk. 'I don't know for sure – really JC, I don't – but I suspect it's because of Artane,' he said. 'There may be people on the board who can't get past it.'

John absorbed his words in silence. It was as he had always feared, but it still felt like a kick in the teeth. Prejudice against former industrial-school inmates was alive and well in modern Ireland.

'The shadow of that bloody place never goes away, does it?' he said to Treasa that night.

But if prejudice against industrial-school boys continued, there was no denying that things were changing dramatically around their home in Mulhuddart.

These days, Treasa sighed when she threw open her bedroom curtains. It didn't matter that daffodils were swaying in the morning breeze, and that beams of warm sunlight flooded the room. All Treasa could see was the crowd of people gathered at the bus stop right outside their front gate. 'The sooner those trees grow, the better,' she said.

'They're fast-growing, Treasa. In a year or two you won't be able to see that bus stop at all,' he said, buttoning his shirt and joining her at the window. They looked out towards the rows of saplings they had planted.

Treasa blinked in confusion. She looked at John. 'Where *are* our bloody trees?' she said.

It was the last straw for Treasa when they realised that their carefully chosen trees had been dug up and stolen during the night. For years, she had despaired as she watched the suburbs sprawl like a concrete cancer across their once rural idyll. By the 1980s, Mulhuddart's green fields were gone, replaced by vast housing estates.

Treasa was fed up with the traffic, the anti-social behaviour, and the graffiti on her garden wall. Most of all, she was fed up with that bus stop outside her front door. 'We have to get out of here for our own sanity!' she exclaimed.

John and Treasa agreed it was time to start again with a new job and a new home. Within weeks, John was offered a teaching position in County Wicklow, so they directed their search for a house there. Both were excited when they discovered the old station house was up for sale near Miss French's home in Kilternan.

'What do you think, Miss French?' John asked, after they had viewed the property together. 'It's a lovely old place, and we thought it would be nice to be able to hop on the train and get straight into the city if we needed to.'

From the start of their search, they were drawn to Kilternan. They were familiar with the area, it was still unspoiled, and Miss French lived there. John hadn't seen Miss French as often as he would have liked when they lived in Mulhuddart, and he felt guilty about it. Her older brother, Robert Butler Digby-French, a lecturer in English at Trinity College Dublin, had died aged seventy-seven in 1981, and she now lived on her own.

John thought it would be ideal if he moved somewhere closer to her, and this lovely old house was only a mile down the road from Newtown Verney. He valued Miss French's opinion, but she didn't seem enthusiastic about the station house's Victorian charm. 'Yes, it's pretty,' she said. 'But is it really what you and Treasa want? You said you wanted to be out in the country, but it's right by a road, and you'll have trains going past several times a day.'

John and Treasa felt deflated. Maybe Miss French was right. Back at the house, she surprised John by asking to speak to him in private in the drawing room.

John was immediately concerned, but he followed her to where she had a site map of her house and garden laid out on her desk. She pointed to an area outlined in red on the document.

'I don't know how you feel about this,' she said, 'but I have to sell a site in the garden if I want to keep the house, and this is it.'

The plot was in a sunny spot where her sweet peas grew.

'I have inheritance taxes to pay since my brother died,'

she explained. 'This plot is ready to go on sale, but I wouldn't advertise it if you were to consider buying it.'

John was excited about the idea straight away, but Miss French was more cautious. 'It's just an option,' she said. 'Talk to Treasa about it. See what she thinks before you make any decision.'

John told Treasa on the drive home, and he didn't need to persuade her.

'I love Miss French's place,' she said. 'If she's happy with it, and you're happy, then so am I.'

So John bought the site in 1985, and they sold the house in Mulhuddart to fund the construction of a new home. Their plans to move to rural Kilternan continued, even though the job in Wicklow didn't work out.

John thought it was the perfect arrangement. He was happy to be close to Miss French in a beautiful part of the country, and she was delighted that she could pay off her inheritance tax and stay in her home. She also felt secure for the first time since her brother's death: she was seventy-nine, and random attacks on elderly people in the area had frightened her.

Miss French loved having John nearby and also the company of his wife and young family. She insisted on them moving into her rambling old house while they built their own home.

'Oh, I don't know if that's a good idea,' said Treasa, when she heard of the offer. 'Miss French is used to living on her own. How is she going to cope with five kids and two adults moving in on top of her?'

But Miss French was adamant that she wanted them to move in, and John was happy with the idea, so Treasa went along with it. Despite Treasa's reservations, Miss French seemed to thrive in the hectic atmosphere and enjoyed having the kids around her. 'If we're all living together, you're going to have to drop the formality of "Miss French",' she said. 'My name is Eleanor, but my friends call me Nell, so please call me that.'

John and Treasa looked at each other in astonishment, but they changed the habit of a lifetime and did as she'd said.

The old lady remained very private about her finances, but it was clear that she had little income. For some reason she didn't even have a state pension, and relied on small cash amounts she earned from selling baked goods at a local farmers' market.

John and Treasa agreed that they should look after the upkeep in the old house and pay for all the groceries and household bills so that Nell's outgoings were minimal. Still, Nell liked to maintain a supervisory role in the kitchen, which caused the occasional clash between the two women. Nell looked askance, for example, when she saw Treasa present John with a tin of sardines and a fork for lunch. 'A tin?' she exclaimed, adding, in horror: 'And how can you possibly eat fish without a fish fork?'

There were other days when the couple inadvertently upset Nell's sense of social order: she was not pleased to discover builders sitting in her kitchen, drinking tea. 'There's nothing wrong with making tea for them, but I don't know why you had to bring them in,' she complained afterwards. 'I make a dinner for the gardener, but he always eats it in the potting shed.'

Treasa and John glanced at each other and tried not to laugh.

'That woman has a heart of gold, but she has some peculiar ideas,' Treasa said later.

Nell was also very particular about John's diet.

'Look, it's late, Nell,' Treasa argued, one evening. 'We're just in the door, and sausages are the quickest thing to cook for everyone.'

But Nell made it clear that this was a grave dereliction of duty towards her husband. 'Sausages are fine occasionally for you and the children,' she said. 'But everyone knows there's not enough meat in them for a working man.'

Treasa bit her tongue and continued to cook the sausages, stabbing them hard with her fork.

Nell hovered a minute, until she could see that Treasa was not for turning. 'Do you know,' she said, 'I'm a bit peckish too. I might put on something for myself.'

Treasa wasn't fooled when Nell began frying two lamb chops on another pan. She cornered her husband as she brought out the sausages.

'If you touch Nell's lamb chops, I'll kill you,' she told him, under her breath.

When Nell thought Treasa wasn't looking, she slid her plate of lamb chops towards John, eyeing him meaningfully. Meanwhile, Treasa eyed John equally meaningfully and threatened him silently. 'Don't you dare!' she mouthed, behind Nell's back.

The air crackled with so much hostility that John could hardly eat at all.

The new house took longer to build than anyone expected, and the family lived with Nell for nearly two years. The old lady insisted that she was sorry to see them go when they moved out.

'We're moving across the lawn, Nell,' laughed Treasa. 'And you're getting back your lovely house and some of your peace and quiet.'

As the years marched on, Nell grew older and more frail, so John set up an intercom system and alarm between the two houses. 'Okay, Nell,' he explained. 'If for some reason you can't reach the intercom, you have these emergency buttons.' He showed her one beside her bed. 'All you have to do is press this, and we'll come running,' he said.

Only days later, the alarm rang with a terrible clang at 5 a.m.

Hearts racing, John and Treasa leaped out of bed, dashed across the lawn, ran up the stairs and into Nell's bedroom. They found Nell sitting up in bed, drinking a glass of 7Up, with her elbow leaning on the buzzer.

'What are you doing here? And what's that terrible racket?' she said.

One day in 1992 Treasa was working in Donnybrook Crèche and Montessori when she was called to the phone.

'Mam, can you come home?' It was Brian, who was

studying for his Inter Cert exams that morning. 'It's Nell – there's something wrong with her. She's talking funny.'

Treasa rang for an ambulance, alerted Nell's neighbour, left a message at John's school and rushed home. Nell had suffered a severe stroke. John's heart broke when he saw her lying immobile and helpless in the sterile ward of Loughlinstown Hospital.

White-haired and frail, yet line-free and beautiful, she was like a delicate bird in a cage. Eleanor Digby-French passed away in hospital aged eighty-six and was buried alongside her mother, father and brother in Kilternan Church of Ireland graveyard. Many people had seen her as a rather grand old lady, but she was Nell to John, kind-hearted, generous, wise and funny. She was his mentor, his counsellor, his cheerleader and his saviour.

She had always encouraged him to find his real family, but he knew that, even if he found them, they could never mean as much to him as she did. She had taken him, an urchin boy, a stranger, under her wing. She had given him bread and butter and jam, encouragement and love, and become the only true family he had ever had.

The woman who had given him so much in life left everything else to him in death. He inherited her home and her beloved garden and the few material things she held dear. He had never expected it, and it moved him more than he ever thought possible. She had been like a mother to him, and her final loving gesture told him that he had been like a son to her.

We have a photo of Nell, which must have been from the 1920s or 1930s when she was dressed in ermine and pearls for an evening out. She looked as if she had stepped from a Hollywood movie set, she was so glamorous.

It was only after she died that we learned the Digby-French family had many illustrious ancestors. Her family are descendants of the earls of Bristol according to Debrett's *and* Burke's Peerage, *the guides to the titled families of England. One of the better-known members of her family tree was Mary Boleyn, a mistress of King Henry VIII before her ill-fated sister, Anne, became his wife. The Digby-French line descended from Mary's daughter Catherine Carey, suspected to be the illegitimate child of the king and the half-sister of Elizabeth I. If Nell knew of her royal connections, she never spoke of them.*

Over the years, I often wondered why Nell never married. She was a kind and beautiful woman, and I'd heard stories of beaus and proposals. It turned out that her mother, Synolda, a domineering woman who lived until she was ninety, demanded an end to one of Nell's engagements because the man was a Catholic. She put an end to another, claiming she was in ill-health and needed her daughter as her companion.

My parents were at one end of the spectrum, abandoning a child in an orphanage, but Nell's mother was at the opposite by refusing to let her go. It strikes me that parents of all sorts can mess up their children's lives.

19

That Woman

September 1996, Kilternan

Treasa burst into the kitchen waving an envelope bearing the emblem of the Holy Faith Convent. 'It's here!' she said, sinking into the chair beside John's and ripping open the letter. He smiled. She was more excited about getting these records than he was. After all the decades, the Holy Faith Convent had agreed to provide John with the information they held about him. By now, the Church and the state were loosening their stranglehold on the records of adopted people.

St Brigid's Orphanage, located in an old five-storey Georgian building on Dublin's Eccles Street, was long gone, but the same order of nuns held all the records. Here at last was a transcript of those from the day John had been handed to them.

It didn't look like much. When Treasa opened the envelope, all that lay within was one A4 sheet of white paper. It told them the exact date when John had arrived at the orphanage: 12 February 1936, a Wednesday, in the depth of winter. It was the year when King Edward VIII abdicated the British throne to marry Wallis Simpson. But in Dublin it was just an ordinary day, a day when a couple handed over their child to an orphanage.

The page contained the notes: '*The names of his parents were given as William Cameron and Elizabeth Farrell (Maguire).*'

John frowned and looked at Treasa in confusion. 'I don't understand this – why does it say her name is Elizabeth Farrell Maguire?'

His birth certificate recorded his mother's name as Elizabeth Cameron and her maiden name as Maguire. He wondered where 'Farrell' had come from all of a sudden.

'This is crazy!' said Treasa. 'Farrell? Have we been looking for the wrong woman all along?'

The document from the Holy Faith Convent continued: '*The parents passed off as being married but, in fact, were not married. The father, who is a Protestant, brought the child here. He stated that he was an accountant's clerk from County Down and was out of employment. The mother was from County Longford.*'

'Well, at least we know where they're from!' exclaimed Treasa. 'That gives us something to go on at last.'

The records from the orphanage also noted: '*This case was recommended by the Catholic Protection & Rescue Society, South Anne St.*' It was some time later that Treasa discovered the organisation offered aid to mothers who were likely to turn to Protestant childcare agencies with their baby – 'Get them before the other side gets them.' They didn't want any child, even the poorest and most unwanted, to slip out of the grip of the Catholic faith.

Another line noted: 'Nurse (foster mother): Mrs Bennett, 27 St Michael's Terrace, Inchicore'. That came as a surprise to both of them because they had never heard the name before.

'Mrs Bennett must have been your first foster mother before the Mulligans,' said Treasa. 'She must have been the one who reared you from the day you were given to the orphanage.'

John had always wondered about his earliest memory, in which he had sat in a pram under a white blanket in a sunny window. He'd thought he must have been with his mother, but now he realised he was with Mrs Bennett.

Another line noted: '21 July 1938: Changed to Mrs Mulligan, Murphystown.'

'You were only two years and ten months old!' gasped Treasa. 'What a terrible time to uproot a child, never mind putting him in a place as bad as the Mulligans'.'

The final line of John's record, dated 30 March 1944, was an even starker reminder of his fate because it simply stated: 'Sent to Artane School.'

There it was. John's entire adoption history finished with four ominous words: *Sent to Artane School.*

They had to iron out the confusion over his mother's surname, so they submitted a request to the Holy Faith Convent to see the original entry in the orphanage's records.

They were invited into the convent in the Coombe in Dublin to see the ledger. The records, handwritten in faded fountain-pen ink, identified 'Elizabeth Maguire' as John's mother.

However, a line in darker ink was drawn through the surname, and 'Farrell' had been clearly written above it instead.

'It's a different pen and different handwriting, so it was done later, but we've no idea who did it or why,' said the sister in charge, Sister Benignus. 'There's no attempt to conceal the original name, so it looks like someone was making a correction.'

The couple were even more bewildered. John's birth certificate recorded that a woman called Elizabeth Cameron née Maguire was his mother. Meanwhile, the orphanage records stated that his birth mother was Elizabeth Farrell from County Longford.

It prompted them to begin a new search in Longford, but they were dismayed to discover that 'Farrell' was one of the most common surnames in the county. The full title of the county had once been Longphort O'Farrell, meaning 'fortress of the Farrells'.

John and Treasa had no parish in which to begin their

search for Elizabeth Farrell, so they started with the records of St Mel's Cathedral in Longford town. But they hardly knew where to begin. Was John's mother listed under Cameron, Maguire or Farrell? In the end, the search led nowhere.

During summer holidays, John and Treasa continued to travel to Longford graveyards where they scanned lichen-covered stones to find a family connection. But they came no closer to uncovering John's past.

They filed a request under the Freedom of Information Act to get John's records from Artane. The only additional information he received was that he had been detained in the industrial school on a charge of 'receiving alms' or for begging on the street. Knowing that this was a trumped-up charge, John applied for his records from the Children's Court in Dublin. The court transcripts claim that his eight-year-old self was accused of 'receiving alms' on 20 March 1944, at a location recorded as 46 Eccles Street in Dublin.

It was almost a sick joke. The authorities had not only invented the charge, but the address they had used for the supposed crime scene was that of St Brigid's Orphanage where John had been abandoned as a baby. They hadn't even bothered to make the charge look genuine.

September 1996, Longford

John rolled his shoulders, stretched his neck and exhaled. He'd had enough of the cold, dark vault at the back of the church. The sun was shining outside, and he and Treasa were getting nowhere with their search.

'Let's just get out of here,' he said.

They had travelled to Longford to look through the records in St Mel's again. Treasa refused to abandon the search and wanted to give it another try. She was losing heart, though. She shut a book of baptismal records she had been leafing through and heaved it back onto its shelf.

'I wish we knew what we were looking for,' she said. 'Just let me go and thank the sacristan for letting us back here.'

'No luck, then?' the sacristan asked, seeing their downcast demeanour.

'None,' said Treasa. 'I doubt any of these people are still alive now anyway. John is sixty-one years old, but we'd like to find out something about his people. We know his mother is a Maguire or a Farrell, and his father is Cameron, but we've never been able to find a single family member.'

The sacristan shook his head sympathetically. 'It's a terrible thing not to know your people,' he said. 'You'd think it wouldn't be that hard. Cameron is not a common name around here.'

He pondered for a second. 'You know, there's a Mary Brennan in the town here, and I'm nearly sure her mother's maiden name is Cameron,' he said. 'She might be worth calling, seeing as you've come all this way already.'

Half an hour later, Mary Brennan welcomed them into her house. 'What a coincidence!' she said. 'My grandparents were William and Elizabeth Cameron, and her maiden name was Maguire.'

John and Treasa glanced at each other in astonishment.

It seemed like far more than a coincidence. Mary shook her head adamantly. 'No, this Elizabeth Cameron was too old and sick to give birth to John in 1935,' she said.

Treasa was unwilling to give up this promising lead without a fight. 'John's godmother said his mother was quite old to be expecting,' she said. 'We don't really know what age she was when she gave birth to John.'

Mary flicked through a collection of family memorabilia before finding the page she was looking for. 'Yes, it says here that she died on 18 July 1937, aged forty-eight,' she said. 'That was less than two years after you were born, John. She was too old to have a child in those days, and we know she had cancer of the uterus for years.'

That Elizabeth Cameron had to be ruled out as John's mother.

'What happened to your grandfather, William Cameron?' Treasa asked.

Mary's forehead wrinkled as she tried to recall stories she had heard years earlier about her grandparents. 'By the time Elizabeth Cameron died, our mother was twenty and her brothers and sisters were a bit younger. Their father William moved to Dublin, and no one had much contact with him after that.'

John sighed in frustration.

'The names are a real coincidence, but you're looking for another Elizabeth Cameron,' said Mary. 'My grandmother couldn't have been your mother.'

John was utterly disheartened with the search now.

It had looked so promising for a while, yet he was facing another dead-end.

'Let's just forget about this, Treasa,' he said, as they drove out of Longford. 'What good will come of it now? I'm sixty-one, so if my mother was thirty years old when she had me, she'd be ninety-one now. Chances are she's long dead.'

Treasa felt inclined to agree.

September 2002, Longford

'*That* woman's dead.'

'Is that you, Fran? What woman's dead?'

'*That* woman.'

'Fran, what are you talking about?' demanded Mary Brennan, frowning in exasperation. 'Who's dead?'

'The woman our mother always referred to as "*that* woman".'

'Oh, *that* woman. How do you know?'

'It's in the Deaths in the *Irish Times*. It says Elizabeth Cameron has died.'

'But she wasn't a Cameron!'

'Well, she's in the *Times*. Cameron née Farrell.'

'Elizabeth Cameron? I've never thought of her as Elizabeth Cameron. I wonder . . . I meant to tell you, a couple came here years ago asking about an Elizabeth and William Cameron. He said he was their son. They thought her maiden name was Maguire, but I said it couldn't have been our grandmother.'

'No, but it could have been *that* woman.'

'That's what I'm thinking now, but our grandfather and *that* woman had a girl, didn't they?'

'Sure, we don't know what went on. They might have had a boy too. Someone ought to tell him she's dead. If he's her son, he has a right to know.'

September 2002, Kilternan

Niamh hardly heard the phone because the rain was hammering so hard on the windows. She pulled her cardigan tighter around her as she hurried down the hall to answer the insistent ring.

'Hello, you don't know me, but my name is Fran Dean,' the voice on the other end began. 'I think I'm related to you.'

Niamh almost froze with the shock, realising that this might be the call her father had hoped for all his life, and he wasn't at home.

When his car finally pulled into the drive, she ran to fling open the front door. 'Dad, I thought you'd never get home,' she cried, her eyes wide and frantic. 'This is going to come as a shock. I think someone from your family has called.'

John felt his legs melt under him. He managed to make his way to the kitchen table where he sank into a chair. He tried to absorb the details of Niamh's story, but the information was overwhelming. If he understood her properly, he had relatives. Many relatives. He had people.

'But, Dad, listen, here's the bad bit. She thinks your mother has just died. She saw it in the Deaths column. She thinks it's her.'

John held his head in his hands, trying to process this latest mental bomb blast. 'So I'm going to a funeral?' he asked, hearing the tremble in his voice but unable to do anything about it. 'My mother was still alive until now, but now I'm going to her funeral?'

Niamh saw her father search her face for a denial that she couldn't give.

John pushed aside the thought of his mother. He chose to focus on the fact that he might have an actual blood relative, someone who had phoned his house. He was sixty-seven years old, and he'd never met anyone in his life to whom he was related, apart from his children. Now he might have found someone. And there were more people, according to Niamh. Many more, perhaps.

And his mother? He hadn't expected her to be alive, so to find others related to her, others who had known her or his father, was a miracle. The disappointment and the grief over his mother could come later.

Soon after, Treasa arrived home, and John was glad to hear Niamh relate the story of the phone call again in case he had imagined it.

He began to understand that he might never have found his family if he and Treasa hadn't gone to Longford years before, if they hadn't talked to that sacristan, if the sacristan hadn't pointed him in the direction of Mary Brennan, if they hadn't met Mary, if she hadn't mentioned them to her sister, Fran, and if Fran hadn't gone to the trouble of looking through the phone book to find him in Kilternan.

The links were so fragile, yet they had held. John was on the brink of discovering the mysteries of his life.

He sat, still dazed, and behind him he could hear Treasa saying again and again that the phone number was engaged. She couldn't get through to Fran, his new relation, his first relation ever.

'Where did she say she lived?' Treasa asked.

'Clonskeagh,' Niamh said.

John sat at the table, lost in some dark abyss. Treasa knew he was too shocked to process all this at once. She ran her fingers down the phone directory, snatched her keys, pulled his photograph from the wall and ran for her car.

She left John staring into space, lighting cigarette after cigarette, trembling with anticipation, nervousness, fear, happiness, hope.

His mind raced as Treasa drove towards the only person who had ever claimed to be a blood relative of his, a woman whose eyes filled with tears as soon as Treasa showed her John's photograph. 'Oh my God,' the woman said, gazing at the picture. 'There's no mistake. He's the image of my grandfather, William Cameron.'

Part II

To tell the remainder of this story, I must rewind the clock and travel back a full three years before I was born because by 1932 the events that would shape my life were already in train. The people who were to decide my fate and that of several others were already orbiting about one another.

How much heartbreak and agony could have been avoided if my mother and father had never met? But they did, and they battled an equally unyielding force of nature in my mother's husband.

Those three people whirled around each other, blowing hell-winds of passion and fury, and leaving a swathe of destruction in their paths. Then they would never speak about it again. My mother certainly never did. Neither did Hugh nor William to my knowledge.

They buried memories of those events in deep, sunless recesses where no light was ever allowed to penetrate. As the years passed, they became unwitting allies of sorts, gatekeepers to the twisted secrets and guilt of the past. They shut the door on that chapter of their lives and moved on from it all, including us, their children.

No doubt they would see me telling their story as betrayal, but they're beyond hurting now. Only the living feel pain.

In the decade after receiving that fateful phone call and finding the first of many relatives, my family and I have unearthed significant amounts of material about my past. Through this, I have managed to piece together some of the story that shaped my life. Of course, there are still many missing pieces in the jigsaw puzzle. I can honestly say I still don't understand why any of the three of them did what they did. Without a doubt, there are motives and explanations from the black events of the 1930s which are lost in the mists of time.

We have amassed a lot of information gleaned from a variety of sources, including legal documents, letters, newspapers of the time and the memories of family and neighbours. However, I found the only way to put coloured flesh on the bones of these facts is through the imagination. I hope the reader will see that the following narrative is not so much about making up the story, but more about making the most of the material we found. I have decided to recount this part of the story with the help of a witness to it: the midwife.

My midwife is a hybrid of Mary Walsh and Mary Doyle,

both real-life nurses, one of whom I met and who delivered me, and both of whom were involved with all the major protagonists in this tale.

The only transcripts of actual dialogue between the people in this story are a few exchanges recorded in newspaper court reports. As a result, the conversations and interchanges, even a few minor characters, are, by necessity, imaginative reconstructions. The timelines, the locales, the events and almost all the characters are factual and accurate, to the best of my knowledge.

20

The Affair

The affair was the talk of Granard town and beyond. What started as squinting suspicions and a trickle of whispers became a torrent of salacious tattle by the winter of 1932.

There was hardly a soul across the county who hadn't heard about Lizzie Major's cavorting with a married man. *And her poor husband, God help us, away in America, trying to put bread on the table for the family.*

Mrs Dunne, the shopkeeper, shook her head and sighed as she wrapped the butter in brown paper. 'It's a fright, Nurse, a fright, disgracing her mother and father's good names . . . and her with two small children too.' She paused to let her gimlet eye flicker over Nurse Doyle. 'Have you tried having a word with her, Nurse?' she asked, scanning the young woman's face for a reaction.

Mary had almost to prise the package from the shopkeeper's grip before dropping the butter into her basket. 'Oh, I never pay attention to idle gossip, Mrs Dunne,' she said, with an air of tedium that she hoped would bring an end to the prattle.

But Mrs Dunne grabbed her own throat with her hand. 'I'm the last one for gossip, Nurse Doyle!' she said, with an air of injured affront. 'I'm worried about the woman, that's all. And her poor parents and those two little craythurs.'

Mary didn't fall for the bait. 'Is that the time?' She feigned surprise as she glanced at her fob watch. 'I have to get back to the dispensary. What do I owe you, Mrs Dunne?'

Mrs Dunne's nose lifted, and her lips pursed at this patent snub, but the younger woman pretended not to notice. Mrs Dunne spread gossip with the same relish that she slathered creamery butter on her bread.

Mary breathed a sigh as she stepped out onto Granard's blustery main street. Her navy wool cape whipped around her as she hurried back to the dispensary, and she had to clap her free hand to her cap as a gust of wind threatened to tear it from her head.

It astounded her how fast news of all sorts could spread in the area. Once when she had pedalled furiously all the way from a birth in Edgeworthstown she had found Mrs Dunne already knew the weight of the child.

Everyone marvelled at the speed of information since Radio Athlone had gone live in the summer, and a handful of prosperous people in the town rushed to buy one of the new-fangled wireless sets. But Mary believed a wireless could never beat the speed of word-of-mouth in the county. Longford was a cesspool of gossip and slander, and Lizzie Major was the centre of it right now.

She recalled how Lizzie, usually so gay and mischievous, had appeared so frightened the last time she had seen her. 'What am I going to do, Mary?' she had pleaded. 'John Donohoe is trying to ruin me. He and John McGrath are telling everyone they saw us canoodling in the old Mallon cottage in Dromeel.'

Mary thought Lizzie was foolish to think she could meet her fancy man there, but she didn't say it aloud. The bachelors were known to spy on courting couples who used the tumbledown cottage for their trysts.

'They followed us on their bikes,' Lizzie told her. 'Those two oul ferrets pedalled after us for all they were worth. What's wrong with these people? They couldn't see William, so they tried to shine their lamps on his face.' Lizzie half-laughed and sobbed as she recalled the chaotic scenes that ensued. 'I threw my coat over his head, and poor William nearly ended up in the ditch,' she said. 'In the end, we had to climb old Nelligan's gate and run across the fields with our bikes to get away from them.' Lizzie looked at Mary in bewilderment and pleaded with her again: 'What will I do, Mary? They're going to ruin me.'

Mary repeated what she had said from the very first time Lizzie had confided in her. 'Give up William Cameron, Lizzie. Give him up while you still can.'

Then Lizzie said what she always said: 'Oh, God, you're

right, Mary. Nothing is worth this. I swear I will, Mary. I swear I will.'

But nothing would break her from William Cameron.

A whirl of dust followed Mary into the waiting room before she had a chance to shut the dispensary door. Several pairs of dark eyes regarded her when she turned around. 'Afternoon, everyone!' she said, with more cheer than she felt. She laid down her basket so she could undo the buttons on her cloak.

Thomas Reynolds's hacking cough rent the air, and Mary saw Mrs Davis edge away uneasily. Thomas suffered from bronchitis, but everyone had a terrible fear of consumption, as they called it, and the sanatorium. Tuberculosis, a scourge and a death sentence for many, was rampant.

Mary's gaze settled on a woman with doleful brown eyes dominating her peaky face. 'Mrs Kirwan, are you here to see me?' Mary enquired, with an inclination of her head.

The woman nodded.

'Come on in with me so,' said Mary, with an encouraging smile, glad to be distracted from thoughts of Lizzie Major.

Mrs Kirwan cradled the youngest of her brood, while two more toddlers hung out of her skirts. Her eldest two were at home with her elderly mother.

'How are you, Mrs Kirwan?' Mary asked, closing the door behind them.

'I just need a tonic, Nurse. I'm so tired all the time,' she said. 'Something so I can keep up with the farm and the children.'

The dark circles under her eyes and her general pallor

spoke of her exhaustion. Mary could see that the woman was worn out, but with five children aged under six and another on the way, it was little wonder she was weary.

She needs a break from having babies, not a tonic, thought Mary. She thought of a nursing friend in England who had written to tell her about a new form of natural birth control. It was called the rhythm method and had been developed by a Catholic doctor. Yet even if she had had the knowledge or means to provide family planning for her patients, it was a taboo subject. And if the word 'contraceptive' was even mentioned in the dispensary, Canon Markey would descend on them like the hammers of Hell.

There was no appetite for godless notions like 'family planning' in Ireland, especially since the Eucharistic Congress that summer. Religious fervour was at an all-time high, and the latest papal encyclical called on the faithful to procreate more saints and servants of God.

'You're anaemic, Mrs Kirwan,' said Mary. 'I'm going to prescribe iron salts, a bottle of Guinness a day and bed rest, but I want you to see Dr McEvoy as a precaution.' She recognised the panic in the woman's eyes, so she added: 'Don't worry about the cost. It's just a precaution, so there'll be no charge.'

Mrs Kirwan looked dazed as Mary shepherded her and her children towards Dr McEvoy's office.

The afternoon passed quickly, and Mary had already seen off the last of her patients when Dr McEvoy rapped on her open door. He had an old mackintosh over his arm, a hat in one hand and his medical bag in the other. He was ready to leave. 'Glad you're still here, Mary. I'm calling to the Kirwan place before I head home. I think I need to make it clear to Mr Kirwan that his wife gets bed rest, but I just wanted a quick word with you before I go.'

He cleared his throat and glanced back over his shoulder into the waiting room, even though he knew the place was empty.

'I wonder if you've heard about these goings-on with your friend Mrs Major?' he asked, his tone hushed.

Dr McEvoy was a genial man who went beyond the call of duty for his patients. But even before his wife died, he had been solitary, with little interest in the intrigues of a small country town.

Mary bristled at the doctor's description of her as a 'friend' of Mrs Major. 'I wouldn't say Mrs Major and I are friends,' she said. 'She went to school with my oldest sister, but there are ten years or more between us.'

'Yes, but everyone says you two talk all the time,' said Dr McEvoy.

Everyone says. Mary sighed to herself. There wasn't much that went on in this town that everyone didn't have something to say about. But she had become a sounding board for Lizzie, even her confidante. Now she wished she had followed her instincts and stayed out of it. 'Well, of course I talk to her. She's my patient, and her children are my patients,' she said.

Dr McEvoy seemed hardly to listen as he ruffled his hair with one hand. 'The thing is, I met Dr Morris last night,' he said, referring to the GP for Longford town, a long-time friend. 'Does Mrs Major know she's knocking around with a man whose wife is very sick?'

Mary shuffled the pages of a file on her desk.

Dr McEvoy went on: 'Dr Morris is worried that she might hear about this malarkey with her husband.'

Mary never looked up, and her reply was noncommittal: 'That's understandable.'

The doctor glanced longingly towards the dispensary door, but he persisted. 'Dr Morris said the man has a clatter of children and is a Protestant to boot.' He glanced at his watch. The last thing he wanted to do was discuss Lizzie Major's affair with a married man. 'Look, Mary, I promised Dr Morris that I'd do something about it,' he said, 'but I can't talk to Mrs Major. It would be better coming from another woman. Would you go over to the Farrell place and reason with her? Try and knock some sense into her before things end up a right damned mess.'

He cupped the back of his head with one hand and stretched his neck in a gesture of weariness. Mary didn't have the heart to say that reasoning with Lizzie Major was likely to be a waste of breath. She nodded her assent. 'I've got to make a few calls out that direction anyway, so I'll go in the next week. I'll let you know how I get on.'

The doctor brightened, relieved that he could leave it all in Mary's capable hands. 'Excellent, many thanks. Goodnight so, Mary,' he said, as he left the room.

She heard the dispensary door slam and, seconds later, the putter of his Model A Ford coming to life. Then he was gone.

Mary would never say it to him, but she feared things were already 'a right damned mess', and nothing she could do would change anything now.

My daughter Fiona read one of the first drafts of this book, which included the story of the two old bachelors chasing Mrs Major and her lover. Fiona said it sounded very far-fetched. I had to assure her that the two men gave evidence about the incident in court soon after. Be assured, too, that the parish priest of Granard, Canon Markey, and Dr McEvoy were also real people who became embroiled in Lizzie Major's story.

Elizabeth Major's private life came into sharp focus just as religious devotion and the power of the Catholic Church reached a peak in Ireland.

The Eucharistic Congress of the summer of 1932 has gone down in the annals of Irish history as one of the most spectacular public events of that century in Ireland. At a time when Dublin had a population of just 500,000 and the population of the entire country was less than three million, more than a million worshippers flocked to the Pontifical Mass in the Phoenix Park.

The highlight on 26 June was a live broadcast by Pope Pius XI from the Vatican, which was transmitted via the biggest public-address system in the world at that time. Loudspeakers were strung across the Phoenix Park, along the Liffey quays, down O'Connell Street and across the city centre, turning Dublin into one big open-air Mass.

By 1932, the Catholic Church was an impregnable force of law in the Irish Free State, and Elizabeth Major, the woman who was to become my mother, was recklessly breaking all its rules.

21

Roose

November 1932

Dark clouds rolled over the countryside, and heavy rains flooded the roads for days. A week elapsed before Mary was able to honour her promise to Dr McEvoy and set off for Lizzie's home in the townland of Roose.

She mounted her High Nelly that morning under an iron-grey sky, hoping that the rain would hold off. As the macadam surface of Market Street ended, she felt the familiar jolt of her tyres hitting the dirt roads. It was a six-mile journey to Roose in the rural hinterlands of Granard.

Torrential rain combined with horse-drawn carts ensured that the road surface was badly churned and rutted in spots. Mary had to dismount several times to get around the black pools of rainwater rippling in the wind, and she knew the water would lie there until the first sunshine days of spring dried them out. The horizon was wild and lonely, studded with bare trees and reeds swaying in the boglands. There was no sign of life in the fields, apart from handfuls of foraging sparrows, finches and crows.

She wasn't long on the road before she met Matty Murphy driving his donkey and cart towards Granard. He tipped the peak of his cap in salute. 'Begob, it's a terrible road back there,' he called, indicating over his shoulder with a jerk of his head. 'Keep an eye out for me teeth, Nurse.'

'I will to be sure, Mr Murphy,' she said, laughing because it was a long time since Matty Murphy had had teeth.

With a lazy flick of the reins and a grunt of 'Hup, y'oul bugger,' he continued on his way.

Life for those who lived beyond the town was as rough as the old road. The people were subsistence farmers who toiled from early morning until dark, with no running water, no electricity and poor sanitation. The women bore the daily toil of drawing buckets of water from the well or from streams at the end of the field. They lifted heavy kettles off the open fire for hot water to fill the washtubs or to scrub the milk churns. Most of the people lived in low-slung thatched cottages, which looked charming when freshly whitewashed. Unfortunately, those picturesque exteriors belied the dark, cold, damp and smoky conditions inside.

Mary was grateful to live in the town where life was more comfortable. Terraced houses were warmer, and many roofs were tiled now rather than thatched; they had WCs outside their back doors and those with fancy kitchen ranges had a source of hot running water.

Best of all, the electricity board had connected Granard to the Shannon Scheme in the past year, transforming the townspeople's lives. Now, with a flick of a switch, the people had light. Not everyone was pleased, of course. Old Mrs Doherty on Church Street had slammed her door in the face of the wiremen. There was no way, she swore, they were going to burn her alive in her bed with their new-fangled light on a string. And where in the name of God, demanded some others, did they think people were going to find ten pounds a year to pay for light on a switch? And why should they bother when they had perfectly good oil lamps?

But the people living outside the towns didn't have the luxury of choice. Once the sun went down, the fire in the hearth, paraffin lamps and candles kept the inky darkness at bay.

On the way to Roose, Mary dropped in to see a Mrs Connolly and her new baby. The mother had preferred to use the services of the local handywoman, Mrs Barrett, for the birth. The old woman was still popular despite efforts to stamp out the practice of unlicensed midwives. Handywomen were being prosecuted in some counties, but Mary knew better than to make an official complaint about Mrs Barrett. She would alienate herself in Granard if she turned on one of their own. Mothers died in childbirth all the time, and the infant death rate was more than 10 per cent in some areas, but the tradition of handywomen was difficult to break.

About three miles from Granard, Mary heard a motor rumbling behind her. She dismounted to watch Canon Markey drive by in his ruby and black Baby Austin with the young curate, Father Mahon, clutching the wheel.

The canon gave a regal wave from his passenger seat, but Father Mahon focused his eyes on the potholed road.

The good father was probably on his way to a fine silver-service lunch in the Longford Arms Hotel, thought Mary. Granard's parish priest enjoyed a very different lifestyle from that of his flock.

The sound of the motor faded until all she could hear once again was the rattle of her bike over the uneven roadway and the wind rustling in the hedgerows. She wondered what she would say to Lizzie this time. The woman had ignored all the advice she had previously given her, so she knew this was a fool's errand. But she had to try one final time and fulfil her promise to Dr McEvoy.

Unlike many in Granard, Mary felt some sympathy for Lizzie. She was a married woman in name only because she hadn't set eyes on her husband in years. Still, the locals were unforgiving. There were no excuses for a woman to commit adultery.

And what about her poor mother and father's reputation? Had she no thought for them at all? Having an affair with any married man was an appalling scandal, but the fact that the man was a Protestant made it an even more heinous crime.

Not for the first time, Mary wondered if Michael and Julia

Farrell, Lizzie's parents, knew what was going on. They were a well-respected couple, although some accused the father of spoiling his two daughters to excess.

Lizzie was now the only daughter. They had lost the younger, Julia, to emigration. There were few employment opportunities for women in the Irish Free State, so Mary felt lucky that her father could afford to pay for her nursing studies in the Coombe in Dublin. After qualifying, she had got a position of outdoor nurse with the Queen's Institute of District Nursing. A year ago, she had become dispensary midwife and district health nurse in Granard, part-funded by the Longford Health Board.

Most women weren't as fortunate. Julia Farrell had gone to America in search of a position in domestic service just months after her sister married Hugh Major. Even though the Great Depression was worldwide, there was always a demand for young Irishwomen in middle-class homes in big cities like New York and Chicago. Hugh Major came from a respectable farming family down the road in Cartron, just outside Granard town. But Hugh was no farmer. He had spent the previous decade working as a butler in a grand house in New York.

Elizabeth Farrell was twenty-five years old, and Hugh Major was forty when they married on 24 June 1924. Their first child, Hugh Junior, was only three months old when his father sailed back to America in August 1925. Mr Major returned in the spring of the following year to settle his late mother's estate. By the time he sailed from Cobh to New York again, on 19 July 1926, Lizzie was expecting their second child, Veronica. The little girl, whom everyone called Maisie, was now almost six years old and had never met her father.

'Oh, he sends remittances every so often,' Lizzie had told Mary the previous year, 'but any time I've written asking him when he's coming home, he replies that it's not the right time. It's *never* the right time.'

'These are hard times,' Mary said. 'Men have to make ends meet. Lots of them emigrate for work.'

But Lizzie's expression had twisted with scorn. 'We have enough here. We have my father's two farms if Hugh had been willing to work them, but he wasn't.'

Lizzie gazed into the fire, and Mary saw sadness in her eyes.

'We didn't rub together well,' Lizzie said. 'There were arguments, lots of them. Believe me, he's a hard man to live with. In the end, there was no discussion. He was off back to America, just like that. Make no mistake, he suited himself, and there was nothing we could do about it.'

It wasn't natural, Mary thought, a man staying away from his wife and children for seven years. He could have sent for them to join him in America, but he hadn't. Mr Major was not as blameless as the town gossips made him out to be.

As Mary neared the turn-off for Roose, she heard the crunch of bicycle tyres behind her, and Paddy Walsh rolled up alongside her on an old drop-handle machine. A tall, lean man in his early twenties, he worked for his elderly uncle on his farm outside Edgeworthstown. 'Fair morning, Nurse Doyle,' said Paddy. 'Where are you off to?'

'I'm on a call to the Farrells in Roose.'

'And I'm on my way to do some work for Mr Farrell. I met him at Mass, and he said the shed roof leaked buckets last week.' Rummaging in his jacket pocket, he pulled out a ten-pack of Woodbines. He offered her a cigarette, but she declined. Her paltry salary didn't allow her to take up expensive habits like smoking.

Paddy released his grip on the handlebars and cupped nut-brown hands to his face to light his cigarette. He blew out a plume of smoke, exhaling with pleasure. 'So how are you enjoying Granard, Nurse Doyle?' he asked, his bike weaving to slow to her pace.

'The name's Mary, or do you want me to call you Mr Walsh?'

He laughed. 'Yerra, I've been called plenty worse, but Paddy will do. So, Mary, how are you liking Granard?'

'I enjoy the work,' she said. 'It's kind of nice being my own boss – the hospital matrons were dragons. I've a lot more freedom now, but I've a lot more responsibility too.'

'Do you get home much?'

'Not as often as I thought I would,' Mary admitted. 'It's supposed to be a fifty-six-hour week, but I never seem to have a full day off. It's a two-hour cycle to Longford, so it's hard to get away.'

As they reached the Farrells' farm, Mary was surprised to see the canon's motor parked on the grass verge outside.

'It's all action at the Farrells' place today,' said Paddy.

It was only as they dismounted that they heard raised voices in the yard. Obscured by the hedgerow, Mary hesitated, not knowing whether to go forward to the gate or to retreat down the road. Paddy was stopped in his tracks too.

'. . . disgraceful behaviour!' she heard Canon Markey roar.

'It's no business of yours who I talk to, Father.' Lizzie's voice was shrill. 'I'm a married woman with two children, not some chit of a child.'

'I came here in good faith,' Canon Markey brayed, looking at Mr Farrell, 'hoping that you could do something about your daughter's conduct. Her philandering is the talk of the town and her poor husband in America, putting food on all yeer plates.'

'Divil all the food he puts on my plate, Father,' she heard Michael Farrell shout. 'And divil all the philandering going on either. That man came to see me about a boundary issue and then a greyhound, and the next thing my daughter is being slandered as a slattern.'

'Little wonder the lassie is as shameless as she is when her own father behaves like a blackguard,' bellowed the canon.

'Get off my land, right now!' Mr Farrell yelled. 'You're lucky I don't fling you out on the road by the pin of your Roman collar.'

'Mr Michael Farrell, I've never been so insulted in my life!' the canon howled.

'Insulted? You're insulted?' cried Farrell. 'You storm into my house and call my daughter a hussy and accuse her mother and father of letting her run wild over the county, and you say you're insulted! Get off my land now, before I throw you off!'

'Make no mistake, I'll be writing to Mr Major to let him know what's going on behind his back,' thundered Canon Markey. 'The depravity and wickedness in this house are a sorrow to the whole town.'

The canon stormed out the gate, his face dark with anger, the curate scuttling on his heels.

'You'd be better writing to him to tell him to come home and look after his family, like any normal husband,' yelled Farrell, in his wake.

The canon barely glanced at Mary and Paddy standing in mute shock on the roadway. He flung himself into the motor and pulled the door with a bang after him.

The curate shot them an apologetic look as he dashed to the driver's side of the car. He scrambled in and, with a rev of the engine, pulled off at speed, road grit crunching.

Mary stood frozen, gripping the handlebars of her bike, afraid to move in case their presence was discovered. She could hear Lizzie and her mother, Julia, crying hysterically now.

Paddy's mouth was a grim line, and he ran his fingers through his shock of copper-coloured hair. 'Be the holies,' was all he said.

My mother was born Elizabeth Farrell, on 5 April 1899, in the townland of Roose near Moatfarrell in County Longford. Her younger sister Julia Mary arrived three years later on 18 June 1902.

According to research by the National Archives of Ireland, in 1911 Dublin had the worst housing conditions of any city in the United Kingdom. The levels of poverty in rural areas of Ireland during those years were also possibly worse than those in the rest of Western Europe.

With no son to take over the family farm, my maternal grandfather, Michael Farrell, signed over the farm to his elder daughter's husband.

Like most Irishwomen of the time, my Aunt Julia had few options open to her apart from emigration. Country women who stayed at home were doomed to a life of unpaid drudgery on farms belonging to their fathers, husbands and brothers. In Julia's case, it was her brother-in-law.

Even though emigration was always associated with Irishmen, official figures from the early years of the state show that twice as many Irishwomen as men were emigrating. The few jobs that were open to women often required hefty apprenticeship fees of fifty pounds or more or were unpaid apprenticeships in which they had to serve their time. More often, women were paid a wage far less than their male equivalents, an amount that was often insufficient to live an independent life.

Even joining a religious order, an avenue to respect and status for women, was restricted to the well-heeled. Postulants were expected to bring a dowry of up to five hundred pounds to their convents. Alternatively, they became lay sisters, which meant they spent their entire vocation as skivvies to the 'proper' sisters who came with a dowry.

My Aunt Julia left for America on the SS Mount Clay *on 25 March 1925, nine months after Hugh Major took over the farm. She never saw her family again.*

22

A Plan

27 April 1933

'There isn't any doubt now, Lizzie. You need to think about leaving.' Mary's tone was urgent, but she spoke quietly. 'There'll be too much trouble if you stay.'

Lizzie sat by the hearth in tears. 'I kept hoping it wouldn't come to this,' she said. 'God, I'm such a fool, Mary. What am I to do?'

Mary hadn't many options to offer her. 'Is there any family in Dublin or England who'll take you in?'

Lizzie gazed at her clasped hands and shook her head.

Mary knew it was unlikely, but she asked anyway: 'Can William afford to keep you somewhere until you have the baby?'

Lizzie shook her head again with a sob.

Mary took a deep breath and spoke the inexorable truth. 'It's the mother-and-baby home, so.'

Lizzie's head swivelled towards her, and her glistening eyes were suddenly hard. 'No!' she said, with gritted teeth. 'I won't be bundled away and treated like a common harlot by that shower.'

Mary was startled at the violence of her reaction. They had first suspected Lizzie's predicament a month earlier.

'Did you know,' Lizzie said, 'that it was my husband who introduced me to William in the first place?'

Of course Mary knew. Everyone did.

A land boundary dispute had broken out between the Farrells and their neighbours, and Mr Major had dispatched his wife to consult with Reynolds' Solicitors in Longford town.

On a bright day in early September, Lizzie had dressed in her Sunday best for the legal appointment. Even though she had been raised on a farm, she had had a passion for lovely clothes from childhood. 'I have Julia demented asking her to send me stuff from America,' she used to say, when people admired her fashions.

At first glance, some might have mistaken Lizzie for a plain woman with sharp features. She was pleasingly tall and slim, but with a pointed nose and thin lips she would never be a classic beauty. Yet when people looked again, they noticed her burnished chestnut hair, which she arranged in an elegant chignon at the nape of her slender neck. The halo of wisps that escaped it added a feminine softness to her angular face and frame. And there was something about the sweep of her long, dark lashes and the curve of her smile. Lizzie never appeared without lipstick, so she always had a touch of big-city glamour about her. Her sister's parcels from America contained daring shades of crimson and scarlet for Lizzie's lips.

Even when Lizzie trudged around the farm in her housecoat and gumboots, her lips were smeared with red. Of course, local busybodies scorned her vanity and called her a 'painted woman', but Lizzie refused to give up her lipstick.

The day she went for her legal appointment, she spun about the floor for her parents' approval in her favourite floral tea dress. 'What do you think? Am I ready for Longford town?'

'You look like a slip of a girl, Lizzie. On me oath, like a girl,' her father said, with pride.

Even now, her eyes bloodshot, and wearing an apron fashioned from a flour bag, Mary thought Lizzie looked younger than her years. And there was elegance about her, something undeniably beguiling.

The solicitor's clerk, William Cameron, thought so too. He was stunned to meet this farmer's wife with her colourful dress, sparkling eyes and bright red lips. She was like no woman he had ever met in Longford before. And he glowed with pleasure at the prospect of meeting her again at the Farrell farm where he had the task of measuring the disputed boundary.

Until then, Lizzie's most persistent admirer was old

Matty Murphy. He liked to lean on the gate watching her as she worked the fields her father owned near Dromeel. 'Let an old man die happy, and give us a kiss, Lizzie Farrell,' he'd shout.

'Not as long as I've got a pitchfork,' she'd reply, and Matty would throw back his head and laugh heartily.

Matty always said that Mrs Major 'looked like a film star' at Mass every week. But Mary attended Mass in Granard, and the Farrells attended Clonbroney church, so she never saw this weekly metamorphosis until the day she bumped into Lizzie in Longford town.

It was an autumn day, and Longford's main street was strewn with leaves that skittered ahead of her in the breeze. It was Mary's first free Saturday in months, and she was happy to be back in her hometown for the day. As she made her way to the draper's, she saw a striking couple approach. The woman was tall and slender and wore a hip-skimming skirt with a kick-flare hem, and a matching belted navy jacket. A sweet navy cloche completed the look and framed the woman's angular face in its gentle curves. Mary had to look twice before she recognised Lizzie. She was in earnest conversation with a slender, well-dressed man in a smart camel coat and brown trilby. How exotic they looked in these drab country-town surroundings, Mary thought. It was as if Lizzie had stepped out of a fashion plate from Paris. Little wonder that people eyed her with curiosity.

'Mary!' Lizzie cried, smiling in pleasure when she saw the nurse. 'Look at you, all pretty in your civvies! Isn't it great to get dressed up once in a while?'

Mary wore a belted gaberdine coat and a black beret. She had never felt less pretty in her life. Lizzie's companion removed his hat, revealing flaxen hair slicked high over his brow.

Mary guessed he was in his forties, older than she'd thought from a distance. He proffered his hand and a dazzling smile. 'Good Lord, Elizabeth,' he said. 'Not another beauty who's been hiding away in Roose?'

'No, not from Roose,' said Lizzie. 'This is Nurse Mary Doyle from Longford, but she's living with us in Granard these days. Mary, can I introduce you to Mr William Cameron?'

'*Very* pleased to meet you,' William said, and Mary wondered if she imagined he held her hand a fraction too long.

'William works with Reynolds' Solicitors,' said Lizzie. 'He has very kindly come in on a Saturday to go over some old maps of the farm.' She gestured to the folder under her companion's arm. 'Problems with the boundaries. You don't want to know,' she said, with a tinkling laugh. 'Will you join us for tea?'

With a sweep of her dark eyelashes at Mr Cameron, she added: 'Where are we going, William? I hope I didn't get all dressed up for nothing.'

Mary saw the familiarity between them straight away. She noted how the name 'Elizabeth' rolled off his tongue and how he almost stroked her with his affectionate gaze.

'Will the Longford Arms suit, Madame?' he purred, and Lizzie beamed in return.

'Much as I'd like to, my mother would kill me,' Mary

replied, with a smile. She didn't miss the flash of relief that crossed William Cameron's face.

When Mary called to the Farrell house in Roose weeks later, she noticed the light in Lizzie's eye and how she used every opportunity to mention William Cameron.

There wasn't much that could be kept secret in a country town, so Mary wasn't surprised when she heard the rumours about them. But rumours, even if well founded, were one thing. A baby was another. This baby was irrevocable proof of sex outside marriage, and the penalty for that in Ireland was a heavy one for women.

Yet here was Lizzie, once again rejecting the only sensible advice she could give her. Mary sighed with frustration. 'Think of your mother and father and think of little Hugh and Maisie,' she said. 'You have to do something before you start showing.'

Lizzie threw back her head. 'And what happens if I vanish for a few months? Don't you think everyone won't know anyway? What do I say to my mother and father? What do I write and tell Himself? His brother is down the road.' Lizzie rose from her stool at the hearth. 'If I leave this place now, I might as well walk down the main street with a big belly.'

Mary was out of ideas. 'Do your mother and father know anything?'

The women could hear Mrs Farrell cleaning the milk churns in the yard, and they knew Michael Farrell was out mending fences.

'My mother says I was foolish to be seen on my own

with William Cameron, but she doesn't believe a word of the gossip,' said Lizzie. 'But that oul yoke Bernie Smith in Aughamore complained to my father that he caught us in Flaherty's barn.' She wrung her hands, then folded her arms. 'Dadda sent him packing, but he knows,' she said. 'He hasn't said anything. He's angrier with my so-called husband than he is with me. But, God, it would finish them both off if they found out about this baby.'

Lizzie took a deep breath and wiped the tear streaks from her face with the backs of her hands. 'I need to finish the washing,' she said, lifting the kettle from the fire. She poured the steaming water over clothes steeping in the washtub. A washboard and a bar of Sunlight soap waited for her on a three-legged stool. She would spend the rest of the day scrubbing clothes until her knuckles bled raw.

Mary gathered up her things to leave, knowing she had achieved nothing by her visit. She had hoped to persuade Lizzie to seek shelter in a mother-and-baby home, but the woman was adamant that she would not take help from the nuns.

Then Lizzie seemed to gather her thoughts again. 'Hugh can never know,' she said. 'If he finds out, he'll throw us all onto the side of the road.'

Mary paused. 'You don't know that, Lizzie. He's lived a long time in America. He might be more understanding than you think.'

But Lizzie shook her head. 'I didn't know him for long, but I know the kind of man he is. He hasn't been here in seven years, but he still controls us all in this house, and he won't be made a fool of. He'll destroy us if he discovers I'm having another man's child.' Her blue eyes flashed at Mary. 'But I have to do something. When do you think this baby will arrive?'

'Going by your dates, end of December, early January at the latest.'

Lizzie stared at Mary, a glint of steel in her expression. 'I've nothing left to lose now, I suppose,' she said. 'It's time I wrote to Mr Major.'

Mary was relieved that Lizzie had a plan at last. She hadn't much choice but to appeal to her husband. After all these years of neglect, the man would surely do the decent thing and help the mother of his children in her hour of need.

Pregnancy was nearly impossible to avoid among sexually active adults in 1930s' Ireland. Contraception was still technically legal in the country up to 1935, but no one would supply it for fear of the clergy.

If she had lived in England, Elizabeth Major would have had access to the Marie Stopes Clinic and other clinics that were transforming the lives of married women. The prevalence of Catholic dogma ensured that there was no family planning movement in Ireland.

Irish women of means could have 'gentlemen's families' with the help of physicians in London. A few doctors in the leafier areas of Dublin also discreetly supplied the cervical cap, the sponge and other devices. Resourceful people smuggled in condoms from Northern Ireland, along with banned books and tea. But the reality for most of the population was that contraception was unobtainable. The prospects looked grim for Elizabeth Major, pregnant by adultery. Pregnant single women who had money slipped away to London or Dublin to have their babies secretly and give them up for adoption.

Many who fell foul of the strict morals of the day faced incarceration in mother-and-baby homes and the Magdalene Laundries. Falling pregnant outside marriage was scandalous and dangerous for any woman, but it was especially hazardous for Elizabeth Major, who risked losing the family home.

23

Mr Major

20 May 1933

Mrs Whitney bustled into the kitchen and landed her laden wicker basket on the table with a thump. 'He's coming home,' she said, breathless. 'He's on his way now.' She whipped off her headscarf with a tug of the knot under her chin, and silver curls sprang to life around her face.

Mary's brow wrinkled in confusion. 'Who's coming home?'

'Mr Major!' said Mrs Whitney, watching Mary's reaction as she slipped off her pea-green coat. But Mary continued reading the *Longford Leader*.

That girl wouldn't let her right hand know what her left was doing, thought the old woman. 'Anyway,' Mrs Whitney continued, 'Edward Major said they'd received a telegram from Hugh Major saying he was boarding a ship home. They're collecting him at the station on Tuesday. What do you think of that?'

'I think it's about time,' said Mary, not looking up.

'Aye,' said Mrs Whitney, sliding into the chair in front of Mary and lowering her voice, 'but why is he coming home now?'

Mary kept her eyes focused on the front-page headline, which read: 'Longford's £40,000 Share of Sweepstakes'. 'I have no idea.'

'Well, I wouldn't put it past someone here to have stirred up trouble. Someone might have written to Mr Major,' said Mrs Whitney, in a hushed tone.

Mary continued to read the newspaper.

Mrs Whitney glared, convinced that Mary was feigning disinterest.

'Well, it's a holy terror what is going on these days in this town!' She harrumphed.

Mary rustled the paper and smoothed the front page. 'It says here that forty thousand pounds from the Hospital Sweepstakes is to be given for a new hospital in Longford with X-ray machines,' she said. 'This new Sweepstakes is a great thing all the same, isn't it, Mrs Whitney?'

The landlady got to her feet to empty her basket. 'You can pretend to be all holier than thou, Missy, but you don't fool me for a minute. I know you're as interested as everyone else is around here. Maybe more so.'

Mary couldn't help laughing at her landlady, her lips

puckered tight with indignation. 'I'm tired of all the sanctimonious busybodies in this town, that's all,' she said. 'Everyone is all sympathy for Mr Major, and they want to see Mrs Major tarred and feathered.'

'You can't blame the people this time, you really can't. Yon bucko is an oul Protestant, so you can't expect too much from the likes of him, but she's from good Catholic stock. It's a terrible carry-on altogether.'

Mary steered the conversation to safer ground. 'Hugh Major, what's he like?'

'Him? Well, to be truthful, he was always a bit of an odd fish,' Mrs Whitney said, with a fleeting frown of disapproval. 'He took after his father, old James Major, I'd say, but he's passed fifteen years now. The other boys – Edward and James – are friendlier sorts. They take after their mother Bridget, Lord rest her soul. Hugh is the type who might pass you on the road and not bid you the time of day.'

Mary wondered why, being the eldest, Hugh had not taken over the family farm.

'I suppose the land is not for everyone. The Majors came in with Cromwell as soldiers and tradespeople – they were brewers, wine merchants and adventurers. His great-aunt, Dinah Major from this town, was one of the first settlers in America's Wild West. Maybe the land wasn't in his blood.'

'So, what has he been doing in America, do you know?'

'We'd never have heard except he stayed with Patrick Ward out there for a while. He's Mrs Ward's son, a cousin of the Majors. Mr Major stayed with him until he got a job in service.' Mrs Whitney unpacked her messages as she talked. 'He did well for himself in the beginning, becoming a butler for a big noise in New York called John Pierson. He was a general in the Union Army in the civil war and a big business tycoon, with mansions all over the east coast.'

Mrs Whitney threw a side glance at Mary to confirm she had her attention. 'Mr Major worked in their Manhattan house with eight servants – almost all of them Irish. Imagine, the Piersons and their son were the only people in the whole house, and they had eight servants looking after them. Aye, and the rest of us lucky to have shoes for Mass of a Sunday.'

'So what brought Mr Major back to Ireland in the first place? How did he first meet Lizzie Farrell?'

Mrs Whitney had to pause a few seconds to recall. 'He came back about eight or nine years ago. I don't know why he left New York. He was nearly forty, and maybe he thought it was time to get a wife and settle down. He just turned up here, out of the blue, in the spring of 1924.' She leaned forward, warming to the subject as the memories flooded back. 'There was great excitement because everyone expected a homecoming night. You know, with dancing and singing and a barrel of porter. That's what the Americans are supposed to do, but Yankee Major never put his hand in his pocket. And, with all his fine clothes, he carried on like a swank. People didn't forget that, you know.'

'And how did Lizzie meet him?'

'Oh, that was at one of Willie Kelly's céilí nights,' said Mrs Whitney, with a smile. 'Sure, you haven't lived until you go to one of his house parties. He charges a shilling and puts on a barrel of porter and sets up a card room out the back. There's dancing until sunrise.' She laughed as she added: 'Canon Markey goes mad when he hears about it in confessions afterwards. Mr Major showed up at one of the céilís, and once he set eyes on young Lizzie Farrell, that was it.'

Mary could imagine the attraction Lizzie held for Mr Major. She had a vivacity that was enchanting, and when she looked out from under her sweeping dark lashes, the effect was devastating. She had seen Lizzie's slim hands, their scarlet tips fluttering gracefully as she talked to William Cameron. She could imagine the spell she wove, her gilded bangles twinkling in the candlelight that night. Lizzie's natural confidence must have reminded Hugh Major more of an elegant New York socialite than a farmer's daughter. But Mary found it harder to imagine what had attracted Lizzie to the older, surly Mr Major. He was a plain, short man by all accounts. Maybe, after his travels, he appeared more urbane than other available men around the county.

'It was a short courtship. They married in Clonbroney church months later in June 1924. That was some night. Michael Farrell threw a party to remember out in Roose. Lizzie danced all night, but everyone remarked how Mr Major didn't set foot on the floor.'

She had to think for a moment before she went on: 'I believe it was the very next day he shifted all his belongings from his brother's and moved to the Farrells' house. Old Farrell was glad to have a younger man around because he was nearly sixty then and the arthritis was slowing him down.'

Mary still found it odd that Major would leave his young bride and children and move back to America. 'Did no one think it unusual that he took off to America like that and him only newly wed?'

'Maybe he didn't have as much money as was rumoured. A lot of married men have to emigrate for work.'

Mrs Whitney's gaze became unfocused as she tried to recall the details. 'Much later, I heard rumours that things weren't good between them. They said it was a bad match. He was too old and stuck in his ways, and Lizzie Farrell was too flighty. But sure, not every match is made in Heaven, and we have to learn to put up with it.'

The old lady filled the kettle. 'It wouldn't have done her any harm if her father had laid a stout stick across her backside a few times instead of spoiling her,' she said.

Mary's landlady gathered her thoughts for a moment. 'But say what you like about Mr Major, he never stopped sending the remittances. He works as a chauffeur now – drives a fancy car through New York, according to Mrs Ward.' She nodded to herself and tapped the side of her nose. 'And we'd all know if the money orders stopped arriving. He's always done his duty by her. She can complain that he doesn't send her enough, but he's still the breadwinner in the house.'

Mary felt exasperated. 'But he's gone seven years. That's not right!'

Mrs Whitney nodded. 'He should never have married her. It wasn't fair on a young girl to tie up her life like that and leave. But there are plenty more like him who, once they see the Statue of Liberty, can never settle here again. Everything at home looks backward and small to them. All they can see is the dirt and the mud, and they hear small-town talk and find it suffocating. I'd say that's what happened to Hugh Major. He didn't fit in back here, and he realised it when it was too late.'

'So why is everyone so hard on Mrs Major?'

'Lizzie Farrell made her own bed, just like her husband. He's never forgotten his responsibilities. Her duty is to her children and not to be running around like some trollop with a Protestant.'

Mary wasn't going to be drawn into defending Mrs Major. So, the two sat, listening to the tick of the clock and the turf sods collapsing in the range.

''Twill be interesting anyway,' Mrs Whitney sniffed, 'Mr Major coming back after all this time.'

Mary was relieved that no one in the town seemed to know of Lizzie's condition. That news, at least, had escaped their attention so far. 'I wonder how Lizzie's doing, now that she's heard he's coming home,' Mary mused.

Mrs Whitney threw her a mischievous glance. 'Little wonder how she's doing. She's busy reciting the five glorious mysteries that Mr Major hasn't heard any of the goings-on here.'

We never really found out what brought Hugh Major home from America in 1924. We know he was back only a short while before he married my mother.

Arranged marriages were still common in rural areas at the time but we found nothing to suggest that they were 'matched'. Single people also commonly met at crossroads dances where they gathered for set dancing. They may have met at a house dance, which were popular at the time, and Willie Kelly was known for hosting them in the area.

We can trace Hugh Major's journeys to America through the ships' passenger lists, Ellis Island arrivals forms and US immigration records. The records also reveal descriptive details: he had grey hair, was five foot seven inches tall and weighed 115 pounds.

24

Deceit

5 July 1933

'You're crazy, Lizzie. Honest to God, pure crazy!'

Mary slapped the palm of her hand to her cheek and blinked rapidly in disbelief. She didn't trust herself to say anything more.

Lizzie's eyes were blue and steely, and her voice was cold and low. 'I have no choice,' she said, enunciating each word with a quiet calm, her eyes defiantly boring into Mary's.

'As sure as there's a God,' Mary said, 'you'll not get away with this, Lizzie.'

Hugh Major returned to Roose on 23 May 1933, and there was a collective intake of breath in the local community. The population of Granard and beyond was on tenterhooks to see what would happen next.

'Sparks will fly,' Mrs Whitney predicted grimly, and her friend, Mrs Ganley, clucked and nodded in solemn agreement.

Days later, there was much nudging and whispering when Hugh Major and his brother rode down the main street on their shafted cart. Mary heard about Mr Major's return to town as she browsed the hardware in Dunne's Grocery.

'Aye, Himself and the brother were in Larry Kiernan's,' said Mrs Ganley.

'Kiernan's, was it?' Mrs Dunne said, her eyes narrowing at the mention of the rival grocer's.

The store, L.D. Kiernan's, was run by the family of Kitty Kiernan, the woman once engaged to the late republican hero Michael Collins. The assassination of Collins in August 1922 was one of the darkest episodes of the Irish civil war, and the entire town had sympathy for Kitty, who had been due to marry 'the Big Fellow' just weeks after his death. The family, with strong republican connections, was much admired. It was a source of much frustration for Mrs Dunne that she could never be heard to speak badly of the Kiernans.

As well as owning the grocery, the Kiernans ran the Greville Arms Hotel, a hardware store, a bakery, a timber-undertaker's shop and Kiernan's bar. *Their greedy fingers are in every pot in the town*, thought Mrs Dunne. She would have liked to feign disinterest in the Majors' shopping expedition, but she was too curious.

'They bought, let's see, paraffin oil, candles, a sack of

flour and six pounds of sugar,' said Mrs Ganley, counting off the shopping items on her fingers.

'So how long is he home for?' Mrs Dunne asked impatiently. 'What did he have to say for himself?'

'Divil a bit. Larry Kiernan's wife said that while she was weighing the sugar, she welcomed him home, like any civilised person would, and she asked him how long he'd be here for. She said he looked through her as if she wasn't there.'

'No!' gasped Mrs Dunne.

'To be sure he did. Edward Major, God love him, did his best to cover for the brother, but Mrs Kiernan said she blanked the other bucko after that.'

'No call for that sort of rudeness!'

'None at all, and she only asking a polite question.'

'So,' said Mrs Dunne, her eyes gleaming, 'do you think he's staying at the brother's house?'

'Not a bit of it. He was driving the Farrells' pony and cart today, so he's at home with the wife. And not only that, I met Conor Quinn on the way down here, and he says he's seen him out walking their fields in Roose.'

Mrs Dunne raised an eyebrow. 'He's a more understanding husband than most, so,' she said, with an exaggerated wink.

'You're a terrible woman, Mrs Dunne!' chortled Mrs Ganley.

Their laughter ended abruptly as Mary upset the broom handles. Mrs Dunne, who had forgotten that she was in the shop, eyed her friend in silent warning. 'Can I interest you in these new tonic wines we've had delivered, Miss Doyle?' she asked.

Mary was relieved to hear that Mr Major had moved back in with his wife. She had worried as to how he would react after Lizzie's letter reached him, but this news was positive. 'No, thank you, Mrs Dunne,' she replied, advancing to the counter, with her shopping errands for Mrs Whitney. 'Did I hear you say Mr Major is home, Mrs Ganley?'

Mrs Dunne cocked a quizzical eyebrow. *The cheek of that one. She wouldn't let you know the time of day herself, but she has no problem earwigging in our private conversation.*

Mrs Ganley seized the opportunity to continue with her tale of Mr Major's return. 'Oh, yes, Bridget saw Himself in town too, and she said that he was very well got up in his back-belted jacket. Grey plaid it was, so she said.'

'A back-belted jacket, no less?' said Mrs Dunne, already forgetting her irritation with Nurse Doyle.

'Aye, it's called a sports coat,' said Mrs Ganley. 'That's what Bridget says, and she's seen them in the picture house. She was in Stafford's talkies in Longford again last weekend.'

'Oh, very swish!' said Mrs Dunne. 'With their back-belted jackets and their talkies and the divil knows what. Well, there's no keeping up with you young people, is there, Miss Doyle?'

The following Sunday, the Majors were the talk of the town again after they attended Mass in Clonbroney.

'Linking arms they were, coming into the churchyard,' said Mrs Mahon, her eyes still bulging at the notion of it.

'No!' said Mrs Whitney, with a gasp. 'Linking arms, no less?'

'Oh, it was a fine show. The Majors were like Darby and Joan and he in America for the past seven years.'

'And Herself cavorting in the hayshed with the quare fella every Friday night!' added Mrs Whitney.

The two women hooted heartily at that one.

'Aye, both of them at Mass,' said Mrs Mahon, when she settled down again. 'And Lizzie Major smiling on his arm like butter wouldn't melt . . .'

'Do you think Mr Major knows, Mrs Mahon?'

'Well, holy God, if he doesn't, he's the only one then.'

Mary was as surprised as anyone to hear about the Majors' united front at Sunday Mass. It seemed Lizzie didn't know the man she was married to after all. Hugh Major was a kinder person than she believed. Didn't he rush home as soon as he got Lizzie's letter? Instead of throwing her on the side of the road, as Lizzie had feared, he was playing the role of a devoted husband.

It was the baby Mary felt sorry for because she knew few husbands would accept another man's child into their home. She expected the Majors would announce plans to go to Dublin or London any day soon, and no one would ever know of the existence of a baby if they returned later.

A few weeks after Mr Major's return, Mary was pleased to see Lizzie waiting in the dispensary queue. She stood out from all the others in the waiting room in a cream cotton dress with a pink rose print and her bright red lipstick. Her condition was still not evident.

'Well, you're a sight for sore eyes in that lovely frock, Mrs Major,' said Mary. 'Are you here for a check-up with me or Dr McEvoy?'

'It's you I'd like to see,' said Lizzie, with a beaming smile.

The two grinned like conspirators when they were alone in Mary's consulting room.

'It's so good to see a friendly face again,' said Lizzie. 'You wouldn't believe the looks I'm getting from some people in this town.' She appeared to be in high spirits despite the censure of the townspeople.

'How have you been?' Mary asked, her voice low. She knew ears would be straining in the waiting room, hoping to pick up any snippet from their conversation.

'Well, it's not been easy, but we're getting along,' Lizzie said. 'Hugh is a bit of a heavy presence in the house, so I'm glad to have an excuse to get away today.'

'What's the excuse?'

'To have your medical opinion,' said Lizzie, with a smile. 'I've been so sick these mornings that I may be in a family way.'

Mary frowned in confusion. 'You *may* be in a family way? You know you are.'

'Aye, but it's time to make it official,' said Lizzie.

'Oh!' said Mary, a smile of delight spreading across her face, 'I'm so glad. So Mr Major has agreed to raise the baby as his own?'

It was Lizzie's turn to look confused. 'Of course he'll raise the baby as his own. He's no reason to think it's not his.'

Mary had to gather her thoughts for a few seconds. 'You haven't told him?' she said.

'About the baby? Of course I haven't! Are you mad? I told you what he'd do to us.'

'You're going to pretend that child is his?' said Mary, her voice rising several octaves, despite herself.

'He never needs to know,' said Lizzie, her voice low and steady. 'Maisie arrived late, and this one will do the same. Babies arrive late all the time, don't they? Even a few weeks will do it, and he will never know. Not for sure. No one ever will.'

'You're crazy, Lizzie, honest to God. Pure crazy!'

Mary's shock rendered her speechless for a minute. Her mind raced. She had to convince Lizzie that this plan was madness.

'As sure as there's a God, you'll not get away with this. The man is not stupid. The people around here can't help themselves, so he'll hear about William Cameron.'

But Lizzie put her hand on Mary's. 'I've thought about this,' she said, her eyes hard. 'I've had plenty of time to think about it. This is the only way.' She broke into a bright smile. 'Look, Mary, don't worry. I know how to make him happy. I'm a devoted wife now and let him have his way with everything. I never row with him, although God knows it's hard at times.' She smiled with satisfaction. 'It doesn't matter what those busybodies say, he won't believe a word of it.'

Mary stared at her in horror. 'Oh, God, Lizzie, please

think about what you're doing. It's still not too late to come clean and tell him.'

'My mind is made up, Mary. My husband will hear the good news about his third child today.'

'This child is due late December. Your husband came home at the end of May. Think about it, Lizzie – your timing is a full two months out.'

Lizzie tossed her head in exasperation. 'With a bit of luck, the baby will be late, like my last one, and when it arrives, I'll say it's premature,' she said. 'Look, this is the only way to keep a roof over our heads. I have Mamma and Dadda and the children to think about too.'

Mary slumped in her chair. She was lost for words, but her stomach churned with anxiety. 'I want no part of this, Lizzie, none at all. The affair is one thing, but this . . . no.'

'Oh, please don't judge me, Mary. True as God, I've had my fill of the village idiots with their whispering and finger-pointing.'

Mary saw the set of Lizzie's jaw, the determination in her eyes, and knew she couldn't reason with her. Mary was confused. It was clear now that Lizzie had never confessed her adultery or thrown herself on Hugh Major's mercy. 'So how did you persuade Mr Major to come back to Ireland after all these years?' she asked.

'I sent him a strongly worded letter. I said that my reputation would be in tatters if he didn't come. I'd been too long on my own, and there were old men around here trying to ruin my name because I refused their advances.'

'And he came back because you wrote that?'

'Reputation and name are important to Mr Major. He's a proud man, and I'm his wife so he would never stand for anyone impugning my virtue. If I look bad, it reflects on him.' She laughed hollowly. 'I should have thought of it before, but honest to God, I'm not sure I ever wanted him back.' Her eyes were downcast now. 'I told him everything he wanted to hear, that I missed him, that I wanted him back, and that the place was falling apart without him. How could he refuse me?'

'And Mr Cameron – how does he feel about his child being reared by another man?'

'Poor William has enough problems,' said Lizzie. 'The medical bills for his wife never stop. Even though they haven't a marriage in the proper sense, he is in a bind with her. We're all in a bind.' She reached out again and squeezed Mary's hand. 'I shouldn't tell you, but I'm meeting him later,' she said, a new gleam in her eye. 'Out beyond the Leahys' place, where no one will know. But I promise you, it'll be the last time I see him.'

Mary stared at the woman beaming before her, oblivious of the danger she was in. She really is crazy, she thought. Pure crazy.

To be frank, we don't know what Elizabeth Major wrote in that letter to her husband. We do know that she wrote to him, and we know that whatever she wrote, it proved to be persuasive. It prompted him to return home immediately after spending seven years living on the other side of the Atlantic.

25

The Baby

7 July 1933

Mary hung her cloak in the hall and wrinkled her nose at the smell of fish frying on the pan. Why did Fridays seem to come around so often? 'I'm turning Protestant, Mrs Whitney,' she said, as she dropped gloomily into a kitchen chair. 'I want bacon. I'm not abstaining from meat any more.'

'Wash out your mouth with soap, you heathen,' said Mrs Whitney. 'It's a penance, so eat that fish, and offer it up for the holy souls.' The landlady slapped a plate of herring, turnip and a potato bursting out of its jacket in front of her disgruntled lodger. 'There's more news about Mrs Major too,' she said, huddling over the table in front of Mary.

Mary stuck a fork into the fish dejectedly. 'Go on so. What's she supposed to have done now?' she asked, with little enthusiasm.

'She's only been running around with that oul divil again,' said Mrs Whitney. 'Honest to God, and her good husband only back from America. It's all over town.' She tapped the table with a forefinger for emphasis. 'Paddy Clarke in Garrowhill says he saw her with Cameron on the road. And he shouted at them not to be making a disgrace of themselves!'

Mary's fork dangled in mid-air as she listened in fascinated horror.

'And not a word of a lie but Mrs Major tried to turn into the Finnertys' place with some excuse that they were calling about a greyhound. What did oul Clarke do? He shouted to Mrs Finnerty to shut the door on them adulterers, and she did!' She hooted with laughter. 'He made a holy show of them did Paddy. He says he told Mrs Major to go home to her husband, and he stood there until she cycled off. He said he'd follow them all day and night if he had to. He wasn't going to stand for that sort of carry-on.' She added: 'He says he even watched the Protestant fella until he got on a bus back to that poor wife of his.' Mrs Whitney struck the table with her hand for emphasis. 'Can you believe the brazenness of it?'

There wasn't much Mary could say. Lizzie Major was the one woman who could leave her dumbstruck.

27 December 1933

Hoary frost clung to the ground outside, and the blazing fire in the range couldn't vanquish the chill in the kitchen. Mary finished starching her uniform. Her Christmas break was over, and she had several calls to make around the area the next morning.

She heard a rapping on the front door, but Mrs Whitney darted out of the parlour before she could answer. *For an old lady, she's fast on her feet,* thought Mary, raising her eyes to Heaven.

'Come in, young man, before you catch your death of cold,' she heard Mrs Whitney say. 'It's the handsome Mr Walsh to see you, Nurse Doyle.'

The unscheduled call from Paddy filled Mary with concern. His uncle had bad bronchitis, which wasn't clearing despite Dr McEvoy's efforts. 'Is Denny okay?' she asked, as all three of them met in the hall.

'Denny's the same,' Paddy assured her. He glanced at Mrs Whitney, but the old lady was going nowhere. 'It's Mrs Major,' he said at last. 'Michael Farrell asked me to fetch you. He says the baby's coming.'

Mary's heart sank. Lizzie was out of luck, and her baby was arriving right on time. She saw Mrs Whitney mentally totting up the months since Hugh Major's return.

'It doesn't look good for the baby's chances, does it?' said Paddy. 'It's way too early. Poor Mr Farrell looked sick with the worry.'

Mrs Whitney's knowing expression said she wasn't fooled for a minute, and Mary guessed that Lizzie's father wasn't deceived either. She hadn't shared Lizzie's secret with anyone, and she felt bad seeing Paddy's anxiety over the Majors' baby.

'Will you cycle on to the doctor's, Paddy, and let him know?' said Mary, lifting her wool cape from the hook in the hall. 'I'll get my bag and head straight out.'

It was almost four in the afternoon, and the light was nearly gone. Mary checked the carbide lamp on the bike and took off for Roose. When she reached the turning for the Farrells' home, she saw Julia Farrell holding up her Tilley lamp and waving frantically at her. Shrouded in a shawl, Julia was a fever of anxiety.

'Thank God you're here, Nurse, thank God. This is so bad – the baby will never survive, will he? Is the doctor on his way? The poor baby has no chance, has he, Nurse?'

Poor Julia has no idea of Lizzie's secret either, Mary realised. 'Miracles happen all the time, Mrs Farrell,' she replied.

The Farrell home was a neat two-storey dwelling with a kitchen, a parlour and three bedrooms. They were better off than many because Mr Farrell had had a salaried post as a relieving officer in Granard in his younger years. His job, and that of his father before him, was to distribute aid to the less fortunate. They were all that stood between the poor and the workhouse.

These days, Mr Farrell had forty-two acres in Roose, about half of which were arable, and he also had a farm in Dromeel with twenty-five acres of poorer land. He had a small pension, but money was tight: arthritis had set in, and he could no longer do much around the farm.

The two women brought a cold blast of air with them as they entered the house. Mr Farrell sat by the fire, rosary beads entwined in his fingers. 'God bless you, Nurse. You're a welcome sight indeed,' he said, but he looked sombre.

'She's up here, Nurse,' said Mrs Farrell, kneading her hands and motioning towards the stairs. 'She's been asking for you.'

Before Mary could follow, Hugh Major emerged from the shadows, his eyes dark and his face inscrutable. He was a small man but had a powerful presence, a big neck and a jutting chin. 'I want to know what's going on,' he said, his tone cold. 'This can't be right. She shouldn't be having this baby now.'

'It sometimes happens, Mr Major,' said Mary, pulling off her scarf and cloak. 'Please God everything will be well anyway.'

'I want to see Dr McEvoy,' he said, standing in her way.

'I've sent a message, so he'll come when he can,' she said. 'But I need to attend to Lizzie *now*.'

He glared at her but said no more. Turning on his heel, he strode to the kitchen window and stood, his back ramrod straight, staring into the night. Julia glanced from Mary to Michael nervously before she turned for the stairs, Mary following.

From the bedroom door, Mary could see that Lizzie's labour was advanced. A sheen of sweat covered her face in the cold candlelight.

'I'm glad you're here, Mary,' she panted. 'Mamma, I'm fine now. Let us two get on with it.'

Julia's fingers fluttered to her throat with uncertainty, but she left the room and they heard her light steps descend.

'I'm in trouble, Mary. Big trouble,' gasped Lizzie. 'I hoped the baby wouldn't come for weeks. He's suspicious. Someone's been pouring poison in his ear.'

'Let's concentrate on having a healthy baby,' said Mary, taking Lizzie's pulse. 'Nothing else matters for the moment.'

But Lizzie grabbed Mary's wrist and her eyes glittered black in the light. 'This baby is premature,' she hissed, through gritted teeth. 'Premature. That is the only word I want to hear you saying to my husband.'

'Premature,' repeated Mary, calmly. 'I know what to say.'

This was not the time for an argument.

'Let's concentrate on birthing this baby, Lizzie. It won't be long now.'

As the baby girl's cries rang out in the night air, Mary experienced the familiar rush of happiness. She held the wobbling head beneath her steady hand and gazed at the child with pleasure. The baby was robust and kicking, waving her pudgy fists.

Mary heard the clamour of footsteps on the stairs, feet that were drawn by the baby's cries. Julia Farrell almost fell into the room, and she sobbed with relief when she saw the child. Hugh Major hovered in the doorway behind her.

'Thank God, thank God, she's a little miracle,' Julia cried. 'Oh, look, Hugh, the child is fine. Oh, Lizzie, she's a beautiful girl.'

But Hugh Major's expression was stony as he looked at the baby. He left the doorway without a word, and they heard his heavy footsteps descend the stairs. Julia looked from Mary to Lizzie in confusion, then followed him.

Lizzie hardly glanced at the baby that Mary placed in her arms. She looked at Mary wild-eyed and pleaded in whispers: 'Tell him! Dear God, tell him! You've got to tell him.'

But the sound of a motor in the yard alerted them to Dr McEvoy's arrival. Lizzie's eyes darted around the room as if she was searching for an escape route, and Mary heard the heavy silence in the kitchen as the doctor entered.

'I'm so sorry, I got here as soon as I could,' she heard him say, before he sprang up the stairs, two at a time. Jim McEvoy entered breathless and peeling off his coat.

His eyes rested on the perfect baby dozing in Lizzie's arms, and his eyes flew to Mary. For an instant he was flustered.

'Everything's in hand, Doctor,' said Mary. 'It's a healthy girl, and Mrs Major is well.'

'Excellent,' he said, recovering his composure. 'Congratulations, Mrs Major. I'll look the baby over while I'm here.'

Mary and Lizzie listened in silence when the doctor returned to the kitchen. They heard him being cut short as he attempted to congratulate the Farrells and Mr Major.

'A word outside, Doctor,' Hugh Major said, his words clipped.

The women heard the muffled sounds of the men talking

in the yard. Lizzie stifled a sob with her fist and stared into the blackness outside her bedroom window. Then they heard the doctor start his motor, and the wheels crunching over the frosty ground.

Lizzie said nothing more. Mary made sure the newborn child latched on to her mother's breast before she left. During that time, she noted that Lizzie took no pleasure in the child and that Hugh Major never returned to the house.

26

Feud

January–March 1934

Hugh Major never spent another night under the roof of that house in Roose. Within days, everyone in the county knew he had moved into his sister Delia's home on Moxham Street in Granard.

For many weeks, there was no communication between Mr and Mrs Major. Then one day, when Elizabeth Major and her mother were in town, and Mr Farrell was confined to bed, Hugh returned to the farm and removed all the livestock.

'Begob, he drove them all, cattle, the horse, pigs and bonhams, everything, off the farm,' said their neighbour, Mrs Quinn. 'He only left the oul cow, which couldn't walk all the way back to Cartron.'

Mrs Major marched to the constabulary station in Granard the next day to lay charges against Mr Major for stealing their stock.

'The guards said there's no case to pursue,' said Mrs Whitney. 'Mr Major is the owner of the farm and has the deeds to prove it.'

Una Major was baptised in Clonbroney church a month later, with Hugh Major notably absent at the font. Mrs Major publicly swore that he could deny it all he wanted, but the child would bear his name because he was her father.

Mrs Farrell despaired of the situation and pleaded with the priest in Clonbroney to mediate between her daughter and Mr Major. But the priest returned from a visit to Mr Major with the man's response ringing in his ears.

'If I never see that woman again, it will be fifty years too soon,' he said.

Without remittances from America, or livestock to provide food or cash, Lizzie survived on credit from the storekeepers. 'Send the tab to my husband at Moxham Street,' she said, in Kiernan's store, loud enough for everyone to hear.

The people of the townland shook their heads and were united in their belief that Mrs Major was a brazen hussy. However, Mr Major's next move appalled everyone. He posted an advert in the *Longford Leader* stating that he would no longer honour 'any bills of credit on the account of Mrs Elizabeth Major, née Farrell, of Roose in the Barony of Granard'.

Rumour-mongering was one thing, but it was quite another to have the scandalous goings-on in their town advertised for the whole county to see. The respectable people of the town and beyond were shocked by this public escalation of the Majors' marital feud.

'There's no call for the man to do that,' said Mrs Whitney, clucking her tongue. 'Washing dirty laundry in public like that.'

'No call for it at all,' agreed Mrs Dunne. 'He doesn't even seem to have a care for his children, leaving them to starve with their grandparents.'

Mrs Major burned with rage over the advertisement. She responded by marching into C.J.P. Farrell Solicitors in Longford town to launch a legal suit for maintenance against Mr Major.

10 April 1934

Mary plunged the dressings into the dispensary's sterilising unit and put the syringes on to boil. Then she started a letter to the County Board of Health to apply for a taxi budget. She knew her services could be much more effective if she used the local hackney in emergencies.

She had only dipped her pen into the inkwell when she heard a knock on the door. She found Michael Farrell outside. 'Come in out of the rain, Mr Farrell,' she said. 'Is there anything the matter with the grandchildren?'

He entered, dragging his cap off his head and running his hand through his thin hair. He looked ill at ease. 'No, no, the children are well, Miss. It's our Lizzie,' he said. 'She's taken to the bed, and we're worried about her. She's not eaten a bite for days.'

'Should I ask Dr McEvoy to see her?'

'She says she won't see him ever again. She likes you, though. We thought you might come out and see her, because she's not herself at all, Nurse.'

Mary could see the worry lines etched in his brow and felt sorry for the old man. His life was in turmoil at a time when he and his wife should be relaxing their bones by the fire. 'I finish the clinic here at noon, and I'll be straight out after,' she said, squeezing his arm reassuringly. 'Ask Julia to have some hot water on the boil if she can manage it, and I'll get Lizzie cleaned up and out of bed.'

Dr McEvoy was going in that direction, and he offered to drive her most of the way to Roose that afternoon. 'What's going on with the Farrells?' he asked. 'I trust the premature child is well.'

Mary smiled. 'The baby is fine, but Lizzie has taken to the bed.'

'She's been through a lot since the birth. I imagine she has a touch of melancholy.'

The American Medical Association had removed post-natal depression from their diagnostic manuals ten years before. Mary and Dr McEvoy knew that, officially, the condition didn't exist. Yet they had witnessed enough tears to know that melancholy often coincided with childbirth.

Mary received a rapturous reception from Mrs Farrell, but the grey in the older woman's hair and the lines on her face were more pronounced. The stress of her daughter's very public marital troubles was taking its toll.

Mary found Lizzie's room in darkness with a blanket over the window shutting out all the light. With one sweeping motion, she tore down the blanket, and Lizzie lifted her head in irritation, blinking and squinting in the bright light. Her pupils were pinholes in bloodshot eyes, and without her trademark lipstick, her face looked pinched and pale. Mary had never seen her in such a mess.

'Get out,' Lizzie said wearily.

'Indeed I won't after coming all the way out here,' Mary replied.

With another sweep, she whipped off all the bedclothes, prompting Lizzie to rise in outrage. 'Get out of this room and out of this house, Mary Doyle.'

'Not before you wash, get dressed and clean up this room.'

Lizzie's face crumpled, and she began sobbing. 'Please, Mary, leave me alone.'

Mary rinsed her washcloth in the bucket she had hauled up the stairs and, using a bar of carbolic soap, began scrubbing her patient.

She brought up more hot water to wash and rinse Lizzie's hair. Then she handed her a comb as she rifled through her wardrobe and gathered clean undergarments, a bright red dress and patent leather shoes. 'My goodness, you have such lovely things, Lizzie,' she said, with envy.

She stripped the bed and remade it with fresh sheets as Lizzie got dressed. When her patient was finally ready,

Mary applied a slick of vibrant red colour to her lips. 'Now there's the Lizzie Major I know,' she said, standing back to admire her handiwork. Lizzie looked as if she'd lost all her usual spark but Mary ignored that. 'If we hurry, we'll meet Hughie and Maisie coming out of school. Wouldn't it be a nice surprise to have their mother waiting outside for them?'

Mary felt sorry for the children: Hugh was nine years old and Maisie was seven, but their mother and father were neglecting them.

'I'm not going,' said Lizzie, her voice rising to a wail. 'I don't want to see anyone. I can't stand how they look at me.'

'Lizzie Major, do you want people to say that you fell apart after Hugh Major left you? You have your red dress and your red lipstick, so you might as well get out there and be the scarlet woman they all expect!'

Lizzie didn't return a smile. 'I don't have the strength to move these days. Honest to God, I don't, Mary.'

'We're only walking the half-mile down to Clonbroney and back, that's all,' said Mary. 'You need the fresh air, so you're going, whether you like it or not.'

Mrs Farrell lit up as she saw her daughter out of bed for the first time in weeks. 'It's a tonic looking at you in your lovely dress,' she said, clasping her hands, tears brimming in her eyes.

Lizzie said nothing, but Mary gave Julia a reassuring wink as she pushed Lizzie out the door. The rain clouds of the morning had cleared, and the two women felt the warmth of early April sunshine as they strolled to Clonbroney.

'Now, what has you so bad, Lizzie?' asked Mary. 'I know you get a bit melancholic after a baby but staying in bed for weeks at a time is not like you at all.'

'Everything is gone bad and it's all my fault.'

'There's an answer to most problems.'

'We should be planting now, but we've nothing to plant, and we don't know if there's any point anyway,' said Lizzie. 'We don't know how long more we can keep the roof over our heads.'

Mary linked Lizzie's arm. 'Look, you have children together,' she said. 'No court will allow him to throw you out on the road. The house has been in your family for generations.'

Lizzie hesitated, and then the tears began to fall again. 'There's more. I haven't told anyone yet, but I got a letter a few weeks ago from his solicitors saying . . . Oh, Mary.'

She stopped to wipe the tears from her cheeks with the backs of her hands and swallowed a sob. 'The letter says Hugh Major has started proceedings in the Irish High Court to divorce me.'

27

Legal Suit

22 May 1934

Locals crushed into Granard District Court to hear Mrs Major's case for maintenance against her husband.

'Like flies around a jam jar,' sniffed Mrs Whitney, though she barely resisted going to the court herself.

Mary, like the rest of the county, pored over the intimate details of Mr and Mrs Major's marriage split in the reports published in the *Longford Leader* and the *Anglo-Celt*.

The *Leader*'s front page bore big block capitals that read 'MATRIMONIAL DISPUTE' and sub-headlines that read: 'Husband's Grave Allegations' and 'To Seek a Divorce'. Meanwhile, the *Anglo-Celt* ran the story with the headlines, 'Matrimonial Troubles' and 'Painful Case at Granard'.

The report was indeed painful, thought Mary, but she still read every word of it. She was astonished that Lizzie had managed to summon the energy to attend the case at all – her mood had been so low for months now. But she did and, by all accounts, she looked well or 'brazen', depending on who was telling the story.

Mr Major's solicitor, Patrick J. Connellan, attempted to stop the case altogether by stating that divorce proceedings in the High Court in Dublin were already under way.

Mrs Major's solicitor, Mathew Farrell, objected, claiming that the case for maintenance was urgent. District Judge Mr Sandes said he would hear the evidence before deciding for or against an adjournment. As was reported in a local newspaper at the time:

> Mrs Elizabeth Major, applicant, was called to give her deposition.
>
> In reply to Mr Farrell [her solicitor], she deposed that she was married in 1924. Her father's farm was made over to her husband. Since then, her husband had been several times in America, being absent seven years entirely.
>
> He went to America in 1926 without giving her any notice. He returned and remained at home three weeks and went back to America again and was absent nearly 7 years.
>
> She said he returned last May and lived with her until December 27 when witness

gave birth to a baby. Her husband left the house on the day the baby was born and never returned. There were three children. The eldest being 9 years and the second 7 years and the baby born on December 27.

Since her husband left, witness was supported by her father, who had a small pension. She wrote to her husband to tell him that proceedings were being taken.

She received for a reply that he disputed parentage of the baby, and he was taking proceedings in the High Court

Mr Sandes (Judge): What sum do you mention [for maintenance]?

Mrs Major (Plaintiff): I would want £2 per week.

Mrs Major was questioned by solicitor Mr Connellan on behalf of Mr Major.

Mr Connellan: Did your husband send you money from America?

Mrs Major: Yes.

Mr Connellan: In 1927 did he send you £67?

Mrs Major: I have no idea of the amount.

Mrs Major admitted also receiving money in the years 1928, '29, '30, and '31, but said she did not know if the money averaged about £60 [per year].

Mr Connellan: What settlement was made

at the marriage? Did your husband bring in £500 to the place?

Mrs Major: Yes.

Mr Connellan: And also had your father and mother and sister the right of support on the place?

Mrs Major: Yes.

Mr Connellan: What cattle were on the land when Mr Major went in there?

Mrs Major: A cow and calf.

Mr Connellan: What cattle did he take off the lands?

Mrs Major: He took off seven yearlings and a horse.

Mr Connellan: Did he leave anything on the place?

Mrs Major: Yes. A cow.

Mr Connellan: The cow was there?

Mrs Major: Yes.

Mrs Major's father, Michael Farrell, was called to the stand.

Mr Farrell admitted that the cattle were bought by Mr Major, but that he stripped the land and left no means of livelihood on the farm.

Mr Connellan: They were his cattle.

Mr Hugh Major was called to give his deposition. The defendant gave evidence

[that] he married into the place in 1924 and left the lands free of charge and debts. He said the farm contained 46 acres, but only about 20 acres were workable.

Mr Sandes: I will have to know why the farm is not worked?

Mr Major: I left the farm.

Mr Sandes, addressing Mr Major: You suggest you would support the two children?

Mr Major: Yes.

Mr Sandes: What would you think reasonable?

Mr Major: £1 a month.

Mr Sandes: For two children?

Mr Connellan: They are living on the farm.

Mr Sandes: But the defendant won't go there or work the farm because his wife is on the land . . . he has left the land because he suggests he is not the father of the child. I must hold that he is the father until the [High] Court decides otherwise.

Mr Major argued that he had already given his father-in-law £500 and he spent £350 on the place and sent plenty of money home from America.

Mr Sandes asked Mr Major: What offer will you make?

Mr Major stated he was already paying £1 a week for himself and had no means of earning money.

Mr Sandes: £1 a week for yourself? Then how much will it take to keep a woman and three children? You had better make a suggestion.

Mr Farrell (Solicitor): Is it your position that you don't want to pay or aren't able to pay?

Mr Major: I am not able.

Mr Farrell: Did you give your wife any notice of you leaving?

Mr Major: No.

Mr Farrell: Do you want to brand this child as illegitimate?

Mr Major: Yes.

Longford Leader, 26 May 1934

Mary could almost hear the gasps at this reply in the court. Hugh Major didn't care about publicly shaming his wife or about branding an innocent child a bastard. However, his belligerent attitude didn't endear him to the court. Even reading between the lines of the newspaper account, she could hear the rising frustration of both Mrs Major's solicitor and the judge.

Mr Farrell: Did you sell the oats on the farm?

Mr Major: Yes. That was to pay a bill.

Mr Farrell: Did Mr Farrell claim a 2-year-old and a yearling?

Mr Major: Yes.

Mr Farrell: You brought them away?

Mr Major: Yes.

Mr Farrell: What did you leave behind?

Mr Major: I left a ton of meal and ten tons of potatoes.

Mr Farrell: That is what you feed pigs with?

Mr Major: Sometimes.

Mr Farrell: Did you issue an advertisement stopping your wife's credit?

Mr Major: Yes.

Mr Farrell: Is there a shop in the country she would get credit in?

Mr Major: I don't suppose there is.

Mr Farrell: You don't care whether your wife lives or dies?

Mr Major: Why should I?

Mr Farrell: I don't want to enter into your matrimonial troubles, but the children must be clothed and sent to school?

Mr Major: Yes.

Mr Farrell: Could that be done on less than 30 shillings a week?

Mr Major: Living on a farm in the country is different to the town.

The Justice said the evidence showed that the defendant had a banking account and spent £1 a week on himself.

Mr Sandes: When would the High Court action be on?

Mr Connellan: The next term.

The Justice said he would make an order for payment of £1 and 5 shillings weekly from May 28.

'Oh, Mr Major was not happy, not happy at all,' said Mrs Dunne. 'He wanted to pay a pound a month for the children, Mrs Whitney. A pound a month the man wanted to pay, and a loaf of bread costing a whole fivepence!'

'He's a hard man, indeed, Mrs Dunne.'

'When the judge said a pound and five shillings a week, he had a face like thunder on him. You should have seen the face on him, Mrs Whitney.'

Mrs Dunne lowered her voice and narrowed her eyes. 'The judge had it in for him,' she said. 'It's the man's manner, Mrs Whitney. If there's a sourer man from here to the Six Counties, I'd like to see him. And there was Mrs Major batting her eyes up at the judge with her face paint.'

'And what was Mrs Major's reaction to the judge's decision?' asked Mrs Whitney.

'Oh, she was like the cat that got the cream then, Mrs Whitney, and she marched out of that court with her head held high. Oh, she's a shameless one, that one, no doubt about it. But I'll tell you this, though,' Mrs Dunne said, folding her arms, a grin of satisfaction spreading on her face. 'Mrs Major shouldn't hold her breath for that maintenance because I heard Mr Major tell his brother that she'll be singing for that money!'

For most of my life, I knew nothing about my mother, not even her name. In 2002, I finally met family members who had known her, and I started gaining some insight into her and her circumstances.

When they told us that my mother's affair and marriage breakdown were written about in the provincial and national newspapers, my daughter Aileen began researching in the National Library of Ireland. It was there that we found the wealth of information and contemporary reports that infinitely increased our understanding of what had happened.

28

Divorce

September 1934

No legal decree could persuade Hugh Major to support Mrs Major or her children. Mrs Major had to resort to filing a suit for arrears in the Circuit Court.

Mr Major was also true to his word about not honouring any credit run up by his wife and family. Granard store-owner Larry Kiernan and his sister Kitty Kiernan sued Mr Major for the sum of £17/15*s* for goods supplied to his estranged wife.

Meanwhile, the townspeople swapped gossip over the many sightings of Mrs Major in the company of the married William Cameron.

'She's running all over the country with that oul divil,'

said Mrs Whitney. 'Honest to God, Mary, she's carrying on like a tramp.'

But Mrs Whitney hadn't much sympathy for Mr Major either. 'He hasn't darkened the Farrells' door to see if Hughie or Maisie have a bite to eat. It's like they don't exist for either of them!'

The old woman got to her feet to take her soda bread from the range. 'I don't know what this modern world is coming to. It's a terrible carry-on, so it is.'

October 1934

Lizzie jiggled baby Una in her arms and pushed the copy of the medical journal, *The Lancet*, back across the desk to Mary.

'Read it for me, Mary. My head is in a tizz with this. All I want to know is, should I do this blood test or not?'

Lizzie was dressed to the nines as usual, but Mary could see the dark circles under her eyes.

'The solicitor says they've never used a blood test in the Irish or British courts before. How does it work?'

Mary shrugged, defeated. 'I asked Dr McEvoy, but this is all so new that he didn't know either. All he had was this article in *The Lancet*.'

Mary ran her finger down the page, while Lizzie cradled the child. 'It says these tests are only about disproving paternity. They can do that in only 30 per cent of cases. It doesn't work for common blood types, so in the other 70 per cent, the man is *possibly* the father but not definitely.'

'So, I'd have to be unlucky for the test to prove that he's not the father?' said Lizzie.

'I suppose so, but I'm no expert,' said Mary. 'How is Mr Major paying for all this? It says here that the testing results are all processed in Germany. It must cost a fortune.'

Lizzie's expression was cold. 'He'll do anything to destroy me. I don't think he cares what it costs. He must have more money from America than he let on, or he's borrowing.'

Mary pointed out a line in *The Lancet*. 'It says that blood testing "is likely to be accepted with extreme caution in the courts of justice". The court might not even accept the tests into evidence.'

Lizzie sighed. 'The solicitor, Mr Farrell, thinks that the case might never go ahead anyway. He says Hugh will pull out when he realises the huge costs involved.'

'So why are you worrying about the blood test, then? Tell Mr Major you won't do it.'

'But if the case goes ahead, Mr Farrell says the other side will say that I refused to do a blood test, and it will look bad for me. Mr Farrell says if I've nothing to hide, I should do the blood test.'

Mary didn't say anything, but her silence spoke volumes.

'Hugh left me with no choice!' said Lizzie. 'Can't you see that? I need to keep a roof over our heads. We'll lose everything if I don't fight him.' She glanced down at Una. 'This is Hugh Major's baby, and come hell or high water, I will deny adultery.'

25 January 1935
'Your Mrs Major is in the news again today,' said Mrs Whitney, peeling off her coat and waving a rolled-up newspaper. 'I got the last *Evening Herald* in town. It says that Hugh Major has started divorce proceedings in the High Court.'

> **Longford Divorce Case**
> In the High Court today, before the Master, a matrimonial suit was mentioned, in which Hugh Major, farmer, of Roose, Moatfarrell, near Edgeworthstown, Co. Longford, petitions for a divorce *a mensa et thoro* from his wife, Elizabeth Major, on the ground of alleged misconduct.
>
> The parties were married at Clonbroney, Co. Longford, on June 24, 1924.
> *Evening Herald*, 25 January 1935

'What is this "*divorce a mensa et thoro*"?' Mary asked. 'Didn't the government bring in a motion to block divorce?'

Mrs Whitney sat by the range, trying to warm her hands. 'Canon Markey says it's something inherited from old ecclesiastical courts in the Middle Ages. He said it's not like an English or American divorce because they won't be able to marry again.'

'So, what's the point of it, then? Mr Major could separate from Mrs Major without paying hundreds of pounds to the High Court.'

Mrs Whitney leaned in. 'It's expensive but, mark my words, that boyo knows what he's doing. If the wife is found guilty of adultery, the judge can't award her alimony or maintenance.'

The old lady's eyes narrowed. 'Believe me, this is better than an American divorce for him. If he can prove that she and that William Cameron have been at it, he's free of her. He can walk away and leave her penniless.'

26 January 1935

'You should have been head of intelligence during the war, Mrs Whitney,' said Mary, scrubbing a few clothes in the Belfast sink. 'You'd have left Michael Collins in the shade.'

'What are ye ravin' about?' Mrs Whitney replied. 'Do ye want to hear what's goin' on or not? I only said poor Mr and Mrs Farrell are in a right state about the High Court proceedings.'

Mary smiled. 'I don't know what I'm going to do without you when I leave here,' she said. 'You'll have to write me a full bulletin every week.'

Mrs Whitney used the poker to prise open the blackened range lid, then threw a few sods of turf onto the fire.

'If you ask me, you'll be bored livin' in a God-forsaken place like Wexford,' she said. 'You think it'll be all grand being Mrs Walsh, but there'll be no divorces and gaddin' around with married Protestants.'

'You're right, Mrs Whitney,' laughed Mary. 'Enniscorthy will be very dull after Granard.'

Mary had mixed feelings about leaving her job and her

life in Granard. Paddy's Uncle Denny had died and left him the farm but he'd decided to move back to Enniscorthy when his father asked him to take over the family farm. 'My brother won't come back from America now, and it's a bigger farm and far better land. I'd be a fool not to take up the offer,' he explained, before he asked Mary to marry him. He said that the proceeds from his uncle's farm in Edgeworthstown would help them build their own house on the farm in Enniscorthy.

Mary set a date for the wedding a full year away, but now as the day hurtled towards her, she grew more anxious. The public-service marriage ban meant that she couldn't keep her job. But with the authorities clamping down on handywomen, she hoped to find work as a private-hire midwife in Wexford. Still, she resented giving up the job she had. And she knew she would miss her landlady, Mrs Whitney, who was good-humoured and kind-hearted, as well as an endless source of gossip.

Her landlady continued to prattle about the Farrells. 'Their solicitor said the case was only a rush of blood to Mr Major's head, and it wouldn't go ahead,' she said. 'But didn't I say to you that there's method in his madness? He's making sure he never has to pay her a penny in maintenance.'

'How can the Farrells even afford Mathew Farrell Solicitors?' asked Mary.

'Mathew Farrell was on the board of guardians for the workhouse, and old Mr Farrell knows him from his time as the relieving officer. But even a solicitor can't afford High

Court costs.' Mrs Whitney shook her head. 'Hugh Major is going to pauper himself and the Farrells,' she said. 'And it's all their daughter's fault.'

18 February 1935
Mrs Major's solicitors began a counter-attack against Hugh Major, and the affidavits started flying between the parties. Elizabeth Major's claimed in hers that she 'never committed adultery with the said William Cameron' and that Hugh Major was the father of the child, and had deserted her and her children 'without any just cause' and without support, despite the maintenance order granted by Granard District Court on 22 May 1934.

1. . . . The Petitioner failed to maintain the said payments, and there is now due to me £30, 10 shillings for arrears . . . Proceedings are still pending.
2. So far as I am aware, the Petitioner has no assets out of which the costs of these proceedings can be paid other than the farm at Roose over which my parents who are both alive have rights of residence and maintenance.
3. I believe that these proceedings were begun by the Petitioner for the purpose of avoiding the payment under the said maintenance order and not because he has any grounds for divorce against me. As I have no resources

> of any kind out of which to pay any costs, I did not instruct my Solicitor to defend these proceedings . . .
> *Excerpt from Legal Affidavit, 18 February 1935, of Elizabeth Major to the High Court of Justice of Saorstát Éireann.*

In Hugh Major's affidavit of 20 February 1935, he outlined his May 1933 return from the US, where he had gone in 1925 'solely for the purpose of earning money with which to support my wife and children', describing the details of that support.

> From the day of my return from the United States, I resided in my house at Roose in the County of Longford with my wife and family and her parents until the birth of her child born on December 27, 1933. I say positively that I am not the father of the said child, and as a consequence of certain information which I received from Dr McEvoy who attended my wife on the birth of the said child, I went to reside at Granard in the County of Longford and have not since returned to my said home at Roose . . .
> I say further that I sent to my wife on December 14, 1934, a sum of £4 which . . . was returned to me by her solicitors on December 23, 1934.

It is untrue to state as is alleged in the affidavit of my wife that these proceedings have been taken for the purpose of avoiding payment . . . A letter written by me and dated February 23, 1934, to Messrs C.J.P. Farrell & Co . . . gave notice of these proceedings and asked for the custody of my two lawful children, Hugh Major, and Mary Veronica Major . . .

Excerpt from Legal Affidavit of Hugh Major to the High Court of Justice of Saorstát Éireann, 20 February 1935.

In her response on 22 February, Elizabeth 'denies that she has committed adultery with William Cameron' and states 'that the Petitioner is the father of the child born to the Respondent on December 27, 1933'. It goes on to say that Hugh Major 'unlawfully separated from and deserted the Respondent on or about the 28th day of December 1933 and has not lived with the Respondent at Roose since that date . . .'

Wherefore the Respondent humbly prays: That this Honourable Court . . . will pronounce a Decree that the Petitioner receive this Respondent as his wife and render to her conjugal rights and . . . the costs of the proceedings.

Excerpt from High Court filing to the President and judges of the High Court of Justice in Saorstát Éireann from the Respondent, Elizabeth Major, 22 February 1935.

Mr Major was forced to provide his wife with the costs of defending herself in the divorce. Within days, his legal team filed a High Court document saying that he, along with his brother Edward and Thomas Lynch of Muckerstaff, Coolarty in County Longford, had raised the money and paid eighty-eight pounds to the courts for the legal costs of defending Mrs Major against the petitioner, Hugh Major.

May it please your Lordship,
I have . . . ascertained that eighty-seven pounds and nine pence is a sufficient sum of money to be paid into court by [Mr Major] . . . to cover the costs of (Mrs Major), and I beg to report to your Lordship accordingly.

Excerpt from a document from the Taxing Master of the Court to the Judge of the High Court regarding court costs for the Respondent, Elizabeth Major, 22 February 1935.

HIGH COURT APPLICATION

An application was made in the High Court, Dublin, yesterday, on behalf of Mrs E. Major, Roose, Edgeworthstown, Co. Longford.

Mrs E. Major is the Respondent in a matrimonial petition by her husband, Hugh

Major, Granard, who is seeking a divorce on the grounds of alleged misconduct.

It was stated that the Respondent denied the Petitioner's allegations, claimed that he had deserted her, and asked for an order for the restitution of conjugal rights.

Irish Press, 23 February 1935

'Be the holies, Mrs Major is lookin' for her conjugal rights,' said Mrs Dunne, jabbing at the newspaper on her counter.

'Is she not gettin' enough of those rights from the quare fella?' said Mrs Whitney, reading over her shoulder.

'You're an awful woman, Margaret Whitney,' said Mrs Dunne, chuckling as she removed her spectacles and polished them on her cardigan. 'They're makin' a holy show of themselves now, him with his highfalutin' divorce and her demandin' her conjugal rights. What next?'

Mrs Whitney shook her head yet again. 'When I think of those three poor scraps up there in that house . . . What are these two thinking of at all?'

Mrs Dunne read the next paragraph aloud: 'If a spouse fails to comply with a decree for restitution of conjugal rights, a statute provides for committal to prison for a period not exceeding six months.'

Mrs Whitney snorted. 'I'd say he'd do sixty years rather than share a bed with that woman again, and, by God, who'd blame the man?'

From what I understand, divorce a mensa et thoro *was abolished after more than a hundred years with the Judicial Separation and Family Law Reform Act in 1989. The Latin phrase translates as 'divorce from table and bed' and it was essentially a legal separation that sanctioned two married people to live apart. Such 'divorces' were very costly because the decrees had to be granted by the High Court and so were beyond the reach of most people, except the rich or the very determined.*

Hugh Major was clearly a very determined man because he was not a rich one. Applications for divorce a mensa et thoro *were rarely made to the High Court, and they were granted even more rarely.*

This divorce did not dissolve the marriage, it simply relieved the petitioner from the obligation to cohabit with the respondent. It also meant that once a spouse obtained this divorce, if they subsequently died then the other was precluded from taking any share in the estate. More importantly, if a wife was found guilty of adultery, no order for alimony could be made in her favour.

Hugh Major must have acquired the best legal advice in his bid to rid himself of his wife. Divorce a mensa et thoro *was the only legal way he could divest himself of financial responsibility for Elizabeth Major for the rest of his life. It was also the ultimate revenge since it necessitated proof of her adultery in a very public forum. Mr Major clearly saw this costly separation as a worthwhile investment.*

Meanwhile, Elizabeth Major took proceedings as a deserted spouse to apply for the restitution of conjugal rights. I'm not sure if this was to humiliate Hugh Major or to demonstrate to the court her willingness to fully reconcile with her errant husband. Possibly it was both.

29

High Court

High Court, Day 1: Monday, 25 March 1935

As soon as Mary saw the dome of the Four Courts on Dublin's skyline, her heart sank. She had only ever seen the classical building in pictures and never dreamed she would have to enter this bastion of Irish law. She had been dreading this day since she received the summons from Hannan & Connellan law offices on behalf of Hugh Major.

Dr McEvoy could see how nervous she was. 'Remember: answer truthfully, and there's nothing to be afraid of,' he said, as they walked towards the court. But he was unaware of how much she knew. She would sink Lizzie and her family if she told the truth.

She and the doctor booked into Ross's Hotel on Parkgate

Street the night before the case. Mary should have revelled in spending her first night in a hotel, but anxiety over her deposition meant that she hardly slept. Dr McEvoy kindly footed her bill until Mr Major's solicitors had reimbursed their expenses. For that she was grateful, because every spare penny was going towards her wedding only a week away.

At times like this, she felt furious with Lizzie. *I should be getting fitted for my dress instead of shaking like a leaf and spending my days in a courtroom*, she thought.

She took a deep breath as she and the doctor stepped through the imposing doors and entered the great Round Hall. At first, she saw only a sea of faces, but then she discerned Lizzie in the crowd. Even though she was standing with her father and two barristers in their white collars, black gowns and wigs, she had never looked more alone. Heads jerked in her direction, lips thinned, and men whispered. Mary knew Lizzie felt the eyes of everyone boring into her.

She wore a sober grey jacket and fitted skirt, and she had wound her hair up in an elegant chignon. But her face was pale, her eyes sunken and there was no paint on her lips. Lizzie's head swivelled, and her gaze connected with Mary's. They approached each other, meeting in the middle of the Round Room, two women in a sea of men.

'How are you feeling, Lizzie?' Mary asked. Asking the question felt faintly ridiculous. It felt even crazier that it had come to this. They were in the High Court in Dublin on opposite sides of an infamous divorce case.

'I feel better than I did half an hour ago,' said Lizzie. 'I don't think I was ever so sick. I didn't think I'd make it here.'

Mary noted Lizzie's grey pallor and bloodshot eyes. 'I'm feeling green around the gills myself,' she said, 'and I'm only here as a witness.'

Lizzie glanced around the hall. 'I don't think we're supposed to be talking at all, but sure I've no one in Granard left to talk to,' she said, with a wan smile. 'He's called everyone as witnesses, half our neighbours, you, the doctor.'

'Who are all these people?' Mary asked, looking around in awe at the crowd.

'Law students, members of the public. The newspaper coverage has attracted a lot of attention,' said Lizzie, grimacing. 'These divorce cases don't come around often. No one has ever seen blood tests brought up in evidence.'

Lizzie nodded towards a sudden gap in the hall, and Mary saw Hugh Major among a tight knot of men. Lizzie spoke through gritted teeth. 'Would you look at Himself? Any time I feel afraid, all I have to do is look at him. Little cock of the walk, but if he thinks he's going to break me, he's wrong. I rue the day I married him, but he'll not get our home, if I have anything to do with it.'

She seemed mentally to shake herself before indicating her suit with a downward wave of her hands. 'My first time in Dublin, and I'm wearing sackcloth grey. The barrister told me no lipstick, no paint. He wants me looking like a nun in mourning.'

Mary caught a glimpse of a man she recognised. He stood alone, hovering near the entrance, apparently reading a newspaper, but stealing glances at Lizzie. 'My God, is that Mr Cameron? Has Mr Major called him as a witness too?' she whispered.

Lizzie examined her hands. 'Our side called him because they think the judge needs to hear him deny the allegations. He has to do it for his own wife's sake too.' She raised her voice for all to hear: 'Mr Cameron and his wife are good friends of my parents, after all.'

Defiant to the last, thought Mary.

A group of men with notepads shoved their way through the crowd as the clerk of the court approached to open the courtroom door. Reporters, Mary realised, her heart missing a beat.

'Why not admit to the adultery and let him have his divorce, Lizzie?' Mary pleaded quietly. 'Bring a stop to it now before he drags your name through the mud.'

'He dragged my name through the mud when he walked out on the night of Una's birth,' Lizzie said scornfully. 'He's not taking my father's farm from us.'

The crowd moved as a herd, once the clerk had unlocked the courtroom door. Lizzie grabbed hold of Mary's arm.

'Say as little as you can, Mary, that's all I ask,' she whispered in her ear. 'And remember, whatever you say against me, I will deny it.'

Then she melted into the crowd that was fighting its way into the courtroom.

LONGFORD DIVORCE SUIT

He was in America for several years before he returned to Roose May 23, 1933. His wife gave birth on December 27, 1933.

When he challenged her with unfaithfulness, she denied it, and he told her that while he was away, Canon Markey had spoken to her about her conduct but that she only insulted him.

When the priest spoke to parents and asked them to make her conduct herself, they had also insulted him.

She denied this and asked him [Hugh Major] not to take legal proceedings.

She suggested that a blood test should be taken of the baby and he agreed promising that if it was favourable to her, he would not look for a divorce.

This test had been made by Dr McGrath, the state pathologist, and Dr Dockeray.

Mr Campbell [Counsel for Mrs Elizabeth Major]: Is it your case that your wife first suggested a blood test?

Mr Major: It is. I believe that she mentioned it first. I knew little about the thing although I lived in America before and after I was married, she lived in the country all the time and had not been as far as Dublin even during her life.

In reply to further questions, the witness, Mr Major, said that Mr Cameron was a married man with a grown-up family.

He said he did not know that Mr and Mrs Cameron were friendly with the respondent's father and mother.

Irish Times, 26 March 1935

COUNTY LONGFORD DIVORCE SUIT

Mr J McGrath, State Pathologist, said that with Dr Dockeray, he had carried out a blood test.

This was the first occasion on which this particular test had been tendered as evidence in Irish or English courts.

Doctors were appointed officially by the German courts to carry it out, and it was also used in the American, Danish and Russian Courts.

Irish Press, 26 March 1935

RESULT OF BLOOD TEST

Dr John McGrath, State pathologist . . . gave evidence of a blood test that he had carried out with Dr Dockeray.

It showed that Hugh Major belonged to the O.N. group, the respondent Mrs Major to the O.M. group and the child to the O.M. group.

No conclusion could be reached from the 'O' formation of the groups.

The father was of the group 'N' and would and must invariably transmit the 'N' factor to any child of his.

The mother must, of course, transmit the 'M' factor and a child of the two must be of group 'M.N.'

The child was of group 'M' only, and her blood did not contain the 'N' factor.

Because of this, Dr McGrath stated, Hugh Major could not have been the father of the child.

Irish Times, 26 March 1935

Lizzie's head dropped as the courtroom erupted into cheers and jeers. An irate Mr Justice Sullivan demanded silence and his tipstaff rose and called for order in the court.

Hugh Major gave a satisfied smile as those around him patted him on the back. Not everyone in the court understood Dr McGrath's testimony, but the conclusion was clear. This new-fangled scientific evidence from America had made a liar of Mrs Major.

The judge adjourned the hearing for the day. Before the tipstaff had a chance to call 'All rise,' Hugh Major was shaking hands vigorously with his counsel. Mr Major's witnesses, mostly local farmers, were jubilant too, as they left the court.

Lizzie Major's barristers, Mr Campbell and Mr Odell,

looked grim as they packed their files into battered leather briefcases. Mary glimpsed what seemed to be a terse exchange between the two before they addressed Lizzie and her father, Michael.

Lizzie stood to leave but grabbed the pew end of a bench to steady herself. She looked waxen and sick. *It's little wonder*, Mary thought. She felt drained and exhausted herself. She had been in a state of heightened anxiety all day, fearing that she would be the next to be called to give evidence.

Dr McEvoy was reassuring as they put on their coats in the Round Hall. 'After the results of that blood test, I doubt they'll need us at all,' he said.

Mary felt hopeful as a clerk for Mr Ó Briain, the barrister for Hugh Major, approached them.

'Mr Ó Briain apologises that he wasn't able to call you to the stand today,' he said. 'We don't know if the judge is going to admit the blood test evidence, so we have to ask you to come back in the morning.'

Mary felt that tightness in her chest again, and knew she wouldn't sleep for yet another night.

Up to the early twentieth century, there was a saying 'Maternity is a matter of fact, paternity a matter of opinion.'

By the late 1920s and early 1930s, blood testing had begun to appear in paternity cases only among the very wealthy in America and the Soviet Union. Major v. Major was a landmark case, introducing blood tests for the first time in a paternity dispute in the courts of the UK and Ireland. Mr

Major's legal team employed a form of blood testing, called serological testing, which was cutting-edge and developed only in the 1930s.

My mother was unlucky that her husband had even heard of these tests, and somehow had found the means to pay for them. Even a year or two earlier, they hadn't existed, and no one would have been able to prove her lies.

The newer blood test could disprove parentage in about 40 per cent of cases, giving my mother's lies a 60 per cent chance of success, but it wasn't to be. Her name was plastered all over the national and provincial newspapers, but those were days before news photographers in Ireland. So, as far as we're aware, there isn't a single shot of her, Hugh Major or William Cameron going into or out of the High Court.

30

High Court, Days 2 and 3

High Court, Day 2, Tuesday, 26 March

DIVORCE SUIT

John Donohoe gave evidence . . . that in October 1932, with a man named McGrath, he saw Mrs Major and a man coming down a laneway from the direction of a ruined house at Dromeel.

As the couple passed them, Mrs Major concealed her friend's face with her coat.

He got a bicycle and pursued them, and when he attempted to shine the light of a bicycle lamp on the man, Mrs Major again covered his head with her coat.

He could not identify the man, but he had no doubt that the woman was Mrs Major.

The witness said that the ruined house was frequented by courting couples of the district . . . but he denied that he and McGrath made it a practice to spy on them.

Similar evidence was given by John McGrath.

Weekly Irish Times, 30 March 1935 reporting on events of 26 March

FOUNTAIN PEN AND TWO SHILLINGS: EVIDENCE IN MATRIMONIAL SUIT

Bernard Smith gave evidence . . . that he was caretaker of a farm at Aughamore near where Mrs Major lived.

On a night in March 1933, a dog barked, and he went out to the hayshed. He saw Mrs Major and Cameron in the shed.

He told them that that was no place for them to be; that the owner of the shed was a 'contrary' man and that if he knew that anything wrong was happening there, he would 'give him [Smith] the road' next morning.

Smith said he returned to his house and with his wife went back to the shed where they again saw Mrs Major and Cameron.

Evening Herald, 26 March 1935

'What happened next, Mr Smith?' asked Mr Major's counsel, Mr Ó Briain.

Bernard Smith, a balding, portly man, shuffled uncomfortably in a brown suit that looked two sizes too small for him.

'They left the barn this time, but the next morning Mrs Major arrived at my house,' he said.

'Would a social call like this have been normal, Mr Smith?'

'She never called to us before.'

'So why did Mrs Major call that morning, Mr Smith?'

'She said that her first cousin Maisie Farrell was staying with her, along with a schoolteacher from County Westmeath, and they were at the farm last night. She said the schoolteacher had lost a fountain pen and two shillings, and she asked me to look for the pen and return it to her secretly if I found it. She said her cousin wouldn't like it to be known that she was there.'

'Did she offer an inducement to return this pen, Mr Smith?'

'She said a big pig had been slaughtered at home and that she would see that I got some of it.'

'And did you find the pen?'

'Yes, I found it in the field, and I returned it to Mrs Major that day.'

'And did you get payment?'

'The pig? No, I never saw a bit of it,' he said, prompting laughter in the courtroom.

'So, did you see this Maisie Farrell and this schoolteacher

from County Westmeath in the barn that evening, Mr Smith?'

'No, I didn't.'

'Who did you see that night?'

'Mrs Major and Mr Cameron.'

'Could you have missed Maisie Farrell or this teacher? Could they have been hiding in the barn?'

'No. There was no one else there.'

'Could you have been mistaken when you identified Mrs Major and Mr Cameron in the hayshed?'

'Mrs Major tried to persuade me that I saw her cousin in the barn with this man, but I'm not blind. I'm not mistaken.'

Mr Odell, junior counsel representing Mrs Major, rose to cross-examine the witness. Mr Smith inserted a finger behind his shirt collar and tugged at it as if for air.

'Mr Smith, you are a farm manager, is that right?'

'Yes.'

'Is it not true, Mr Smith, that Mrs Major's father, Michael Farrell, reported you to your employer recently?'

'Yes.'

'Why was that?'

'He claimed that I wasn't maintaining the fences properly.'

'How did you feel about that?'

'I was angry because it wasn't true.'

'Angry enough to concoct this story about his daughter being in the barn when you and your wife saw two other people entirely?'

'No. I'm telling the truth. I know who I saw.'

Patrick Clarke, Garrowhill, said that . . . in July 1933, he met Mrs Major and Cameron on the public road and spoke to them.

They tried to enter a house, but he told the owner not to admit them. He waited until Mrs Major cycled off and saw Cameron enter a bus going in the opposite direction.
Irish Press, 27 March 1935

Dr J. McEvoy gave evidence for the petitioner [Mr Major], the last witness in regard to the baby in the case.
Irish Independent, 27 March 1935

When they called Dr McEvoy to the stand, Mary's heart beat hard and she dug her nails into her palms to steady herself. She expected Mr Major's barrister to call on her next.

She watched as Dr McEvoy gave his testimony about the birth of baby Una. He was resolute. When asked if he believed the baby could have been premature, he gave a slow shake of his head and stated solemnly that Mrs Major's child was a full-term baby.

The barrister, Mr Ó Briain, reiterated to the court that Mr Major had returned to Ireland on 23 May 1933.

'In your medical opinion, Dr McEvoy, in which month was this child conceived if she was born full-term on December the twenty-seventh?'

'Some time in mid to late March,' the doctor replied.

'So at least two months before Mr Major returned from New York on May the twenty-third?'

'I believe so, yes.'

As Mary braced herself to be called, Mr Ó Briain announced that he had concluded his witness evidence.

Instead, Lizzie's counsel, Mr Odell, rose before the court again. A tall, lean man with a hooked nose and long fluid limbs, he moved with balletic grace and presence in the room.

> Mr Odell [barrister for Mrs Major] described the petitioner, Mr Major, as a man of peculiar character and an intensely suspicious nature.
>
> He said Mr Cameron was friendly with Mrs Major's parents and had a common interest with her father in greyhound raising . . .
> *Irish Press*, 27 March 1935

Mary saw Mr Major's colour deepening as Mr Odell painted him as 'peculiar' and a suspicious man. But he snorted out loud when Mr Odell said that Mr Cameron was a friend of Mrs Major's parents.

The courtroom visibly stirred when Mr Odell called his client, Mrs Elizabeth Major, to the witness stand.

Lizzie strode to the stand with assurance but her hand trembled as she placed it on the Bible and she repeated the oath: 'I swear by Almighty God that the evidence I shall give shall be the truth, the whole truth and nothing but the truth.'

Mr Odell swept up to her and without hesitation asked: 'Mrs Major, were you unfaithful to your husband, Hugh Major?'

Lizzie's face hardened. 'I was not,' she said, and her answer, ringing clearly around the hushed courtroom, prompted audible gasps. Even Mary gave a slow, disbelieving shake of her head, wondering at Lizzie's shamelessness.

The Justice, Timothy Sullivan, called for silence in the court. Mr Justice Sullivan was President of the High Court and renowned as one of the most eminent and respected judges in Ireland. A kindly, old-fashioned and dignified gentleman, he bristled at the open hostility in the courtroom towards this ashen-faced woman in the witness box. Lowering his spectacles, he spoke directly to Lizzie. 'If at any stage, Mrs Major, you feel this getting too much for you, let me know, and we'll adjourn for as long as you need,' he said.

Mary couldn't feel as much sympathy for Lizzie as the Justice. How could anyone lie with such defiance when the weight of evidence was piled against her? But then she saw Lizzie's eyes flicker towards Hugh Major, the blaze of pure loathing in them.

Mr Odell continued with his client's evidence. 'Is it true, Mrs Major, as your husband has testified, that you introduced the idea of doing a blood test to prove paternity of the child?'

'No,' Lizzie said adamantly. 'I never heard of such a thing in my life until my husband suggested it.'

Mr Odell asked her about Bernard Smith and the story of the fountain pen.

'I was not in the barn that night,' she said. 'Mr Smith has a grudge against my father, and he is making up the entire story.'

She couldn't fail to miss the indignant murmurs and head-shaking in the courtroom. Her voice choked as the questioning continued, and her wan pallor became more evident.

Mr Justice Sullivan raised his hand, bringing a halt to Lizzie's barrister's enquiries and adjourned the hearing until the next day.

Lizzie didn't need lipstick to charm the men, thought Mary, as she watched her bolt from the courtroom.

Mary approached the harassed-looking clerk working for Mr Major's barristers in the Round Hall. The man's tie was awry, and he was laden with papers and files, but he looked apologetic when he saw her. 'Mr Major's counsel has decided they don't need to call you for evidence after all,' he said. 'I'm sorry for all the inconvenience of bringing you to Dublin.'

Mary almost beamed with relief. It seemed that after the doctor's confident medical opinion, the testimony of a mere midwife wasn't necessary. She felt she could breathe easily for the first time in days.

Across the Round Hall, she saw Mr Odell and Mr Campbell sweep away, their gowns billowing behind them, leaving

Lizzie in their wake. She looked so forlorn and ill that Mary forgot her earlier anger and approached her. 'How are you, Lizzie?' she asked, keeping her voice low, amid the swirl of curious clerks, solicitors, the general public and reporters. 'They say it will all be over tomorrow.'

Lizzie squeezed her eyes shut for a moment and opened them with relief. 'I felt sick again for a moment in there. It comes and goes in waves.'

'It's the strain, Lizzie. I swear, I don't know how you can stand it.'

'It's nothing to do with the strain, Mary,' Lizzie replied, with a smile.

Then she squeezed Mary's upper arm and whispered in her ear: 'I felt the baby kick for the first time today.'

Mary could only stare at her in response.

'Oh, I know it's not ideal, but we're leaving together after this ordeal is over. We need to move somewhere people will let us live our lives.'

Mary wanted to scream at her. *What about Mr Cameron's family? What about your children and your parents?*

But Lizzie was oblivious. If she hadn't been so pale, she could almost have been described as jaunty. It was the end of a gruelling day in court, in which she had been portrayed as a floozy romping in a hayshed, yet she was unbowed.

Mary found it hard to speak during the long journey back to Granard, fearing she might blurt out Lizzie's secret if she spoke at all. Dr McEvoy interpreted Mary's silence as exhaustion and was sympathetic. 'You really didn't need this circus when your wedding is in a few days, Mary,' he said. He sighed in exasperation as he drove down twisting country lanes. 'I watched that woman in court, and I wondered what on earth goes through her head,' he said. 'Taking up with a married man was bad enough, but now to be lying in court and denying adultery – what is she doing?'

Mary shrugged, still dazed after her latest encounter with Lizzie. 'I don't know, Doctor,' she said. 'I really don't, except I think she might be mad.'

'She must be. Anyone who could swear an oath and say what she said after all that evidence against her . . . The case is as good as over. Mr Major will have his divorce.'

High Court, Day 3, Wednesday, 27 March
As the third day of proceedings began, it looked bad for Mrs Major, but Mr Odell was determined to go down fighting, so first he called William Cameron to the stand.

> **LONGFORD DIVORCE SUIT**
> The hearing was concluded of the matrimonial suit in which Hugh Major, Roose, Moatfarrell, Edgeworthstown sought a divorce from his wife . . .
>
> . . . William Cameron also . . . denied the suggestions made against him regarding his association with Mrs Major.
>
> *Irish Times*, 28 March 1935

Mr Odell called another witness who claimed that the scandalous hayshed evidence by Bernard Smith was a lie to wreak revenge against Mrs Major's father.

LONGFORD DIVORCE SUIT

[Witness] James McDonagh said that he was in Bernard Smith's house the night Smith had sworn that he found Mrs Major and Cameron in the shed.

Smith, when he came back, said that there were a couple in the shed all right but that he did not know who they were.

Later, Smith told him [McDonagh] he would get 'even' with Farrell for reporting him to his employer by saying that Mrs Major [Farrell's daughter] was the woman in the shed.

Irish Times, 28 March 1935

In a last-ditch attempt to stymie Mr Major's case, Mr Odell made a legal bid to overturn the evidence provided by the blood test. However, Mr Justice Sullivan insisted that his ruling would be based on the evidence of the witnesses and the alleged acts of misconduct, although he would still admit the blood test evidence.

LONGFORD DIVORCE SUIT

Mr Odell . . . addressed the Judge on the . . . admissibility of the evidence of . . . the blood test.

The Court was asked for the first time in the legal history of Great Britain or Ireland to permit . . . [a new type of] evidence . . . to show that the father was not the father of his child born in wedlock.

Mr Justice Sullivan said that science advanced from year to year. [He said, one day] it might be possible for medical men [all over the world] to agree that some decisive test had been found by which it was possible to say whether a certain man was the father of a child.

[He said] Counsel was asking him to adhere to the practice already laid down, but he was not going to hold that the practice could not be altered . . . as scientific knowledge progressed.

He had no hesitation in admitting the evidence, but . . . he was not going to decide the case on the paternity of the child, but rather on the evidence . . . of the alleged acts of misconduct.

Irish Times, 28 March 1935

Mr Justice Sullivan then added that his judgment didn't imply that William Cameron was involved in the alleged acts of misconduct, nor did it rule on the legitimacy of Una Major. He did, however, find Mrs Major guilty of misconduct in the hayshed and the charge of adultery had been proved.

LONGFORD DIVORCE SUIT

Mr Justice Sullivan, in the course of his judgement, said that the case was a tragic case in many respects.

It was regrettable that the petitioner, shortly after his marriage, went to America to earn more money for his family . . .

[The judge] was satisfied that if that separation had not occurred, the necessity for divorce proceedings would not have arisen.

In coming to this conclusion, he wanted it to be understood that it had not been necessary for him to base his decision on any question of the legitimacy of the child . . .

He held that he was entitled to infer that Mrs Major was guilty of misconduct in the hayshed . . .

He was not satisfied that the evidence justified him in coming to the conclusion that Cameron was the man there.

He would hold that the misconduct was committed with a man unknown.

As regards the other incidents . . . he could not hold that he could infer that misconduct had been committed with Cameron.

Accordingly, he granted a decree of divorce.

> He allowed the respondent her costs up to the amount that had been lodged by the petitioner as security.
> *Irish Times*, 28 March 1935

The judgement of the President of the High Court on 27 March, 1935 stated:

> The judge . . . found that the charge of adultery alleged in the said petition had been proved and thereupon the judge by his final decree pronounced that the Petitioner, the said Hugh Major, be and he is hereby divorced and separated from bed, board and mutual cohabitation with the said Respondent Elizabeth Major by reason of the adultery of said Respondent . . .

Elizabeth Major was a poor farmer's daughter, raised in a rural backwater, who had never been out of County Longford in her life. The High Court should have been a terrifying ordeal for her, yet she faced down a hostile courtroom, the clergy, lawyers, barristers, journalists, even the President of the High Court.

She took the stand and swore an oath in the High Court that she had not committed adultery. She unashamedly continued to swear that that was the truth, even after pioneering scientific blood tests had proved that her husband could not be the father of her child, Una Major. And she continued her protestations even after a string of witnesses testified that they had caught her cavorting with my father in haybarns and ruined cottages. She stood her ground, even though the entire time she was in the High Court, she was three months pregnant with me, the second child of her affair.

I can only assume her motivation was to save the family farm and home. I have no intention of glorifying her or her actions, but clearly the woman was a force to be reckoned with. She was an iron lady before the term was ever heard of, and this lady was not for turning either.

It should also be noted that the Justice, Timothy Sullivan, presiding over the court, was a prescient man. He refused to rule against the use of blood tests in that case and in future court cases. He said that one day there might be a paternity test that would be accepted all over the world. He was proved right when DNA testing started in the 1980s. It is also clear that he was a kind man. He showed some sympathy for my mother in an era when many men would not. He refused to brand Una an illegitimate child, despite the blood tests. He also pointed a finger at Hugh Major when he said that had he not emigrated shortly after their wedding, this whole sorry saga might never have happened.

31

Enniscorthy

Mary stood back and surveyed her white mayflower blooms with satisfaction. Even as she gathered them from the hedgerows, she knew Paddy would tease her about 'titivating' the place instead of doing a proper day's work on the farm.

Leaving her father-in-law's house and setting up her own home on the site next door was a distant dream. Money was tight, and Paddy and his father, Hugh, were too preoccupied making a living on the farm to spend much time constructing a house.

Days earlier, Paddy had attended a Fianna Fáil meeting, which was addressed by the Minister for Agriculture Dr James Ryan, in Gorey. Farmers, angry that they could no longer make a living, had heckled him. It was de Valera's government that had sparked the ruinous trade war by withholding land annuity payments to Britain. The British retaliated by imposing swingeing trade tariffs on Irish imports, and farmers saw the market for Irish beef disappear overnight. The Irish government responded by imposing its own tariffs on British imports. 'Burn everything British but their coal' was the official slogan. But the campaign was as effective as a midge buzzing around a bullock, and Irish farmers were being ruined.

'All the minister could do was brag about how the government is making Ireland an independent and free country,' said Paddy. 'Monty Breslin shouted it would be a free country all right, free of people with the amount of emigration going on.'

There was no improvement in the price of livestock despite the coal–cattle pact with Britain.

'We have to change the farm from grazing to tillage. The potato trade is steady, thank God,' said Paddy.

But tillage was labour-intensive and time-consuming. Paddy and his father were out all morning with the saddle-harrows, loosening the soil and lifting the weeds for the early potato crop. He said they'd have a long wait to find a buyer for the farm he'd inherited outside Edgeworthstown too. 'Sure you couldn't give away a farm now,' he said. 'The land is going derelict all over with the old dying off and all the young emigrating.'

Mary looked around the hundred-year-old farm kitchen

and fire and sighed. The stone-built farmhouse was damp, and the stairs creaked with age. Her life of luxury with Mrs Whitney, electric light and running water was now a distant dream.

Still, when she stood at the half-door, she enjoyed views of the oak forest and woodland nearby, and the meandering Ballyedmond river at the farm's borders. She looked with pleasure on the apple trees in the small back garden, which were laced with pink blossom.

She missed her job, but she enjoyed her new life with Paddy. His father, who had been a widower for ten years, couldn't have made her feel more welcome and never stopped apologising for 'letting the house go'. She even found her first client, a lady in nearby Monageer, whose baby she would deliver the next month.

The sound of the dogs barking alerted her to the postman's arrival. Paud Grainey rolled up on his bike, whistling, and leaned in over the half-door. 'A grand morning, Mrs Walsh.'

'It is indeed, Paud. Will I wet the tea for you?'

'No rest for the wicked, Mrs Walsh. I've got a full bag on today,' he said, slapping the bulging leather satchel strapped across him. 'I've another one from Granard,' he said, squinting at the postmark on the envelope. 'You'll be able to give me all the news the next time I'm here.'

She recognised Mrs Whitney's fine, spidery writing on the envelope, as she waved off Paud. She realised with a pang that she missed her friend's company.

'I hope that you are in good health, as I am here, and I

hope you are not too bored as Mrs Walsh, the farmer's wife,' she wrote, and her words made Mary smile. Mrs Whitney had warned her of the perils of moving to the country, the worst of which was boredom. 'Nothing but chickens to talk to most of the day,' she'd said, countless times.

Her letter told how Willie Kelly had been hauled in front of the District Court for holding an illegal dance under the brand new Public Dance Halls Act. 'The poor divil was only trying to raise a few bob for the annuities payment,' she wrote, 'but the sergeant raided the place last Saturday week to find thirty people dancing in the kitchen and fifteen playing cards in another room. Willie, the oul eejit, admitted charging admission of one shilling and holding a card game for a turkey.'

Mrs Whitney added: 'Everyone knows that the sergeant had no choice, and it was Canon Markey who was behind the whole thing.'

Mrs Whitney also enclosed a clipping from the *Sunday Independent* about Mrs Major pursuing her maintenance from Mr Major.

'Her solicitor, Mr Farrell, represented her in court. She didn't dare show her face,' she wrote.

At Longford Circuit Court, Mrs Major, Roose, obtained two decrees against her husband, Hugh Major, Roose, for £25 15/- and £16 5/-.

[These amounts are] due under an order of the District Justice at Granard at the rate of 25 shillings a week under the Married Women's Cause of Desertion Act.

It was stated that a decree for divorce, *a mensa et thoro*, had been obtained by Hugh Major, Roose, in the Matrimonial Court on March 24 last. The amount of the decree would be to that date.

Sunday Independent, 12 May 1935

Mrs Whitney continued:

I don't know if you've already heard, but Mrs Major left Roose only a day or two after your wedding. William Cameron arrived in a big hackney car to bring her away. The motor was all very swanky considering Reynolds' Solicitors showed him the door, and he's jobless now. They said they couldn't keep him because of the scandal in the newspapers, but they really got rid of him because he's a left footer. They said they'd never have given him a good paying job if they'd known he was one of THEM.

Anyway, the day they left, Mrs Major gave Hughie and Maisie a few pennies and told them to take the long way to the sweetshop in Clonbroney. The poor mites, when they came back, she was gone, and they were heartbroken.

Mrs Major told Mr and Mrs Farrell that she'll come back for the children when she's settled somewhere, but sure, where will that pair settle?

Mary thought it was a safe bet that Mr and Mrs Farrell didn't know anything about the latest child that was on the way.

Then sure last week, didn't Hugh Major land over at the Farrells' house and demand Hughie and Maisie. He's brought them to a house he's renting on Granard Street.

She could almost see the old lady frowning as she wrote:

Those poor children don't know whether they're coming or going. They're living with a man they hardly know. He's more than fifty years old and has no idea how to be around them. Sure, what business has a single man with two children?

Mary thought of the earnest ten-year-old Hughie and solemn little eight-year-old Maisie. She wondered if either parent was thinking about their interests.

Which brings me to this morning. Mrs Farrell called to my door, the poor woman, with that poor child, Una, in her arms. She asked for your address saying Mrs Major wants to write to you. What could I do but give it to her? I hope you don't mind. She says Mrs Major is staying in lodgings in Ballymahon and is trying to find a job. She was still sympathetic to that woman and says her daughter was run out of town!

Mary knew that, given Lizzie's condition, she could never have stayed in the town. Nor would she be able to look for a job for a long time. She wondered how she would survive if William Cameron was unemployed.

If Lizzie refused to go to a mother-and-baby home, she would have to go to Dublin. Mary had heard that there were free antenatal clinics for the poor in Dublin. The St John Ambulance Brigade had also set up four welfare dining rooms in Dublin, which fed hundreds of expectant mothers.

Mary thought Lizzie hadn't an iota of common sense, and that William Cameron was just as irresponsible. But she would write to Lizzie and try to explain that the best chance of survival for her and the baby lay in Dublin.

I know from my own experience that the Church had an unhealthy stranglehold on society in those days. It saw the growth of cinema, modern music and dancing as a threat to its control. Bishops blamed popular culture on the falling standards of morality among the youth and forced the government to introduce the repressive Public Dance Halls Act in 1935. This draconian new act meant that a dance could be held only with the express permission of the parish priest, the gardaí and the judiciary.

House dances, such as that held by Willie Kelly in County Longford and scores of others around the country, were raided and closed by the gardaí. Those who hosted such dances were classed as criminals. The clergy were concerned about unsupervised dancing of any sort, but jazz music and dancing, in particular, were an occasion of sin.

It's hard to believe now, but in the year of my birth, more than three thousand Gaelic League members marched through Mohill in County Leitrim bearing banners in bold headlines reading 'DOWN WITH JAZZ' and 'OUT WITH PAGANISM'.

While the social life of rural Ireland was being suffocated by conservatism, economic life was even darker. Many small farmers were plunged into extreme poverty by the trade war with Britain.

Some of the best farmland in the country could be found in County Wexford, yet the local papers reported in 1935 that sixty-two farms had gone derelict in Enniscorthy, another thirty-six in Gorey, and fifty-seven were abandoned in the Wexford town area.

During this oppressive era, Elizabeth Major's parents were beacons of enlightenment and tolerance. They stood by their disgraced daughter and cared for their illegitimate granddaughter when many others wouldn't have done so. They were certainly headstrong, rebellious and fearless for their time, like my mother.

If there are any heroes among my family in that era, it's the grandparents I never met.

32

Baby John

Enniscorthy, June 1935

'Come up and see my new home!' cried Lizzie, skipping up the flights of stairs. She seemed to forget that Mary had rented the room on her behalf weeks earlier.

Within days of hearing from Mrs Whitney, Mary received a letter from 'Mrs Elizabeth Cameron'. The signature confused her at first, as did the blithe letter that accompanied it. Lizzie expressed how much she enjoyed living in town for a change, and that she hoped Mary was enjoying life as a married woman. It was only then she revealed that she and William Cameron planned to move to Enniscorthy.

William can't secure work anywhere in the county of Longford. The Valley of the Squinting Windows is alive and well around here.

A friend has recommended William to James O'Connor Solicitors in Castle Street in Enniscorthy. They have agreed to start William on three months' trial on Monday, 3 June, so we'll be neighbours again!

Won't it be fun to see each other again far away from all that nonsense in Granard?

Could we impose on you to secure board and lodgings in the town for us? We only need a small and modest room until William starts earning a regular salary again.

I'd be grateful if you reply using my name as signed. The landlady, bless her, is too blind to read the newspapers, but she would have a heart attack if she suspected we were not man and wife.

Mary didn't know whether to admire Lizzie's spirit or to condemn her for recklessness. The woman's foolishness with William Cameron had upended so many lives. Yet here she was treating it all as a merry adventure. She and William were carrying on as wantonly as if they lived in some godless place like London or New York. He must be as crazy as she is, Mary thought.

Still, she asked Paddy if he knew of lodgings in the town.

'Tom Kinsella's new wife is taking in lodgers above the butcher's on Market Square,' said Paddy. 'She'll be glad to let a room in the oul house because the butchery isn't doing great this weather.'

The Kinsellas' house was ideal, situated a minute's walk from Mr Cameron's new workplace on Castle Street. Mary met with young Mrs Kinsella, who offered board and an attic room for reasonable weekly terms. Lizzie and William moved to Enniscorthy on 1 July 1935.

Mary could barely discern Lizzie's condition as she ascended the stairs ahead of her in a loose flowing skirt. 'I hope the stairs are not going to be too much for you later this summer,' Mary said.

'We're glad to get anything we can afford.' Lizzie wrestled to open the door into their new accommodation. The low ceilings gave the room a claustrophobic feel, and sunlight beating on the roof above made it stifling. A small dormer window beamed a large square of light onto the bed, which dominated the space.

'Look!' said Lizzie, her eyes gleaming, as she flicked the round white switch up and down. She illuminated, then extinguished the bare bulb that hung from the ceiling. 'Oh, I swear I'll never get used to this. It's like magic! The whole house has electric light, and they have plug sockets in the kitchen.'

They sat on the bed, the feather mattress sinking under their weight, wedging them together.

'Did you hear that Mr Major took Hugh and Maisie?' Mary asked.

'Isn't it time enough for him to look after them?' Lizzie

said brightly. 'Let him see what it's like to be left on your own with them.'

Mary thought it odd that she didn't seem to miss the children. 'Do you think he'll let you have them back?'

'Oh, he'll get tired of them. He gets tired of everyone.'

'Lizzie, what about Una? Are you and William going to take her soon?'

'Oh, Mary, let us have a breather.' Her tone was brittle but she laughed. 'We can hardly keep ourselves at the moment, never mind a toddler. Una is fine with her nana and granddad for the time being.'

She patted her belly. 'Not too long now. We're going to concentrate on having this one first. Thank God I can rely on you to be here for the delivery, Mary. And, for goodness' sake, stop calling me Lizzie, I'm Elizabeth Cameron now.'

Enniscorthy, 9 September 1935

The attic room was hot and clammy as the baby's rasping cries rang out. It had been a hard few hours for Lizzie, and Mary exhaled with relief that it was over. She savoured the familiar thrill of cupping a newborn's head in the palm of her hand. Her face was wreathed in smiles. Holding an arrival to the world never ceased to be a glorious thrill for her.

The baby held his arms aloft, fists waving furiously, a small life that was both vital and fragile. He had a layer of downy golden hair on his head.

'Oh, Lizzie, he's perfect, a beautiful little boy,' she breathed, cutting the cord and inhaling his newborn scent.

'Have you and William thought of a name for a boy yet?'

'We're thinking John. John Cameron,' said Lizzie, eyes closed, her face bathed in sweat and her hair stuck in damp tendrils around her face.

Even though the window was wide open, there wasn't a breath of air moving in the room. Lizzie roused herself, as Mary surrendered the baby to her.

'He's a little angel,' said Mary, gazing at the child in admiration. 'Look at those blond curls already. He takes after his dad with his fine head of hair.' She started to bundle up the soiled linens and clean around the room. *Where is Mrs Kinsella? She promised to return with more hot water ages ago.*

'I thought you might call the baby William after his dad,' Mary said, making conversation.

'William already has a boy called after him,' said Lizzie, speaking of her lover's other family for the first time. She indicated for Mary to take the baby from her again. 'William is his second son. He's a trainee accountant, so he's taking after his dad.'

'Have you met any of his children?' Mary asked curiously.

'Good Lord, no!' laughed Lizzie. 'They don't talk to William, never mind me! They haven't spoken to him in ages.'

'Does he not feel guilty about leaving his wife?' asked Mary. 'She hasn't long by all accounts.'

'He can't help the way he feels,' Lizzie said, a sudden light in her eyes. 'We're both glad that we've found a second chance of happiness. You need to grab it where you find it, Mary, trust me.'

Hearing Mrs Kinsella's footsteps on the stairs, their conversation ended abruptly.

'Oh, my goodness, Mrs Cameron, you're keeping me fit today,' Mrs Kinsella gasped, as she backed through the door carrying a basin of water. She placed it on a wooden chair by the bed and exhaled deeply.

Then she caught sight of the baby in Mary's arms and squealed in delight. 'It's here at last! Isn't that incredible, born under our very own roof! Congratulations, Mrs Cameron! Is it a boy or girl? Oh, a boy, and isn't he a handsome divil indeed!'

Mrs Kinsella slumped into the only chair in the room and pulled out a rolled-up copy of the *Irish Press* from the pocket of her apron. 'I brought you today's paper as a keepsake for the baby,' she said. 'It's a good omen, see? The front page is about the Pope.' The headline read: 'Mussolini's Peace Gesture to the Holy See' and it began with the words of His Holiness: 'The entire world desires peace. We are praying for peace.'

Mrs Kinsella added: 'There's another story about a riot on the *Bremen* ship, in New York.'

'The *Bremen*?' said Lizzie. 'I know someone who sailed on that ship from Cobh a long time ago.'

'Oh, who was that, Mrs Cameron? Was it your sister?'

'No, Hugh Major was his name. He was . . . a neighbour of ours,' she said, her eyes dancing with amusement as she glanced at Mary. 'I'd nearly forgotten about him until you mentioned the *Bremen*.'

'Well, they say a few passengers pulled down a swastika flag on the ship, and they were arrested,' said Mrs Kinsella.

The landlady suddenly scrambled to her feet. 'Oh, my goodness,' she said. 'I promised Mr Cameron that I'd go tell him as soon as the baby was born!' She ran her fingers through her hair and pulled off her apron. 'He and my Tom are hugging the bar in Duffy's all day. They'll probably be jiggered by now, but I'll run down and tell him the good news – imagine it's your very first child, and it's a boy!'

Mary couldn't help glancing at Lizzie, who returned her look with a wink.

33

A Safe Place

Enniscorthy, January 1936

Mrs Kinsella spoke in hushed tones as Mary unbuttoned her cloak in the landlady's hallway. 'She's not well at all,' she said, glancing up the stairs, as if Lizzie could hear her four storeys up. 'She's been very morbid, Nurse, for a long time and isn't getting any better at all.'

'Has she seen a doctor?' Mary asked.

'Oh, yes,' said Mrs Kinsella. 'Poor Mr Cameron brought Dr Grant here. The doctor gave her a tonic and told her to pull herself together for the sake of the child, but she's no better.'

Mrs Kinsella leaned in close to Mary, lowering her voice even further. 'The only one Elizabeth will get out of bed for is Father Cartin. She asked me to speak to a priest on her behalf, and he's been very good to her, but she never stops crying, Nurse.'

Mary had set out for the Kinsellas' home as soon as she'd received the hastily written letter from Mr Cameron pleading with her to visit Elizabeth. He wrote that Elizabeth had no interest in either baby John or herself, and he was despairing because she was getting worse.

Mary wondered if Lizzie had heard about Hughie and Maisie's disappearance. Hugh Major claimed that the children were gone to boarding school, but he was refusing to tell anyone of their whereabouts.

'Sure the Farrells know Hugh Major hasn't the money to send them to boarding school,' Mrs Whitney had written. 'So they think he must have put them into a state home.'

Mary heard the baby crying, as Mrs Kinsella rapped on Lizzie's door. 'Elizabeth? Elizabeth, it's me, Sheila, and I have lovely Nurse Walsh who's come to see you.'

Baby John stopped crying, but there was no reply from Lizzie.

'She does this. She won't answer,' hissed Mrs Kinsella, rolling her eyes at Mary. 'Elizabeth, we're coming in to see you.'

The pungent smell reached their nostrils as soon as they opened the door. Mary spotted the baby, his head surrounded by a halo of golden curls, lying in a drawer on the floor. He was wrapped in the blue wool blanket that Mary had knitted as a gift for his birth.

Lizzie was a huddled shape under the patchwork quilt

on the bed in the bitterly cold room. Mary saw that the odour was coming from a bucket of the child's soiled nappies in a far corner of the room.

The child's face was tear-streaked, but his bright blue eyes danced at the sight of the two women. He smiled a gummy smile, his chubby arms and legs jerking in delight at this sudden diversion.

Mary picked up John and bounced him in her arms. As Mrs Kinsella wrestled open the dormer window, Mary shook Lizzie awake and pushed the child into her arms. 'He needs feeding,' she said sternly. 'Let's clean up this room before tackling anything else,' she added, to Mrs Kinsella, who looked in dismay at the task ahead of them.

The two women swept through the room, scrubbing down every surface, hauling up hot water, changing the bedclothes, then bathing and changing the baby.

'Lizzie, you've let yourself go to rack and ruin,' Mary said, as she and Mrs Kinsella tugged her from the bed. 'And you're neglecting John. He shouldn't be cooped up in this room all day. It's bad for his lungs.'

Mrs Kinsella scooped up the baby. 'We'll get out of your way now, ladies,' she said, cradling the child. 'We'll go for a lovely walk, won't we, John?'

Lizzie's eyes were dull and listless, and she moved almost mechanically, as Mary started to bathe her. 'What is it, Lizzie? Is it Hughie and Maisie that's getting you down?' Mary asked kindly, as she ran a warm sponge down Lizzie's back.

Lizzie looked up at her and blinked, and it almost seemed

that she was trying to remember Hughie and Maisie. 'I can't cope with them now,' she said abruptly.

Mary stared at her in disbelief. 'Lizzie! They're locked up in some institution where they don't even have each other for company. God love them, they won't know what's happening to them.'

Lizzie began crying hysterically. Her entire body was torn with so much pent-up emotion that she gasped for breath between sobs. Mary could do nothing but let her cry herself out.

'I can't stand feeling like this,' said Lizzie, after she was spent. 'I haven't felt well for a long time. Father Cartin said I won't feel well until I do the right thing and make my peace with God.'

Mary shook her head in bewilderment. 'Lizzie, isn't it a bit late to be taking the advice of the clergy?'

'I didn't listen before and look at me now!' she cried. 'I can never go home again, and I'm trapped in this place. Father Cartin says the only way I'll ever feel peace again is to reconcile with God and the Church.'

'Well, if it makes you feel better,' said Mary, 'do as he says. Confess your sins and pray for forgiveness.'

'I did, but he's denying me absolution,' Lizzie wailed, her voice breaking again. 'He says I haven't shown proper contrition, and he can't absolve my sins because I'm still committing adultery. He says I can't live with a married man and with a child who was born in sin.'

'There's nothing sinful about any child,' said Mary,

irritated. 'If you were going to have a crisis of conscience, Lizzie, it was a long time ago you should have been having it, not now.' She scrubbed Lizzie a little bit harder. 'You'll just have to live with your conscience and consider yourself blessed to have a lovely boy and his father, who's out working to keep you both.' She caught Lizzie by her shoulders and forced her to meet her eyes. 'You should concentrate now on making a home where you can bring your children back under one roof,' she said. 'They *need* you, Lizzie!'

'You're right, Mary, you're always right,' Lizzie said, but Mary knew that she wasn't listening.

Enniscorthy, 12 February 1936

The ground had a coating of glittering frost, but the sun shone low in the cloudless sky, and a soft breeze ruffled the air.

As Mary set her bike against the lamppost outside the Medical Hall pharmacy on Slaney Place, she saw Mrs Kinsella coming out.

'Just the woman I was hoping to see,' said Mrs Kinsella. 'Have you heard the latest?'

'What news is that, Mrs Kinsella?'

'Mr and Mrs Cameron are moving to Dublin today.'

Mary was momentarily stunned. The last time she had seen Lizzie was only weeks ago, and the woman couldn't get out of bed. 'I haven't talked to Mrs Cameron since the last day I saw you.'

'Well, it came as a big surprise to me as well, I can tell

you,' said Mrs Kinsella. 'They said they're off, just like that, and Mr Cameron has left his job at O'Connor's too.'

'That's a bit sudden.'

'It is, and I'll miss having Mrs Cameron around, to be honest,' said Mrs Kinsella. 'It's nice having another woman in the house to talk to instead of salesmen coming and going. I'm helping them down to the station to catch the eleven o'clock train.'

'I have to pick up a few medications,' said Mary, nodding towards the pharmacy, 'but if you'll hold on a minute, I'll go back with you to say goodbye.'

Mary wondered what their plans were now. Mr Cameron might have found a better job in Dublin. Or perhaps Lizzie had received the maintenance owed to her by her husband, and they could set up home at last.

Back at the house, Mrs Kinsella urged Mary to go up without her. 'I've got to make a start on the dinner,' she said. 'They can let me know when they're ready to go.'

Mary made her way up the staircase, but she had barely time to knock on the door before it flew open and William Cameron stood before her. He was holding John in his arms, and his face fell with disappointment when he saw Mary. 'Oh,' he said. 'I thought it might be Elizabeth.'

'She's not here?' said Mary. 'I came to say goodbye. Mrs Kinsella says you're moving to Dublin.'

'Elizabeth's gone,' he said. 'She took a bag and left early this morning. I thought you might be her.'

'What do you mean she's gone? Gone where?'

'I don't know. She wouldn't tell me,' he said, running his free hand through his mane of hair in exasperation.

Baby John sat alert in his father's arm, his blue eyes watching Mary intently.

'It's that Father Cartin. He's been filling her head with all these ideas about sin and repentance. She says I can't contact her again.' He sighed in frustration. 'I just can't get through to the woman any more.'

Mary was confused. 'She's not bringing John with her?' she asked.

'She wants nothing more to do with him and told me I've to bring him to Dublin,' Mr Cameron said, shifting the child in his arm. 'Father Cartin has arranged for me to deliver him to St Brigid's Orphanage.'

'No!' Mary cried. 'You're not putting him away, are you?'

'What choice do I have?' he replied grimly. 'Some concerned citizen, probably Father Cartin, has alerted my bosses that I'm a Protestant living with a Catholic woman, and they've dismissed me. I might have been able to pay Mrs Kinsella to mind John for a while, but I can't keep myself now, never mind a child.'

Mary reached out to stroke John's face. He grasped her finger with his chubby hand and gurgled with glee. 'Please don't leave him,' she said. 'No matter what the priest says, those institutions are not any place for a child.'

'Oh, but this place isn't an institution. They foster out the babies to families,' said Mr Cameron. 'That's what Elizabeth said, and this is not for good. It's just for a while until she comes to her senses. Father Cartin must have spirited her away somewhere, but she knows she can find me in my sister's in Newtownabbey.'

Mary's spirits were low as she went to leave. Mr Cameron could see her hesitation as she looked back towards the baby, wrapped in the blue wool blanket she had knitted for him.

'It's only for a little while,' Mr Cameron assured Mary, with a smile. 'I don't want to be parted from this little chap. But it's the safest place for him for a few weeks. Sure, we'll take him out of the home as soon as we're back on our feet.'

Epilogue

Elizabeth and William never came back for me, and it took me sixty-seven years to find them – or at least the memories of them. The secrets of my past began to tumble out the day my daughter Niamh answered that fateful phone call from Fran Dean, my niece.

I learned that I had two half-siblings from my mother's marriage, and there were four half-siblings from my father's marriage. Not only that, I also discovered I had one older sister and four younger ones.

From having no family at all, I found myself with a surfeit of riches – a total of eleven brothers and sisters.

Elizabeth Farrell/Major/Cameron

My father, William Cameron, delivered me, as instructed, to St Brigid's Orphanage in Dublin in February 1936. He then went to stay with his younger sister, Ethel Quirey, in Bellevue Park, Antrim Road in Newtownabbey, County Antrim.

No one can account for the movements of my mother for a year or so after she left her lodgings in Enniscorthy. Family members have speculated that she had some kind of breakdown, but we have never been able to confirm that.

All that is certain is that she and my father William were reunited by 1937, and remained together, posing as Mr and Mrs Cameron until he died in 1955. She survived for forty-seven years after the love of her life passed away. In fact, the self-styled Elizabeth Cameron lived until the grand age of 103. She had been buried only days before William's granddaughter, Fran Dean, phoned my house in 2002.

Elizabeth led us on a merry dance for years by adopting the married and maiden names of her lover's wife. My birth certificate recorded Elizabeth Cameron née Maguire as my mother. The first time I saw the name 'Farrell' was in 1996 when I was allowed to view my adoption records for the first time. Someone had corrected the original ledger in the orphanage to draw a line through the name 'Maguire' and write 'Farrell' in another pen above it.

Did my mother come back to correct the record? Elizabeth's second family say it was something she might have done, but I'll never know now.

There were many near misses between my mother and

me down through the years. She worked as a dishwasher in Dublin Zoo's kitchens while Nell French worked there as head of catering. It's even possible we met, because Elizabeth worked in the zoo kitchen during the years that I 'helped' Nell in the zoo shop. And for a brief time, when I worked at Cabra Tech, my mother lived directly across the road from the school. She and my father lived only seven miles from our first family home in Mulhuddart.

There were other coincidences. My daughter Fiona attended St Catherine's National School in Cabra where her best friend was Fiona McWilliams. Fiona's mother told us about an older Mrs Cameron, who lived up the road with her four daughters but, for some reason, we failed to follow up on this information.

My younger son, Brian, became good friends with a student called Alan Byrne while they were both attending Trinity College. Alan turned out to be Brian's cousin, my nephew, and the son of Betty Byrne, one of the sisters I never knew I had, until years later.

Cameron (née Farrell)
Kempton, Dublin and Longford

Our beloved mother Elizabeth passed away at 11.30 o'c on Friday, September 20, 2002, in her 104th year.

Funeral today (Monday).

Mass in the Church of Our Lady Help of Christians, Navan Road to Glasnevin Crematorium.

Donations to St Vincent's Home, Navan Road, Dublin 7.
Death Notice, *Irish Times*

Hugh Major

Hugh Major was unusual for the time, travelling to and from the United States on at least three occasions. We found some details of his life as a butler in the United States Federal Census of 1920, working for the millionaire businessman, J. Frank Pierson. He declares in the census that he arrived in New York in 1914.

We found more about him in the Ellis Island records in New York, biographical details such as his height, weight, hair colour, age and the fact that he lived with his cousin, Patrick Ward, in a brownstone on East 102nd Street in Harlem.

We found no evidence to suggest that Hugh Major ever returned to America after divorcing my mother. We think he lived in Edgeworthstown, where the *Longford Leader* reported in 1947 that he was elected treasurer of the town's Little Theatre Society.

He died in 1968, aged eighty-three, and is buried in St Patrick's old Catholic graveyard in Granard, which is also the resting place of his younger brother, James, who died a year later.

Hugh and Maisie (Veronica) Major

Abandoned by their mother, and then by their father, my half-siblings Hugh and Maisie endured as turbulent a childhood as I did. I met the late Hugh, who lived in Wexford with his daughter, Darina Johnson, some time after Fran Dean's phone call in 2002. Hugh never forgot the day our mother abandoned him and his sister, and he told us the story of the big car arriving and how they were sent for sweets. When they returned, the car was gone, and so was our mother. Hugh said that was the end of the happy childhood he'd known.

Their father, Hugh Major, took them from their grandparents' home soon after, and they lived with him for a few months. He told us that his father sent them away to boarding school after the divorce. Perhaps he, like me, was too ashamed to reveal the truth of his past, because his family discovered that both he and Maisie were put into state institutions at some point after 1935.

My half-sister Maisie Major left Ireland for good when she was released and went to America. She is ninety-three now and has rebuffed any attempts from her siblings to make contact.

William Cameron

My father, William Cameron, died on 29 August 1955, in St Kevin's Hospital in Dublin, now known as St James's. He was sixty-six years old according to his death certificate, which is strangely at odds with his birth certificate.

The records show that he was born at 7 Catherine Street in Belfast on 25 September 1884, which would have made him seventy when he died. His occupation, according to the death certificate, was 'accountant'. It states also that he died of carcinoma of the stomach and secondaries. However, it also reveals that he died of '*tabes dorsalis* certified', which we discovered is an archaic term for syphilis of the spine – an advanced syphilis infection. He might have been infected with the disease twenty or more years before he died, because, despite the image of God-fearing Ireland, the country was in the grip of a syphilis epidemic in the 1930s and 1940s. According to historian Padraig Yeates' book *A City in Wartime*, at the height of the epidemic forty thousand people attended Dublin hospitals for sexually transmitted diseases.

I never learned a lot about my father. Anyone who met him said that he was a charming man, and the other abiding memory of him was that he was always impeccably dressed.

Elizabeth Cameron, née Maguire

My father's wife, Elizabeth Cameron, lived for two years after he was named in the Majors' scandalous divorce case. I can only imagine the humiliation that this private woman endured when her husband made headlines for romping in a haybarn with my mother.

There seems to have been little communication between them after William and Elizabeth's affair came to light. We know there is no mention of her marital name, Cameron, on her death certificate. All the details of her passing are recorded in her maiden name, Mary Elizabeth Maguire.

Elizabeth, also known to her family as Lily, passed away in Lisbrack, County Longford, aged forty-eight on 18 July 1937. Her daughter, Mary Cameron, was by her bedside.

Cause of death is recorded as carcinoma of the uterus and 'cachexia certified', a wasting syndrome associated with cancer.

The Children of William Cameron and Elizabeth Maguire
Sadly, I never met any of my four half-siblings from the marriage of my father to Elizabeth Maguire. They had already passed away by the time I discovered their existence.

Thomas Edward Cameron, known as Tom, was born in 1913 and became a motor mechanic in the new era of the motor car. He died, aged twenty-one, on 23 May 1933 of cardiac failure and pneumonia, according to his death certificate. It also stated that he was 'phthisis certified' – a discreet way of saying he had tuberculosis. By 1933, it was already widely known that his father was having an affair with my mother, so we don't know if William saw his son before he died.

Thomas passed away in the family's rented house on Battery Road in Longford with his mother, 'Lily Cameron', listed as present at his death.

Mary Cameron was born in 1914, so she was twenty-one by the time of her father's public disgrace in the Majors' divorce in 1935. Until the day she died, Mary only ever referred to the notorious Mrs Major, my mother and the woman who stole her father, as '*that* woman'.

Mary married Thomas O'Keefe in 1939 and went on to have four daughters and a son, including Fran Dean, who made that fateful call to us in 2002.

Fran revealed that she knew nothing about the scandal

involving her maternal grandfather as she grew up. She recalls William occasionally visiting her house when she was a small child; she thinks he used to call after doing the accounts of a family near their home. She remembers him as a man in a hat and a long black coat with a red rose in his lapel. She also remembers that he gave her and her sister, Mary, money, even though his second family say he struggled to put food on their table in that era.

Fran said she learned of her grandfather's second family only when she was about eighteen. Her mother, my half-sister Mary, died of a stroke, aged sixty-six, in the 1980s.

William John Cameron was born on 24 December 1915, in Townhall Street in Enniskillen. We know that in 1941, aged twenty-six, he married a farmer's daughter, Kathleen Ludden, who was of 'full age,' or over seventeen.

His residence is recorded as the Mental Hospital, Castlebar, County Mayo, also known as the District Lunatic Asylum, where he worked as an accounting clerk, like his father. The couple's first son Michael W. Cameron was born in 1942.

Christina Cameron, born in 1918, had a tragically short life. At age nineteen, she married Brendan Brennan, the stationmaster for Loughrea, in Longford Cathedral on 22 August 1938. She died only four months later, aged just twenty, on St Stephen's Day 1938, in the Central Hospital in Galway; the cause of death was recorded as endometritis septicaemia and cardiac failure.

Endometritis (not the same as endometriosis) is an infection of the uterus lining, which can be triggered by many causes, including tuberculosis, miscarriage or childbirth. Family members recall that her bereft husband still mourned her passing decades later.

Una Major

My older sister, Una, wasn't even two years old when our parents left her and Longford for ever. We have since heard from friends and neighbours of the Farrells that Elizabeth 'disappeared off the face of the earth' shortly after that. They claim that Julia and Michael Farrell never heard from their daughter again.

There is a reference to Una in a letter penned by our maternal grandfather, Michael Farrell, in Roose, to his younger daughter, Julia, in Freeport, Long Island. The letter is dated 2 August 1939, and he signed off 'best of love from Father, Mother & Baby'.

On 10 January 1940, our grandparents' farm was auctioned after Hugh Major made an undisclosed payment to the couple. By now Michael Farrell was seventy-five, and he, our grandmother and Una moved to a cottage and smallholding in Finglas in Dublin.

Una recalled a day when two men called to their home in Finglas and she heard them talk about her. She said her grandfather was a kind and soft-spoken man, but whatever they said infuriated him, and he threw them out of the house. In hindsight, she believed that these were people from some child protection service. They might have been telling her grandparents that they were too old or too impoverished to care for her.

Our grandparents were indeed poverty-stricken by then. They couldn't afford a white dress for Una when she was making her First Holy Communion. She had to go in a blue one instead and remembered her classmates jeering at her afterwards.

When our grandfather fell ill, they moved back to a rented property in Longford. Michael Farrell died as a pauper, and family members say that his death is registered in a poorhouse or county home in Longford.

Around a year later, Julia Farrell fell seriously ill, and men arrived at the house again. This time they took Una away. She was only nine years old, but she recalled the trauma of that day in vivid detail. She remembered that they had to 'peel' her off her grandmother, screaming. Una was taken to Newtownforbes in County Longford and never saw Julia again. She spent seven unhappy years of her life in Our Lady of Succour Orphanage, home to about 120 girls in the 1930s and 1940s.

The Ryan Report says that medical inspector Dr Anna McCabe visited the orphanage in 1940, a few years before Una's arrival, and noted bruising on many of the girls' bodies in the infirmary. She also expressed her dismay at the filthy condition of the children. 'I cannot find any excuse which would exonerate you and your staff from the verminous condition of several of the children's heads,' she wrote. Una said she spent years scrubbing the floors of the institution and trying to avoid the unmerciful beatings meted out by the nuns.

The rest of the family discovered Una's existence only

by accident. Our younger sisters were at Lough Key Forest Park in County Roscommon in the 1980s when they made a spur-of-the-moment detour to visit Roose.

Betty knocked on the door of a house in the Clonbroney area to ask if they knew where the Farrells once lived. Our mother's secret was uncovered when the woman of the house greeted her with the words 'Oh, you must be Una!'

The resourceful sisters did manage to locate their lost sister, but Una always said Elizabeth's response to the 'surprise' reunion was not a warm one. Our mother's first words to Una sixty years after abandoning her were 'What are *you* doing here?'

Despite her sisters' efforts to include her in the family, Una admitted that her mother always seemed uncomfortable around her and never wanted to be left on her own with her. She never got to the root of why her parents made no attempt to rescue her from Newtownforbes.

By the time I met Una, she was a mother of seven and blissfully married to Michael Hogan. Her daughter Mary subsequently wrote about our first meeting:

When Una met John for the first time in 2002, she walked into the room, sat down beside him, held his hand and looked into his eyes. Together at last, as they looked at each other, they understood the extent of the horrors and the shame of being detained in a state institution. They understood the years of fear and terror of rejection and guilt, of pain and suffering both had endured, because of the actions of their parents.

They sat in silence, two gentle souls, two kind hearts, two kindred spirits, understanding each other . . . not one word was necessary, not one word was spoken. The memory of their first meeting lives on and will always be remembered by those lucky enough to have witnessed it.

Una and I forged a very tight bond from the first time we met, and we remained close right up until she died, aged eighty-four, on 27 November 2018.

I miss her terribly.

Betty, Ada, Marie and Joan Cameron

After Elizabeth and William reunited in 1937, they posed as a married couple, Mr and Mrs Cameron, and moved into a flat in Lower Mount Street in central Dublin.

My sister Betty was born in May 1938, and my second sister, Ada, the following year in July. The family escaped the tenements in Lower Mount Street when Dublin Corporation offered them a home in a new housing development in Cabra. Another sister, Marie, was born in the new house on Kilronan Road in February 1941. My fourth younger sister, Joan, arrived in June 1943, the year before I was sent to Artane Industrial School.

The closest I can ever come to knowing my mother and father is through the memories of my sisters who lived with them. They have recalled that times were hard growing up. Their house in Cabra contained hardly a stick of furniture, and even food was scarce. Yet they look back on their childhood as a happy time, and they remained devoted to our mother right up until her death. Their memories of our father are sketchier. The eldest three were in their teens, and Joan was only twelve when he died. They recall him as an older, kindly man, who suffered ill health for years before he died.

The sisters say they found out through Aunt Ethel, our father's sister, that our mother had two other children, Hugh and Maisie. They think they may have learned about William's other family through her, too.

However, they were startled to discover their older sister, Una, and shocked to hear of my existence days after their mother's death. They were nonetheless generous in welcoming Una and me into their tight-knit family group, and for that I shall be for ever grateful.

I loved finding all these sisters, and Betty and I have forged a tight bond, probably because we are the closest in age. We sadly lost our youngest sister, Joan Cullen, age seventy-two, on 15 April 2016.

Michael and Julia Farrell

My grandparents, Michael and Julia Farrell, were left with a legacy of debt, legal battles and responsibilities when their daughter Elizabeth left Granard after the High Court case. It is hard to imagine what they felt when she never came back.

The Farrells were tied up in legal battles with Hugh Major for many years after the High Court divorce case. They made front-page headlines in the *Longford Leader* in 1936 when they sued Major for £134 in the Circuit Court.

They said the money was owed for maintenance payments, for debts paid on behalf of Mr Major, and for livestock they said their son-in-law had sold. My grandfather claimed a pound a week support, according to the deed drawn up for the marriage of his daughter to Major.

Michael Farrell testified in court that Major had married into the family in June 1924 but had gone back to America a year later 'without consulting his wife or anyone'. When Major returned briefly, 'things did not go too well between the defendant and his wife', and he returned to America again.

My maternal grandfather also discovered that a charge of £200 was registered against his former house and farms by Major's solicitors, Hannan & Connellan. Another charge of £200 was registered in favour of Edward Major, Hugh's brother. It meant that most of the farm's value was owed to the solicitor and Edward Major. My mother also registered another charge on the lands when she could not get the maintenance owed to her by her husband.

My grandfather testified that shortly after Elizabeth left Roose in 1935, Major removed their grandchildren, Hugh and Maisie, from the house.

He said he had a small pension of eight pounds, received every three months, as an ex-relieving officer for Granard. He also held a position as registrar of deaths, which was worth just ten or twelve pounds a year. He said he did not get the full old-age pension from the state. He produced receipts for money paid amounting to £41/7*s.* for bills owed by Mr Major since 1933. He admitted that Mr Major had not asked him to pay the bills. However, he said his daughter warned him that the bills 'might rise another row and cause [Major] to run away to America'.

'I paid them for peace sake,' he said.

Asked where Hugh Major was living, he replied: 'I understand he is living at Edgeworthstown with Mr Noonan, a returned American.'

Michael Farrell was also asked if Hugh Major sent £400 in total to his daughter while he was in America.

He replied: 'I don't know. I never handled a penny belonging to him. I never saw a halfpenny belonging to him in her possession.'

Hugh Major, in response, said he had no intention of contributing a shilling to his father-in-law. The judge, however, awarded my grandfather half the money he claimed.

> Farrell was awarded half the money that he was looking for.
>
> 'Under these circumstances,' the judge concluded, 'I think the fairest thing to do is give judgement for £52 [to Michael Farrell].'
>
> *Longford Leader,* Saturday, 31 October 1936

My grandfather never received this money. In June 1939, a report in the *Longford Leader* claimed that Mr and Mrs Farrell had 'agreed to accept a lump sum' and to give Major clear title of the farms.

In a letter dated August 1939 to his younger daughter, now Mrs Julia Bonniwell, in America, Michael Farrell wrote that he hoped to rent a house from Canon Markey.

> *I approached Father Markey again about the house to see would he set it to me by the year and he won't set it to anyone by the year.*
>
> *The times is too disturbed, and I won't be responsible for putting a yearly rent on it for anyone and 'I will get a suitable kitchen in it, and then I will sell it'. That is the reply I got.*

Michael Farrell's letter also paints a picture of country life and of the ageing parish priest, Canon Markey.

> *Well you would not know what Father Markey would do. He changes his mind so often. He is nearly spent out, and no one will be sorry. He has everyone turned again [sic] him. He had the Sodality Devotions a few Sunday evenings ago at half six, and he fell asleep on his knees and snored. When he woke up, he looked at the boys each side of him and began the same thing over again . . .*
>
> *Except you were up beside him, you would not know or hear what he does be saying. He is away on his holidays in Kingstown [now Dún Laoghaire] and we have the comfort of the world.*
>
> *We do have Father Cosgrove every Sunday from Longford, and he is a delightful preacher, and you would hear him over the whole church . . .*

On 30 December 1939, there was notice that a public auction of Michael Farrell's farms in Clonbroney would take place on 10 January 1940.

By the following July, Michael Farrell was writing to his daughter in America from their new address on North Road, Finglas. He said he was happy to hear of the birth of Julia's son, and he wrote about his and his wife's new life in Dublin and about the produce they grew and reared on their smallholding.

> Well, about this place, we are living in, they are all very nice people and friendly. Every time we churn, they come for buttermilk and give 3d a quart for it.
>
> They think our cow is a wonder the milk is so good and thick. They get buttermilk in the creamery, and it is only like water, and you will get 2/6 a dozen for fresh eggs.
>
> Your mother has 24 hens laying and she has 32 young pullets. It is thought eggs will be sixpence each next winter and spring. Some good Saturday we will go into the city and get our photos and send you out.
>
> This is a very early part of the country. We had new potatoes in the beginning of June, and they are very good and real dry.

Their happy lives in Dublin didn't last long. My grandfather fell ill, and they returned to Longford, where he died, age seventy-seven, in a poorhouse in 1942. My grandmother followed him to the grave a year later. I was seven years old and living in Murphystown at that stage, and they never knew of my existence.

Midwife Nurse Walsh, née Doyle

Nurse Mary Walsh was the midwife who delivered me in Enniscorthy, County Wexford, on 9 September 1935. As I have already related, Treasa and I tracked her down to her address given on my birth certificate, Lymington Road in Enniscorthy.

Even though she was kind, we always felt she held back information from us at the time. Treasa even returned to see her when our daughter Fiona was still a baby, but still failed to extract any more information.

We found Nurse Mary Doyle among a list of witnesses who were summoned to the High Court in 1935 to give evidence on behalf of Hugh Major. She was listed with Dr McEvoy and she appears to have been the midwife who delivered my older sister, Una – the subject of the divorce case.

For the purposes of this book's narration, I have amalgamated the two nurses. The nurse's landlady, Mrs Whitney, and some of her friends in the town, such as Mrs Dunne and Mrs Quinn, are also fictional constructs.

The Mulligans and the Christian Brothers

A few names and identifying details in this book have been changed to protect the privacy of innocent individuals, and the Mulligan family name is one of them. However, my foster parents were very much real people. All the details relating to them in this book are accurate to the best of my knowledge, recollection and research.

For similar reasons, I also changed the names of some of the Christian Brothers. Many of the abusers were never charged or convicted for their crimes, and naming them now, after their deaths, would hurt innocent families.

Author's Conclusions

For many years I tried to unravel the mystery of who I was, and why I was abandoned. I thought if I could just know who my parents were, and meet even one person related to me, I would have all the answers.

And yet after all these years and so many revelations, the mystery remains and has even deepened. Even now, I have no idea who my mother was or what kind of a man my father was. I still can't fathom why they did what they did to us.

These days, old age has inflicted me with Parkinson's and all its symptoms, including balance problems, rigidity and tremors. Last year I was diagnosed with Lewy body dementia. It causes my attention and alertness to fluctuate.

It also causes me to have visual hallucinations – most of them nightmares related to Artane and the Christian Brothers. Those hallucinations are so vivid and real that I relive the same levels of terror I experienced as boy number 11963.

Most people claim to become more accepting and understanding as they grow older. Yet, the older I have become and the more I learn, the less tolerant I feel. My mother did a terrible thing to her children by abandoning us.

I never felt any anger towards her in my earlier years, believing she had had no choice when she gave me up. I'm certainly angrier now.

But then she was a woman who evoked extreme feelings throughout her life and after it. She was loved by many, despised by others. There's no doubt she treated each of her first four children shamefully. She walked away from Hugh and Maisie, never making any attempt to connect with them again. She washed her hands of Una and me in the same brutal way.

I am conscious that double standards are applied when it comes to men and women, so I have no intention of letting the men in our lives off the hook. My father, William Cameron, behaved with little honour, walking out on his terminally ill wife and four children, including one dying from tuberculosis and a child aged seventeen. He was also complicit in my mother's abandonment of two more of his children, Una and me.

Hugh Major was just as bad. He wrested his children,

Hugh and Maisie, from the only home they knew, and abandoned them to the 'care' of the state.

The children were the collateral damage in the antics between these adults. At least four small children's lives were scarred for ever by their actions. We were deprived of our childhood and condemned to be raised in the hellish surroundings of child prisons.

Of course I accept that those were different times, and life was harder then. Ireland was a country of dire poverty, puritanism and religious hypocrisy. But many parents struggled in adversity of all kinds, yet most managed to keep their families together.

After raising my own family, I know I would go through hell and back to protect our children. It's instinct – at least, I once thought it was an instinct in every parent. After all, what kind of person abandons their own children?

In many ways, I always thought what happened was worse for Una, Hugh and Maisie. I always acknowledged that when I talked with Una. She knew a mother's love and her grandparents' love before it was ripped away from her. All three of them knew what it was to have family and a sense of security. They had had it all and lost it all. The betrayal was huge.

It was interesting to discover that Una and I shared the same sense of guilt and shame all our lives. Una grew up feeling she was to blame for her family's break-up. In my case, I felt the shame of being unwanted, a cast-off condemned to a hellhole created by the Christian Brothers.

Yet if Elizabeth Farrell or William Cameron ever shared

any guilt or shame, they never showed it. They were able to compartmentalise their past, shove it into a watertight box and shelve it in a dark and secret corner.

Betty says she remembers that our mother carried a photo of a curly-haired, blond boy in her wallet. She saw Elizabeth taking it out sometimes and staring at it. Betty believes the picture must have been of me because her first son, Hugh, had straight dark hair. Who knows? Maybe my mother did have some regrets.

Yet when her family discovered Una, my mother could have revealed the whole story, but she chose to continue to conceal my existence.

I know she must have gone through a lot during that public divorce. She brought it on herself, of course, but it can't have been easy being vilified and scorned as a fallen woman. She lived in a time when women were repressed and controlled, socially, sexually and economically.

Elizabeth Major was a maverick in many ways, a woman who flouted all the rules when she had an affair with William Cameron. She might have had my grudging respect if she hadn't let her children pay the price of her defiance of the social and religious conventions of the time.

Of course, Elizabeth, William and Hugh were not solely to blame for the tragedy that befell four small children. The religious and state bodies, who had a duty of care to children without guardians, also failed spectacularly.

Yet I still cannot understand how Elizabeth and William callously turned their backs on eight children, then went on to raise four more in a normal, loving family home.

The truth is that even if I had had the chance to meet my mother, I probably wouldn't understand her any better. My sister Una had that chance, and she never received any explanations, any apologies, any excuses. She died with all the unanswered questions that I still have.

In reality, I no longer think much about Elizabeth and William. The human spirit has a way of enduring and of surviving on the tiniest sparks of humanity, and Hugh, Maisie, Una and I did just that. In my case, Eleanor French provided the spark of warmth and care that I needed to survive, and I shall always be grateful to her.

Hugh, Una and I had the joy of finding one another and our younger siblings, Betty, Ada, Marie, Joan and their families. Discovering all these wonderful people, my own flesh and blood, has greatly enriched and enhanced the last years of my life.

Yet our parents are destined to remain an enigma to me. They are little more than shadowy figures in my life. How and why they did what they did, I will never understand.

In the end, I must accept that we can never really know what goes on in the mind of another person and that, ultimately, we all remain a mystery to one another.

Acknowledgements

You can't reach my age or even Treasa's without having to thank a lot of people for making it this far in life!

First, thanks to my niece Fran Dean for making that phone call. If she hadn't thumbed through the phone directory and found us, I would have had a very short story to tell.

To my children, Fiona, Aileen, Shane, Niamh and Brian, of whom we're both so proud, thank you for all your hard work in editing and guiding this book.

Deserving of special mention is Aileen, who worked like a Trojan in researching and overseeing the project – thank you for your dedication, patience and for spurring us on when we felt like giving up. Mam and I appreciate all you've done.

A special note of thanks to our sons-in-law, Fiona's husband Tim Vanderkamp, Aileen's husband Jimmy Rogers and Niamh's husband Tony Seery. Thank you for being part of our family and for all your many kindnesses.

To our grandchildren, Emma, Omai, Aoife, Patrick and Ellie Rose: you are the living embodiment of this family's bright future. I hope that one day you'll dust down this book and learn more about your granddad, grandmother and your past.

I want to send heartfelt thanks to my sisters, Betty Byrne, Ada Healy and Marie Scullay, for welcoming me so warmly and generously. Thank you for being my family.

Thanks especially to my darling sister Betty, the closest in age to me, for your friendship and companionship and for the many fond memories of your husband, Jimmy.

To Nell, my surrogate mother, and to my beloved sisters, Una Hogan and Joan Cullen: you may have passed, but you are always in my heart and sorely missed.

With love to Una's daughters, Bridget Carney and Mary O'Donovan, and her husband, Dan, who are always welcome visitors, along with all Una's large and incredible family.

To Darina Johnson, my half-brother Hugh's daughter, who is always a joy to see. And to all my new nieces and nephews, the sons and daughters of the half-siblings I never had the privilege to meet, it has been an amazing journey getting to know you.

I have so many to thank in Treasa's large and wonderful family. You were my family for a long time before I had anyone: to Treasa's niece, and carbon copy, Ann and husband, Larry Morris, whom we've always been especially close to.

To the Walsh family: Sean and Vera, Joe and Frances, Ray and Brid, Vincent and Celine, Colm and Grace, Tom and Mary, Aine and Mick.

Also, to Maura, with our fond memories of Alf, and to Sean Looby with love to Nessa, RIP. To Nessa and Sean's children, Grainne, Eithne, Orla, Nessa and Derbhla. They lost their mother many years ago, but Treasa has tried to honour her promise to Nessa and has kept an eye on all of them!

To the extended Walsh family, all fifty-two nieces and nephews, it's a privilege to know you all and be a part of this big, vibrant and growing family.

To Joseph and Henry Kinsella: thank you for being great people, for always being at the end of a phone and ready with your help and support.

To my home care team, Caroline, Nicola, Clare, Rena, Marie, Rita, Anna and Litto: you are among the very few blessings of being sick. Thank you for your daily dedication to your work and to me, and of course, thanks for reading the drafts!

To the Parkinson's Association of Ireland: Treasa and I are very grateful for all your invaluable help and assistance.

To John and Imelda Kenny: a special thank you for being there for us all through the years.

To Olive Pierce and Robin Bantry-White, our wonderful neighbours and friends in Kilternan and close friends of Nell.

To Celine and Myles Lawless, more of our incredible friends from Killenagh in Wexford.

To Liam and Marie-France Healy and their family. For their support through the hard times but also for creating wonderful happy holiday memories in France and England. Friends for the past sixty years.

We are blessed again with Deirdre and John McCarthy, our new neighbours in Gorey, kind to a fault and people who can never do enough for us.

In fond memory of Brian and Nelly Hanrahan, our very dear friends: thank you for enriching our lives with so much fun, laughter and companionship.

I can't forget Joe Dwyer, Tim Keane and Des Scott, who have been great friends over the years with whom I had many adventures.

To Tommy Weir, my close friend and unpaid personal adviser in Kilternan!

To George Kavanagh, my childhood pal and one of my few fond memories of Murphystown.

Thanks, too, to Kathryn Rogers, who helped write and edit this book with such care and sensitivity; to Jonathan Williams for believing in the first transcripts of the book, and agreeing to represent it; to Ciara Considine, publisher at Hachette Books Ireland, for enthusiastically bringing it into print.

There have been so many people who have touched my life in the past eighty-five years, especially my partner in love, Treasa, who has been with me through most of it.

My life has become a rich tapestry that's so full of

deep bonds and connections that it would be impossible to name you all. But, rest assured, I'm grateful that our paths crossed and that so many of you kindred spirits float through the pages of this book.

Thank you one and all.

John Cameron